TAKING TURNS WITH THE EARTH

TAKING TURNS WITH THE EARTH

Phenomenology, Deconstruction, and Intergenerational Justice

Matthias Fritsch

STANFORD UNIVERSITY PRESS

STANFORD, CALIFORNIA

Stanford University Press
Stanford, California

© 2018 by the Board of Trustees of the Leland Stanford Junior University. All rights reserved.

No part of this book may be reproduced or transmitted in any form or by any means, electronic or mechanical, including photocopying and recording, or in any information storage or retrieval system without the prior written permission of Stanford University Press.

Printed in the United States of America on acid-free, archival-quality paper

Library of Congress Cataloging-in-Publication Data

Names: Fritsch, Matthias, author.
Title: Taking turns with the Earth : phenomenology, deconstruction, and intergenerational justice / Matthias Fritsch.
Description: Stanford, California : Stanford University Press, 2018. | Includes bibliographical references and index.
Identifiers: LCCN 2018003993 (print) | LCCN 2018005627 (ebook) | ISBN 9781503606968 | ISBN 9781503604940 (cloth : alk. paper) | ISBN 9781503606951 (pbk. : alk. paper)
Subjects: LCSH: Environmental ethics. | Future, The—Philosophy. | Social justice—Philosophy. | Phenomenology. | Deconstruction. | Philosophy, Modern—20th century.
Classification: LCC GE42 (ebook) | LCC GE42 .F75 2018 (print) | DDC 179/.1—dc23
LC record available at https://lccn.loc.gov/2018003993

Cover design: Rob Ehle
Cover photo: Fog over Erlauf valley and Danube, user "Uoaeil" via Wikimedia Commons

Contents

Acknowledgments	*vii*
List of Abbreviations	*ix*
Introduction	1
1. Ontological Problems and Methods in Intergenerational Justice	17
2. Levinas's "Being-for-Beyond-My-Death"	64
3. Asymmetrical Reciprocity and the Gift in Mauss and Derrida	107
4. Double Turn-Taking among Generations and with Earth	154
5. Interment	186
Notes	215
Bibliography	233
Index	257

Acknowledgments

Since starting on this project in 2010, I have accumulated debts that I hope the publication of this book pays forward, in however limited a way. I thank the Alexander-von-Humboldt Stiftung in Germany for granting me a Humboldt Research Fellowship for Experienced Researchers (2010–2011) at the Cluster of Excellence "The Formation of Normative Orders" and the research group Justitia Amplificata at Goethe Universität Frankfurt. The research conditions and atmosphere there were outstanding. Many individuals helped shape my initial thoughts, especially my host professors Christoph Menke and Stefan Gosepath. I fondly recall the helpful conversations with Juliane Rebentisch, Dirk Quadflieg, Thomas Khurana, Dirk Setton, Eva Buddeberg, and many others.

Having returned to Concordia University in Montréal, I happily acknowledge the multi-year financial support from the Social Sciences and Humanities Research Council of Canada (SSHRC). With the help of this research grant, I was fortunate to work with several excellent research assistants, in particular Philippe Lynes, Gwynne Fulton, Kay Rollans, and Michael Giesbrecht. I also learned from many students in courses I taught at Concordia. David Morris gave excellent institutional and scholarly support, as department head, colleague, and friend.

Much of this book was drafted while I was visiting research professor at Kyoto University, Japan (2015–2016). I benefited enormously from numerous conversations with Prof. Hiroshi Abe, who read and commented on extensive parts of the manuscript. Many conversations with Dr. Abe's doctoral students—in particular Yuta Sakazume, Hoko Nakagawa, and Takashi Nukui—helped me to clarify ideas. Seminars and talks at Kyoto's Research Institute for Humanity and Nature, the Regional Office Asia of Future Earth, and the excellent Research Center for Future Design at Kochi University of Technology proved very useful; at the latter two institutions, particular thanks go to Prof. Tatsuyoshi Saijo for his invitations, comments, and encouragement. Other institutions and venues that have been supportive of this project over the years include the Just World Institute at the University of Edinburgh (special thanks to Elizabeth Cripps), the University of Tokyo Center for Philosophy (my thanks to Shinji Kajitani), the Collegium Phaenomenologicum (special thanks to Michael Naas for his invitation), and the International Association of Environmental Philosophy, where several parts of the overall project have had a chance to get a hearing over the years.

The manuscript is, I find, much the better for the comments I received from colleagues who read chapter drafts: with profound gratitude to Len Lawlor, Kelly Oliver, Ted Toadvine, and David Wood. Special thanks go to Lisa Guenther and Samir Haddad, who read the entire manuscript and offered extensive and extremely helpful suggestions. All shortcomings remain mine. At Stanford University Press, I could count on the exemplary and professional support of Emily-Jane Cohen and Faith Wilson Stein.

An earlier and much shorter version of Chapter 3 appeared as "The Gift of Nature in Mauss and Derrida," *Oxford Literary Review* 37(1) (2015): 1–23. My thanks to Edinburgh University Press for permission to reuse. An earlier and much shorter version of Chapter 4 originally appeared in *Mosaic: An Interdisciplinary Critical Journal* 48(3) (2015): 27–45. My thanks to *Mosaic* for permission to reuse.

Last but not least, I could not have written this book without the unwavering and loving support of my family: Katrin, my partner in crime, and our crew, Charlotte, Jasper, Silas, and Julia. This book is dedicated to your living on.

Abbreviations

Page numbers refer first to English translation, then to original French or German text. At times, translations have been modified.

Works by Jacques Derrida

A	*Aporias* (Stanford, CA: Stanford University Press, 1993); trans. Thomas Dutoit from *Apories* (Paris: Galilée, 1996).
AA	*The Animal That Therefore I Am* (New York: Fordham University Press, 2008); trans. David Wills from *L'Animal que donc je suis* (Paris: Galilée, 2006).
AEL	*Adieu to Emmanuel Levinas* (Stanford, CA: Stanford University Press, 1999); trans. Pascale-Anne Brault and Michael Naas from *Adieu à Emmanuel Levinas* (Paris: Galilée, 1997).
AV	*Advances* (Minneapolis: University of Minnesota Press, 2017); trans. Philippe Lynes from "Avances," in Serge Margel, *Le Tombeau du dieu artisan* (Paris: Minuit, 1995).
BS1	*The Beast and the Sovereign*, vol. 1 (Chicago: University of Chicago Press, 2009); trans. Geoffrey Bennington from *Séminaire: La Bête et le souverain, Volume I (2001–2003)* (Paris: Galilée, 2008).
BS2	*The Beast and the Sovereign*, vol. 2 (Chicago: University of Chicago Press, 2011); trans. Geoffrey Bennington from *Séminaire: La Bête et le souverain, Volume II (2002–2003)* (Paris: Galilée, 2010).
DP1	*The Death Penalty* (Chicago: University of Chicago Press, 2014); trans. Peggy Kamuf from *Séminaire: La Peine de mort, Volume 1 (1999–2000)* (Paris: Galilée, 2012).

DP2	*The Death Penalty* (Chicago: University of Chicago Press, 2016); trans. Elizabeth Rottenberg from *Séminaire: La Peine de mort, Volume 2 (2000–2001)* (Paris: Galilée, 2015).
FSC	*For Strasbourg: Conversations of Friendship and Philosophy*, ed. and trans. Pascale-Anne Brault and Michael Naas (New York: Fordham University Press, 2014).
FWT	*For What Tomorrow* (Stanford, CA: Stanford University Press, 2004); trans. Jeff Fort from *De Quoi Demain . . . Dialogue (Avec Elisabeth Roudinesco)* (Paris: Fayard/Galilée, 2001).
GL	*Glas* (Lincoln: University of Nebraska Press, 1986); trans. John P. Leavey and Richard Rand from *Glas* (Paris: Galilée, 1974).
GT	*Given Time: 1. Counterfeit Money* (Chicago: University of Chicago Press, 1992); trans. Peggy Kamuf from *Donner: Le Temps 1. La Fausse monnaie* (Paris: Galilée, 1991).
MP	*Margins of Philosophy* (Brighton, UK: Harvester Press, 1982); trans. Alan Bass from *Marges: De la philosophie* (Paris: Minuit, 1972).
NII	*Negotiations: Interventions and Interviews 1971–2002*, ed. and trans. Elizabeth Rottenberg (Stanford, CA: Stanford University Press, 2002).
OG	*Of Grammatology* (Baltimore: Johns Hopkins University Press, 1974); trans. Gayatri Chakravorty Spivak from *De la grammatologie* (Paris: Minuit, 1967).
PF	*The Politics of Friendship* (London: Verso, 2005); trans. George Collins from *Politiques de l'amitié* (Paris: Galilée, 1994).
PI	*Points . . . Interviews, 1974–1994* (Stanford, CA: Stanford University Press, 1995); trans. Peggy Kamuf et al. from *Points de suspension: Entretiens* (Paris: Galilée, 1992).
R	*Rogues* (Stanford, CA: Stanford University Press, 2005); trans. Pascale-Anne Brault and Michael Naas from *Voyous* (Paris: Galilée, 2003).
SM	*Specters of Marx* (London: Routledge Classics, 2006); trans. Peggy Kamuf from *Spectres de Marx* (Paris: Galilée, 1993).
WD	*Writing and Difference* (London: Routledge Classics, 2001); trans. Alan Bass from *L'Écriture et la différence* (Paris: Seuil, 1967).

WM   *The Work of Mourning* (Chicago: University of Chicago Press, 2001); trans. Pascale-Anne Brault and Michael Naas from *Chaque fois unique, la fin du monde* (Paris: Galilée, 2003).

Works by Martin Heidegger

GA 2   *Being and Time* (New York: Harper Perennial, 2008); trans. John Macquarrie and Edward Robinson from *Sein und Zeit* (Frankfurt am Main: Vittorio Klostermann, 1977).

GA 5   *Off the Beaten Track* (Cambridge: Cambridge University Press, 2002); trans. Julian Young and Kenneth Haynes from *Holzwege* (Frankfurt am Main: Vittorio Klostermann, 1977).

GA 8   *What Is Called Thinking?* (New York: Harper and Row, 1968); trans. J. Glenn Gray from *Was Heißt Denken?* (Frankfurt am Main: Vittorio Klostermann, 2002).

GA 7   "The Thing," in *Poetry, Language, Thought* (New York: Harper and Row, 1971); trans. Albert Hofstadter from *Vorträge und Aufsätze* (Frankfurt am Main: Vittorio Klostermann, 1936–1953).

GA 14   *On Time and Being* (New York: Harper Torchbooks, 1972); trans. Joan Stambaugh from *Zur Sache des Denkens* (Frankfurt am Main: Vittorio Klostermann, 2007).

GA 20   *History of the Concept of Time* (Bloomington: Indiana University Press, 1985); trans. Theodore Kisiel from *Prolegomena zur Geschichte des Zeitbegriffs* (Frankfurt am Main: Vittorio Klostermann, 1979).

GA 24   *The Basic Problems of Phenomenology* (Bloomington: Indiana University Press, 1988); trans. Albert Hofstadter from *Die Grundprobleme der Phänomenologie* (Frankfurt am Main: Vittorio Klostermann, 1975).

GA 29/30: *The Fundamental Concepts of Metaphysics: World, Finitude, Solitude* (Bloomington: Indiana University Press, 1995); trans. William McNeill and Nicholas Walker from *Die Grundbegriffe der Metaphysik: Welt—Endlichkeit—Einsamkeit* (Frankfurt am Main: Vittorio Klostermann, 1983).

GA 65   *Contributions to Philosophy (Of the Event)* (Bloomington: Indiana University Press, 2012); trans. Richard Rojcewicz and

Daniela Vallega-Neu from *Beiträge zur Philosophie (Vom Ereignis)* (Frankfurt am Main: Vittorio Klostermann, 1989).

GA 77   *Country Path Conversations* (Bloomington: Indiana University Press, 2010; trans. Bret W. Davis from *Feldweg-Gespräche* (Frankfurt am Main: Vittorio Klostermann, 1944–1945).

Works by Emmanuel Levinas

CPP   *Collected Philosophical Papers*, trans. Alphonso Lingis (The Hague: Martinus Nijoff, 1987). Original French in *h*: *Humanisme de l'autre homme* (Paris: Le Livre de poche, 2012).

GDT   *God, Death, and Time* (Stanford, CA: Stanford University Press, 2001); trans. Bettina Bergo from *Dieu, la mort et le temps* (Paris: Bernard Grasset, 1993).

LR   *The Levinas Reader*, ed. Séan Hand (London: Blackwell, 1989); original French in *e*: *Éthique comme philosophie première* (Paris: Payot et Rivages, 1998).

OB   *Otherwise than Being, or Beyond Essence* (Pittsburgh: Duquesne University Press, 1998); trans. Alphonso Lingis from *Autrement qu'être, ou Au-delà de l'essence* (Paris: Le Livre de poche, 2008).

TI   *Totality and Infinity: An Essay on Exteriority* (The Hague: Martinus Nijhoff, 1979); trans. Alphonso Lingis from *Totalité et infini: Essai sur l'extériorité* (Paris: Le Livre de poche, 2012).

TO   *Time and the Other and Additional Essays*, trans. Richard A. Cohen (Pittsburgh: Duquesne University Press, 1987); original French in *t*: *Le Temps et l'autre* (Paris: Presses universitaires de France, 2011), *d*: "Diachronie et représentation," *University of Ottawa Quarterly* 55(4) (1985).

Works by Marcel Mauss

G   *The Gift* (London: Routledge Classics, 2002); trans. W. D. Halls from *Essai sur le don: Forme et raison de l'échange dans les sociétés archaïques* (Paris: Presses universitaires de France, 2012).

TAKING TURNS WITH THE EARTH

Introduction

In his masterful monograph on the special challenges imposed on us by the global environmental tragedy, Stephen Gardiner charges existing ethical and political frameworks with "theoretical inadequacy" (Gardiner 2011a, 244), and calls for "deep work in moral and political philosophy" (399). Ethical and political theories, from utilitarianism to libertarianism, liberalism, and nationalist communitarianism (241), should not be "complacent, evasive, or opaque" in face of the ecological crisis. Theories deserve these condemning labels, for instance, when they stop at an "initial diagnosis" that merely says that "climate change is seriously unjust to the global poor, future generations, and nature" (244). To explain what more we must expect, Gardiner compares our theoretical and environmental predicament to feminist responses to the situation of women. The initial diagnosis of patriarchy as fundamentally unjust and inegalitarian occurred, on his telling, roughly one hundred years ago; only then did we gradually get from ethical and political theorizing a "deep analysis" of "precisely what is wrong with patriarchal systems, and how they shape our ways of looking at issues in problematic ways" (243).

For Gardiner, the question that we must ask in the face of dangerous climate change is not only—though that is needed, too—the calculative question of how much we owe to present and future people, a question that dominates the discussion around the global temperature ceiling we must aim to stay under and the distribution of remaining greenhouse gas emissions (see, e.g., Singer 2006, 418). Theory must also not only address ways of overcoming the inadequacy of global political institutions to agree on these questions and find an adequate enforcement mechanism. Rather, we must address the "more basic" problem of the *moral corruption* induced by the "perfect moral storm" in its global, intergenerational, ecological, and theoretical dimensions (Gardiner 2011a, 22, 301ff.). The theoretical storm means that currently available theories of justice are "inept" or "unsuited" for the task at hand (241). Thus, deep analysis is to reflect on how we are related to our contemporaries, in particular non-co-nationals and the global poor (to deal with the "global storm"), to nature (to address the "ecological storm"), and to other generations ("the intergenerational storm"). Gardiner thinks it is the intergenerational storm, what he calls the "tyranny of the contemporary" (143), that tends to be eclipsed the most by moral corruption. This is particularly unfortunate given the central importance of capturing the environmental crisis in terms of relations among generations (145ff.). Intergenerational ethics and politics offers a critical lever in the environmental crisis, not only because of the apparent stark injustices to future people, but also because, initially at least, concern for them promises to bring together, in ways likely unmatched by other facets of the environmental crisis, a broad cross-section of the global public, from environmental activists and ecologists to policy makers and economists as well as the wider community, whose outlook is often more anthropocentric and humanist.

The account of intergenerational justice offered in this book understands itself as contributing to deep analysis. I take this analysis to be ethical in seeking to capture the "wrong" of "intergenerational buck-passing" (148), but also ethical in a broader sense, aiming to get us, in Gardiner's words (243), to *look* at issues less problematically, especially at relations with future generations. Ethical and political theorizing in this broader sense, I will argue beyond Gardiner—and more in line with those who favor broader engagements with social ontology, dissatisfied with what Charles Taylor once called an "ontologically disinterested liberalism" (Taylor 1995, 186; on the "turn to ontology" in moral and political theory, see also White 2000; Calder 2008; Rosenthal 2016)—should reconsider above all what it is to be a human being who is born of a previous generation and leaves the world to future people. If we can above all debunk the presentist phantasm of self-standing individuals and generations—selves and communities that first exist, as if giving birth to themselves, and only then come to have relations with other generations—then we may hope that intergenerational ethics and politics will have roots in how we look at ourselves and our world alongside noncontemporaries. As some empirical research has demonstrated, understanding oneself as not only the present generation but also as the future generation of the past may combat moral corruption and facilitate an accepting openness to demands issued from the future as well as an imaginative anticipation of its needs (Wade-Benzoni 2002, 2009). This may (but need not necessarily) include the sense that one benefited from one's predecessors, a sense that, as social scientists have stressed, plays a significant role in people's pro-futural motivations. Studies show that participants who are asked to make an allocation decision for future generations are strongly influenced by information about how previous participants have behaved—generously or ungenerously—and by the source of the funds to be allocated (whether they were the result of generous gifting of previous participants or not). Summarizing this research, Wade-Benzoni writes that "[t]he data support the hypothesis . . . that the greater the amount of resources perceived as left by previous generations, the greater the amount that will be left to the future" (2002, 1021; see Wade-Benzoni 2009).

Gardiner's deep analysis should not be understood, in my view, to entail a broad endorsement of the claim that intergenerational justice is a radically new problem, calling for completely new solutions. This view is at times presented on the assumption that before industrial modernity, ethics was more or less restricted to face-to-face relations that simply do not extend well to future people (Singer 2002, 9, 19ff.). According to some anthropologists and evolutionary theorists, moralities emerge with kin and small in-groups to which reciprocal conduct is central, but which it would be difficult to extend to non-overlapping future people, especially at a global level (see, e.g., Jamieson 2002; Garvey 2008, 59; for an overview of the evolutionary account of morality in this respect, see Singer 1998).

To be sure, contemporary environmental degradation, as a "perfect moral storm" intersecting global and intergenerational issues, poses new and unique challenges. But short-term thinking and disregard for noncontemporary generations seems rather germane to industrial, capitalist modernity, with its claim to draw its ethical resources only from itself, rather than from inheritance (Blumenberg 1983; Habermas 1988). For instance, Gardiner's own formulation of the intergenerational side of the perfect storm self-consciously presupposes a utility-maximizing, self-regarding, present-centered subject who, as Janna Thompson has charged (Thompson 2013), is assumed to have no lifetime-transcending values (Thompson 2006, 2009). That is why a background theme of this book, beyond the old contrast between society (*Gesellschaft*) and community (*Gemeinschaft*), is formed by references to non-Western and indigenous accounts of selfhood and sociality. This is most explicit in Chapter 3 on socialization and economizing by way of gift practices, which I will develop into an account of asymmetrical reciprocities that contest presentist preconceptions of time, self, and sociality.

Displacing our self-understanding from presentist to generational being means overcoming the social-ontological assumptions of individualism in a specifically intergenerational way. In fact, many of the terms upon which we draw to define ourselves (language, nation, ethnicity, family, and so on) are transgenerational. Despite its ongoing significance, the modern ideal of autonomy should not lead us to overlook the fact that our individual identities merge into a birth cohort and generation, and that our lives are thereby stretched out into past and future. The group-individual binary obscures the interrelation between the singularization and generational collectivization of individuals: we are born as members of a generation whose unity is challenged by every death and every new birth. While this challenge results in the vexed problem of how to individuate a generation (given ongoing dying and birthing, where does a generation begin and end?), it is also an indication of the fact that our being extends into the intergenerational past and the future.

Thus, generational beings are members of groups, cultures, institutions, and environments that transcend the individual intragenerationally (the individual as member of a larger grouping, institution, and environment) and intergenerationally (at least some of these groups, institutions, and environments precede and exceed the lifetime of individuals). The ethical-political point of a nonpresentist self-understanding as generational beings is that we can be, and often are, interpellated, individually and collectively, as members of a generation, with responsibilities that apply uniquely at this level. As a professor at my university, I should worry about handing on the institution, in these days of the corporatization of public education, to the next generation of professors and their students. As a citizen at the age of maturity, I ought to reflect on the democratic heritage in view of passing on political institutions that work well for future citizens in their circumstances. As an earthling (and user of fossil fuels), I must be concerned about climate change, most of whose harms for humans and nonhumans will likely occur quite a while after my death.[1]

These brief examples indicate the path toward a solution to the problem of individuating a generation: as long as intergenerational sharing occurs by reference to an object (university governance structures, democratic institutions, the earth's climate), a crisis in that object may trigger interventionist responsibilities at a given point in time, the starting point for a new generation. As long as the climate is a stable background condition, the question of when the generations that share it begin and end is not a burning issue. Global warming, however, interpellates all those who are adults—however defined, and with varying degrees of knowledge and mitigating, adaptive, and compensatory capacities—as of, say, 1990, the year knowledge of anthropogenic climate change could no longer be seriously doubted as a result of the First Scientific Assessment Report of the Intergovernmental Panel on Climate Change.[2]

Climate change in particular has helped, in recent years, to move the topic of justice for future people (especially non-overlapping) from a marginal to a central problem for society and in the theoretical literature. Global warming has come to crystallize intergenerational and environmental concerns in a particularly urgent way. Former US president Obama put it in a striking way: "We are the first generation to feel the impact of climate change and the last to be able to do something about it" (UN Climate Summit, NYC, 23 September 2014[3]). While we have to guard against political posturing, these words capture the sense that "we"—ranging here from "we US citizens presently living" to "currently living human beings"—are singled out by a special responsibility in our historical situation. Given the data on climate change, and environmental degradation more broadly, we are "the first generation" to have the very real power of massively affecting even distant future generations by business as usual; in addition, we know about these effects, more or less conclusively. As the buzzword "Anthropocene" has it, humans are now considered by many scientists to constitute a geological force in their own right. Despite the increasing prevalence of short-termism and social acceleration (see Scheuerman 2004; Rosa 2010, 2012), today we are "interpellated . . . into unfathomably vast futures and deep pasts" (Bastian and van Dooren 2017, 1). The Anthropocene and its proliferating rivals (Capitalocene, Corporatocene, Chtulucene, etc.; Haraway 2016; Moore 2016) reinscribe recent history in deep time, and confront it with the long-term environmental effects that a much more numerous humanity has on the earth and its ecosystems, from nuclear waste and ocean plastics to greenhouse gases and mass extinctions.

These temporal and terrestrial interpellations, then, call on us to reconceive human power and sovereignty in relation to the geological and atmospheric forces on which we depend, and to rethink present time in the context of long-term intergenerational relations. If the extension of justice from the domestic to the global sphere called for a rethinking of space, then intergenerational issues demand a reconsideration, both social-ontological and normative, of the role of time in human life. Our sense of who we are—as individuals, as citizens, and as human beings—needs to reconnect not only with questions of justice beyond our immediate geographical horizon (environmental issues, after all, typically do not respect state borders), but with intergenerational time frames. While power and knowledge single us out for a special responsibility, we must, at the same time, think of our generation as only one among many generations in a long chain before and after us. This book will present three-party historical reciprocities and taking turns among generations as ways of helping us to achieve this reconceptualization of humans as generational-terrestrial beings, as well as of intergenerational relations themselves.

Other philosophers and theorists have responded to this need for reorientation in recent years. Ever since Hans Jonas's ground-breaking *The Imperative of Responsibility* (1979, English edition 1984), a number of excellent monographs and essay collections on intergenerational justice have appeared, and I have benefited from many of them (Birnbacher 1988; Laslett and Fishkin 1992; de-Shalit 1995; Dobson 1999; Gosseries 2004; Meyer 2005; Tremmel 2006, 2009; Meyer and Gosseries 2009; Gardiner 2011a; Thompson 2013; Gonzalez-Ricoy and Gosseries 2016). Not many of these, however, could be said to offer the kind of deep analysis for which Gardiner calls, an analysis that I just interpreted, and will continue to elaborate, in terms of the social-ontological reconsideration of human subjectivity and sociality. On my account, the time of birth and death is co-constitutive of human agents in their interrelations with each other. As indicated, we are normative beings—vulnerable and agential bodies that are liable to moral criticisms—to the extent we are nonpresentist, generational beings. Understood as natality and mortality, birth and death not only characterize our temporal mode of existence throughout our lives, but they also link us to other generations before and after us.

In making this point, I draw more and more throughout this book on philosophical phenomenology and deconstruction. Given its central emphasis on temporality in the constitution of a human world and in relation to the origin of moral and political normativity—from Husserl's time-consciousness to Heidegger's being-toward-death, from Arendt's natality to Beauvoir's reflections on aging, from Levinas's fecundity to Derrida's objections to the "metaphysics of presence" in favor of the spectral presence of the dead and the unborn—the phenomenological tradition, broadly construed, may be expected to offer central insights into issues in intergenerational justice. Indeed, the work of the two latter thinkers in particular will contribute to the approach I submit here.

Where appropriate, I respond to the existing literature on intergenerational justice, but often on the basis of different philosophical sources and assumptions. A major difference from much existing work on this issue is that I argue that generational time and intergenerational justice should not be viewed as more or less indifferent to one another. Rather, questions of justice ought to be understood as emerging with the time of birth and death, a social time that separates but also links generations. Normative-theoretical proposals regarding the content of intergenerational obligations are proposed here, but only as developed on this social-ontological basis. My hypothesis is that justice should be thought in such a way as to take the temporal connectedness of human lives across birth and death centrally into account. Moral and political obligations include not only a moment of living co-presence, but also point beyond contemporary life to a time both before and after the present. If we properly conceptualize this Janus-faced, dual reference in the present, obligations to those who are not yet born may come to be seen, precisely by foregrounding temporality, as the very hallmark of moral conduct.

On the basis of natal mortality, then, the major objective of this book is to render moral and political relations with overlapping and non-overlapping future people less anomalous than we often take them to be, and to present two overarching models that may help us to think about the shape and the normativity of these relations. The book will make three overall claims: (1) French and German phenomenology, and its elaboration in deconstruction, help us to situate obligations to the future by thinking the emergence of moral relations in connection with human temporality, what I call the time of birth and death. On this basis, the book will elaborate two related models for intergenerational justice, namely, (2) a form of indirect reciprocity (I call it asymmetrical reciprocity) in which we, the presently living, owe future people *both* because of their needs or interests *and* because we received from the past, and (3) the notion of generational turn-taking applied to institutions as well as the natural environment, or what I call the earth. Precisely because the present time of the living is necessarily related to the past as well as to the future, social cooperation and democratic life are best theorized as including from the beginning forms of reciprocity and taking turns among generations with collectively shared "objects." In conclusion, I will argue that the terrestrial biosphere as a key dimension of this kind of sharing (we share the earth with future generations, even very distant future people) is not a passive object of intergenerational sharing, but for its part turns about generations.

Let me now present an overview of the five chapters. Chapter 1 discusses the so-called ontological problems justice for future people is said to face. Given the increasing attention paid to intergenerational justice, I detect a nascent debate as to whether currently widespread moral intuitions and dominant theories of justice suffice to address ongoing environmental damages, especially those affecting the far future. While some argue that extant theories can be tweaked to cover non-overlapping future people, others deny this and call for more radical conceptual changes. Though perhaps not yet to the extent it should, this debate has foregrounded these ontological problems once more, problems that are often seen to render anomalous justice for (at least non-overlapping) future people. In response, I argue that ontological problems call for ontological reconsiderations.

The chapter begins by reviewing and reclassifying the special problems affecting moral relations with future people, from the nonexistence challenge and poor epistemic access to problems affecting interaction and world constitution. I then argue that these challenges call for express investigations of the being of moral agents in relation to time and world, addressing such questions as the role time and generations play in social and normative relations. Most methodologies in this area, however, extend existing (usually presentist) theories of justice, abstract from generational overlap or historical time, or treat intergenerational relations as a special case, divorced from intragenerational justice. Even when there is an explicit recognition of the need for revising current conceptions of morality, the ontological problems thus tend to be exacerbated, avoided, downplayed, or treated in a piecemeal fashion. A guiding assumption remains that a core or nonextensionist theory of justice would not (yet) have to treat generational relations.

Drawing on those strands of the phenomenological literature that take embodiment, interpersonal dependency, and time seriously, I provide a first sketch of the claim that justice becomes an issue for human beings to the extent we are generational beings who are noncontingently subject to birth and death. Birth and death, the argumentative sketch continues, link us to previous and subsequent generations in ways that are socially and morally relevant. If moral normativity arises with generational time, then justice for future people should be seen neither as a special case nor as a problem of extension. Intergenerational justice is thus implicated in intragenerational justice from the beginning, and if we nonetheless single out generational relations in view of responsibility and justice, this theoretical elaboration should address the co-implication of past and future in the present.

Given the centrality of the human time of birth and death to the argument sketched out, in very general form, toward the end of the first chapter, Chapter 2 explores the constitutive role of natality and mortality in much greater detail, with particular focus on the work of Levinas in the wake of German phenomenology. As Heidegger famously argued in *Being and Time*, to be an agent means to grasp one's present time not as "is" but as "to be," suffused with (inherited) potential to be actualized (in the future). The realization of possibilities demands understanding my life as mortal, for otherwise no choice would really rule out another. Further, meaningful autonomous choices depend on individuation and thus confrontation with one's mortal temporalizing, one's "being-toward-death" that no one can take over for the agent.

Levinas agrees but argues in response that death is not accessible "as such"; rather, confronting mortality, even one's own, cannot bypass other people, who are rendered vulnerable by their mortality. Thus, in accessing the death that is co-disclosive of my world of action and comprehension, I necessarily encounter mortal, vulnerable others. On the faces of these others, mortality issues the imperative to let the other live, such that ethical normativity in general begins with the birth of a mortal. On this view, "my" subjectivity is co-constituted by a futural demand to let others have possibilities for life beyond my death. "Being-for-beyond-my-death," "fecundity," "paternity," and "maternity" are some of the terms Levinas uses to characterize the being of subjectivity and the time of interpersonal relations. As I will seek to show, the demand from actual future people on the living is thus not anomalous but exemplary of moral normativity. The demand is called "infinite" not only because the presently living cannot fully acquit themselves of a demand that is co-constitutive of their subjectivity, but because, in taking asymmetrical responsibility for overlapping future generations, the demand transitively extends to children's children, their children, and so on. To take responsibility for those who are to outlive me in the present is thus to equip even more distant future people to address their future-related obligations.

In the interest of further fleshing out these temporal and generational insights toward a theory of justice, as well as to do justice to the feminist critiques of Levinasian "paternity" (from Irigaray to Cavarero), I connect Levinas with both Arendtian and more recent feminist accounts of natality. As understood here, natality means that a human being is not one with its birth or its natural kind, for as creative, free beings that give rise to something new against the background of inherited circumstances, we are not born once and for all but remain in the process of being born. Each time we act to give birth to something new, we draw on the fact that we are not born into a fixed causal chain. For this reason, free agency must be thought as discontinuously linked to one's birth, and thus to one's ongoing (though not fully transparent) relation to previous generations. I thus connect Levinas's "being-for-beyond-my-life" to, in the words of Lisa Guenther, "being-from-others" (Guenther 2008). The futural demand cannot be separated from a debt owed to the past, even if this past cannot be fully represented nor the debt fully tabulated in an economy of intergenerational giving. I conclude the chapter by connecting the feminist critique of Levinas to Derrida's argument that the mortal alterity of the other tends to be misrepresented by Levinas as being beyond empirical history. As a result, if the call to justice stems from historically concrete others, then it cannot just be futural but must also be related to gifts from predecessors.

Taking off from the insights presented at the end of Chapter 2, Chapter 3 presents this book's first model of intergenerational justice. Putting to work the understanding of human time and agency developed in the first two chapters toward answering questions specifically related to intergenerational justice, I introduce a notion of reciprocity that is meant to capture the role that indebtedness to preceding others plays in giving to future others, no matter how asymmetrical and altruistic the gift is taken to be. Human agency requires care and other benefits from predecessors, and dependence on such gifting matters morally in an intergenerational context. Further, some of these gifts (such as language, tradition, institutions, the environment) cannot but be passed on (in a better or worse state, to be sure) to the next generation. Reciprocity among generations foregrounds, in its ontological as well its normative aspects, this linking of the present generation to previous and future generations.

With this goal in view, the chapter connects Derrida's critical reading of Levinas to economic literature on intergenerational transfers, specifically economists who draw on the premodern, indigenous notion of the gift as famously elaborated by Marcel Mauss. Mauss's work thus provides a bridge between Derrida's account of historical time and economists' work on indirect reciprocity. The overall goal is to suggest that the notion of indirect reciprocity—A gives to B who "returns" the gift to C (so, for example, from past to future via the present)—should be elaborated into what I call asymmetrical reciprocity. By asymmetry I intend to denote two further aspects of intergenerational relations: First, if A's gift is co-constitutive of B, then B cannot fully cut loose from the gift by repaying the debt. For this reason, the gift remains inappropriable, excessive, and asymmetrical for B, whose relation to the gift is thus agonistic. Second, the excess remains outstanding and obliges B from a future B will never attain. Speaking of asymmetry in intergenerational reciprocity is meant to capture this ultimate impossibility of clearly assigning the source of intergenerational obligation to either the past or the future. Asymmetrical reciprocity, I will conclude, is thus not as vulnerable as indirect reciprocity to the objection that it cannot account for direct obligations to future people. In this way, Derrida's understanding of the gift as both part of (intergenerational) chains, as well as futurally excessive to them, can both bolster and transform the extant philosophical and economic accounts of intergenerational justice.

In the concluding sections of this chapter, I refine the analysis of asymmetrical reciprocity by responding to potential objections. With the help of the economic literature, I distinguish (as ideal types) four types of reciprocity and related temporalities of intergenerational giving. I relate the account to the empirical findings on "mixed motivations" (neither pure altruism nor pure tit-for-tat can satisfactorily explain intergenerational transfers), and suggest reasons for thinking that indirect reciprocity is not an aberration of direct reciprocity but in fact its condition. Last but not least, I address the charge that asymmetrical reciprocity blurs the distinction between gift and exchange, and thus between the private sphere (in which altruistic gifts would have their dominant place) and the economic market. I argue that the notion of the gift points to the enabling conditions of economic activity, narrowly understood as self-interested exchange. Both gifts of "nature" and from nonpresent generations belong to these conditions, conditions that are too often externalized by market economies.

With this topic of collectively shared goods in mind, Chapter 4 presents turn-taking as the second model of intergenerational justice that elaborates the social-ontological and normative co-implication of past and future in the present. Taking turns is, I argue, more appropriate than asymmetrical reciprocity in cases where the "object" of intergenerational sharing is holistic or quasi-holistic (earth, language, tradition, institutions, and so on). Holistic objects render problematic the substitutability assumption that governs economic discourses of intergenerational sharing and sustainability: for example, substituting improved infrastructure for loss of forests or less disaster-prone climates. That is because their integral structure prohibits or significantly complicates a common assumption in distributive justice, according to which we share objects by dividing them like a cake. In these cases, turn-taking recommends itself as a model of just sharing, especially when the sharers "use" the object at different times. As I will further argue, on account of this holistic and thus preceding nature of the "object" of sharing, taking turns enjoys a certain precedence over intergenerational reciprocity.

The reason why taking turns does justice to the co-implication of nonpresent times in the present and the concomitant entanglements of generations is that, as Derrida argues in *Rogues*, it allows the relative independence of the present without thereby cutting it off from past and future, as linear models of time tend to do. Each time is unique and irreplaceable, but its uniqueness has to be reconciled with the fact that the now, each time, consists only in coming to be from other times and passing away into yet other times. Taking turns, I argue, offers a way of thinking together this relation between irreplaceability and replacement, singularity and multiplicity, or self-assertion in the midst of relations to others and other times. What is irreplaceable each time is its turn, but such a turn consists only in a granting of presence by past and future.

If time does not coincide with itself from the beginning—the present shares its time with the nonpresent past and future—and so consists in taking turns, then this must also be seen to apply to identity, for instance, that of a living organism, an institution, or a collective self such as a democratic nation or a generation. Life forms, singular or collective, exist in the mode of taking turns, with themselves (a past self giving place to a present self giving place to a future self), but also with others, including other generations. In this way, I argue, generations are connected across birth and death by taking turns with the earth and with institutions, especially with democratic ones.

Reflecting on the role of turn-taking for democracies as well as for the environment, I conclude the chapter by highlighting what I see as distinct advantages of taking turns as a model of the intergenerational sharing of quasi-holistic objects. As Allen Habib has argued (2013), unlike sharing by parts or by division, sharing by turns does not require mereological accounting and so no quantitative metric to compare the value of parts to one another. As indicated above, this makes it especially suited to sharing things that cannot be shared by division; turn-taking promises to better respect the holistic nature of certain objects.

Further, turn-taking does not require us to decide whether nature, or the earth, has value in itself to ground duties to—or at least with respect to—the earth itself. Turn-taking disallows welfare trade-offs because it entails duties not only to future turn-takers but to the "thing" with which a turn is to be taken. Turn-taking thereby changes the question of the content of justice: the primary question is no longer, What kinds of things, and how many of them, do we owe future people? but, What is it to take a fair turn with these holistic objects with future people? I conclude the chapter by discussing possible answers to this question.

Quasi-holistic objects like earth and climate, however, *necessarily* precede and outlive generations, and for that reason they are not indifferent to, but co-constitutive of, the very being of generations, the subjects of sharing by taking turns. Failing to capture this co-constitutive role is a problem I see in most models of stewardship, trusteeship, or even Michel Serres's recent renter model (in which nature is conceived as being on rent to its current human users; Serres 2012, 49). We should not think that humans take turns with humans in owning the earth; the very fact that generations do not come on and off-stage *en bloc* precisely means we have to think something larger, an enveloping (preceding and excessive, us-outliving) sphere that is not just an indifferent object but is in fact involved in the very being of the turn-takers. I will suggest that "earth" is one good name for this, as "nature" was in the discussion of Mauss.

To disrupt the humanism that takes the earth to be an indifferent object of intergenerational sharing, then, the final chapter complicates taking turns so as to take into account that the earth also turns human beings about. Individual humans come to be from, and pass away into, the earth, understood as the history and habitat of life. We do not only have generations taking turns with the earth, but individuals being born of earth into a human generation, while returning to earth upon death. Human beings are both "interred" (agonistically belonging to a larger time and space here called earth) and "interring" (responsible for returning others to earth, as in burial). As I argue by way of a reading of Derrida's *The Beast and the Sovereign*, in this second turning (terrestrial rather than intergenerational), earth names the unmasterable, nonpossessable, inappropriable aspect of a preceding and exceeding world from which and toward which human individuals and generations turn, in breathing and eating as well as in birthing and dying. The terrestrial inappropriable—the CO_2 we breathe out, vomit and excrement, our bodies as corpses that we must leave for the next generation as well as hand over to the earth—signals our mortal-natal belonging to a double turning, generational and terrestrial.

In this sense, the terrestrial turning shakes up the linearity and the continuity of the generational turning. The earth's turning sustains, but also crosses and interrupts, the attempts of human sovereigns to remain sovereign despite the passing away of individuals. While there are philosophical and strategic reasons for keeping the two turnings—generational and terrestrial—separate, we should remember their co-implication.

Overall, then, this book presents life as always already intergenerational and in-earthed, interred and interring. Birth and death belong to life so intrinsically that moral, social, and political relations cannot be assumed to take place among the living alone, for the dependencies, asymmetries, and unknowns generated by natality and mortality crucially affect all social relations. The dead and the unborn, as well as the earth, are co-implicated in the presence of the presently living. Asymmetrical reciprocity and double turn-taking express this spectral presence and Janus-faced constitution of terrestrial life; both models of justice rethink human sovereignty in light of earthly relatedness and intergenerational survivance.

1

Ontological Problems and Methods in Intergenerational Justice

In response to the global ecological crisis, intergenerational and climate ethicists debate whether existing moral-political intuitions and theories suffice to address ongoing environmental damages, especially those affecting the far future (Gardiner 2011b; Jamieson 2014; Myers 2015; Kingston 2014). *Grosso modo*, "extensionists" argue that extant theories can be tweaked to cover non-overlapping future people, while "revisionists" deny this and call for more radical conceptual changes (for example, with respect to "collectivizing" responsibility and tying it to the probability of long-term outcomes, rather than just to causal connections). Others argue that due to the "internal logical problems" of existing moral theories when applied to future people and, specifically, climate change, we should not wait for better theories but rather argue for action on climate change in view of common interest (Weisbach, in Gardiner and Weisbach 2016, 257). Thus, this debate foregrounds the "logical" or "ontological problems" that beset many extant theories of intergenerational justice. This first chapter argues that these problems suggest a social-ontological as well as normative response that explores the relation between questions of justice and the human time of birth and death.

I begin by offering a reclassifying overview of the special problems affecting moral relations with future people, including the nonexistence challenge, poor epistemic access, and problems affecting interaction and world constitution. I then argue that, to the extent these problems are indeed social-ontological, they call for express investigations of the ontology of moral agents in relation to time and world—investigations that I think have not yet been carried out in the literature to the extent they are needed. Instead of investigating the role time and generations play in social and normative relations, most methodologies in this area extend existing theories of justice, abstract from generational overlap or from historical time, or treat intergenerational relations as a special case. Even when there is an explicit recognition of the need for "revising morality" (Jamieson 2014, 169ff.), the ontological problems thus tend to be exacerbated, avoided, downplayed, or treated in a piecemeal fashion; a guiding assumption remains that a core or nonextensionist theory of justice would not, or not yet, have to treat generational relations.

With the help of phenomenological and feminist literature, I argue by contrast that justice becomes an issue for human beings to the extent we are generational beings. We are beings who are noncontingently subject to birth and death, and are linked through birth and death to previous and subsequent generations in social and moral ways. Thus, if justice, or moral normativity in general, arises with generational time, then justice for future people should be seen neither as a special case nor as a problem of extension. Intergenerational justice is thus implicated in intragenerational justice from the beginning, and its theoretical elaboration should address the nonlinear co-implication of past and future in the present. Further, generational time situates individuals in a historical lifeworld that is not merely contingent but ontologically constitutive of individuals and their relations. Because of this, lifeworlds, in their ecological and terrestrial embeddedness, should be understood as claiming individuals for their maintenance from the beginning, such that we understand world constitution as necessarily involved in ethics.

With this in mind, the question of justice for future people triggers two equally understandable reactions, both of which should be seen as foregrounding the relation between time and ethics. The first is to abstract from time as many do from space, as we would prefer (more or less) timeless criteria for what is just, and time should be seen as morally irrelevant. The second is to take our historical situatedness seriously, for it is through history and time that we become moral beings and are actually connected to future people. Here I will favor the second approach. For time both relates us (the living) to, and separates us from, future people. That is because between "us" and "them," as the term "the unborn" indicates in part, lies the time of birth and death; we will die and they will be born, but born of us only if we also overlap with some of them so they can give birth to yet others after our death. We may then say that, in a time when theory has undone the primary focus on domestic justice so as to take note of global interconnectedness, it is now time to undo an unreflected priority granted to the living. Reflection on that priority should lead us to conceive of the living as born, giving birth (biologically and nonbiologically), and dying—and thus as intimately connected to the dead and the unborn.

I. Defining "Generation"

As we can perhaps already intimate here, the definition of "generation" we adopt is often crucial in construing sociality: it is a substantive definition. If, for example, we take a generation to only include all those presently living, as opposed to the dead and the unborn, then it may seem a generation is cut off, as if by an abyss, from other generations. On this purely temporal conception (definition 1), there would be only a single generation living at a given time (though of course geographically and politically it may be further divided). The abyss separating different generations—death in the case of previous generations and birth with respect to future people—could seem to divide generations in profound, perhaps even unbridgeable, ways. And on this basis it is only one more step to a conception of generational relations that are marked by the absence of overlap. As we will see, many theories of intergenerational justice (IGJ) interested in modeling the issue in a pure way take this idea of generations coming on the historical stage *en bloc* to be a legitimate assumption for theoretical purposes. By contrast, if we take generations in the familial sense (definition 2) of grandparents, parents, and children, then overlap of generations, their sharing of the time of the living, is crucial. Generational relations in this sense foreground birth, care during infancy and old age, passing away, bequests, and so on. But as some become parents and others do not, and each does so at different times, this familial and familiar sense makes it hard to see how a generation becomes unified beyond the immediate family.

For this reason, a third definition (definition 3) idealizes the second, familial one, and so gives a particular interpretation to what in macroeconomics is known as the "overlapping generations (OLG)" model (Blanchard and Fischer 1989; Barro and Sala-i-Martin 2004[4]). "Generation" then refers to the totality of all those born in a certain time period whose length is determined by the average time it takes for children to become parents and parents to become grandparents (see Birnbacher 1988, 23–24). This length may be twenty to thirty-five years; Wilhelm Dilthey, the great philosopher of life and history, took it to be thirty, and, for the sake of simplification, so will I in what follows (Dilthey 1990, 37). On this definition, "future people" refers to both nonoverlapping individuals (the "unborn" at that time) and overlapping generations (e.g., from the perspective of an age group roughly sixty years of age and up, children and grandchildren—whether or not individuals in that group have children themselves).

For reasons that will emerge gradually in the course of this chapter and the book as a whole, I largely favor this third definition. Overlap stresses some commonalities and reciprocities, but also asymmetries and the significant (and partly enigmatic) facts of birth and death; in addition I think it important to stress that a generation's responsibilities to the more distant future are mediated, in some cases more than in others, by overlapping generations. As laid out in subsequent chapters, highlighting overlap promotes a conception of generational connections as "chains of concern" that I think are socio-ontologically more adequate and normatively more contentful. However, I think it is also important to stress the difference between the living and the nonliving (as the first definition does). In some circumstances, it may also make sense to see all those living, at least at a certain age of maturity, as collectively responsible to the unborn, but I think the third definition can account for this in a more layered way (e.g., G_1, G_2, and G_3 at p_3 are responsible to G_{4+n}, but in such a way that G_4 cannot be bypassed in relating to G_5, thus differentiating the vast and abstract category "the unborn").

It is further imperative to pay attention to the idealizations and abstractions involved not only in the first definition but also in the third

Ontological Problems and Methods in Intergenerational Justice 21

Gen.	period 1	p2	p3	p4	p5	p6	...
...							
G1	———	———	———				
G2		———	———	———			
G3			———	———	———		
G4				———	———	———	
...				...	...	...	

FIGURE 1.1. Illustration of idealized familial generations and their overlap. If each generation is taken to live for three time periods (3 x 30 years), there would be three overlapping generations at any one time. The stipulation of a first period and a first generation is of course not necessary, and indeed, problematic.

definition, for instance, as concerns the starting point of a generation. For of course, at any one time there are individuals who die and new ones who are born. Because of this, decisions about when a "generation" is said to begin, and what justifies thinking it as a unified collective, are contestable and important issues at play in determining, for instance, who is responsible for whom. Overall, my argument—that we are generational beings and the intergenerational relations and the time of birth and death co-constitute who we are—has as a consequence that the division of questions of justice into intra- and intergenerational ones cannot be settled by definition alone, but is itself an eminently moral and political issue that must remain open to contextual specification and political contestation.

As for the question of when a generation begins, a fourth definition of generation (definition 4) in terms of shared cultural experiences and a fifth definition (definition 5) in reference to historical markers, such as large-scale crises, may come into play to determine such starting points. These two senses overlap and intermingle. In the Western world we speak of, for example, the "Lost Generation" (Gertrude Stein and Ernest Hemingway's designation of those who fought in World War I, typically born between 1880 and 1900); the "Baby Boomers" (those born following World War II, roughly from 1946 to 1964, a time that was marked by an increase in birth rates); "Generation X" (born after the baby boomers, so some time from the mid-1960s to the late 1970s / early 1980s); the "Millennials" (also called "Generation Y," as it follows Generation X, with birth years ranging from the early 1980s to the mid-1990s / early 2000s). Notice, however, that the starting points given by these historical markers (World War I or II, etc.) are still not ideal enough to render definition 3 sufficiently rigorous, and also that the typical length of a cultural generation does not correspond to the length demanded by definition 3 (which defines that length with respect to average turnover from children to parents, which would only by coincidence overlap with the temporal distance marked by significant historical events).

While definitions 4 and 5 do overlap, it is also useful to separate them. Definition 4 stresses that generations share a culture, a world that was bequeathed to them by their previous generations. In this sense, Dilthey speaks of "those who experience the same leading influences at the time of their lives when they are most receptive together" (Dilthey 1990, 37). Anne O'Byrne comments: "[A] generation comes to be in the process by which it inherits a world" (O'Byrne 2010, 63). In this sense, a generation comprises those who, as a birth cohort, share a childhood, adolescence, and young adulthood during which formative years they are subject to similar schooling, culture, and historical experiences. The cohort then comes to assume leading roles in society, in economic, social, political, and intellectual contexts and institutions, at about the same time, in turn shaping society in formative ways for the next generation.

This fourth sense of generation is then not just "cultural" but also includes biological elements (a birth cohort that then gives birth to a new, the next, generation) and social-political life (taking over leading roles in society). If I stress the cultural aspect, it is because, in view of what is to come in this and subsequent chapters, it is helpful to understand relations between generations in terms of a third element in which they take place: a culture, an inheritance, a world or lifeworld, a language, institutions, material infrastructure, nature or earth, and so on. This "world" precedes the generations and their relations, even if it does not exist independently of them and their ongoing processes of transmission, which are also forms of renewal and recontextualization. In passing on an inheritance, there is a subterranean dimension that does not come to full awareness, and in this sense resists calculative tabulations: inheritance exceeds the generations it brings into relation.

I have stressed that extant designations for actually existing generations do not coincide with the time periods demanded by the third, idealized definition. Nonetheless, I believe that some historical markers—those connected to generational responsibilities—should play a significant role in defining a generation for the purposes of a theory of intergenerational justice. The primary reason is that we want to know who (which group) has what kind of responsibilities toward which future grouping, and while some responsibilities may be said to be incumbent upon every generation (infant and old age care, education, passing on of a heritage and material transfers, maintenance and upgrading of infrastructure and political institutions, etc.), others are related to specific "historical" tasks, such as combating the threat of fascism in World War II. Much of the current concern over future people has to do, at least in the first instance, not with widespread worries with respect to the general responsibilities all generations would have—though here too one may worry that fast-paced times lead to failures (see Stiegler 2010)—but with specific crises, such as global poverty, national (and intergenerational) debt, and the environmental crisis, which is sure to have very long impacts affecting many future generations. We would then introduce definition 5, according to which a generation is unified by a crisis that encumbers it with a crisis-related task (see Dilthey 1990).

If, for example, we agree that the connection between greenhouse gas emissions and increasingly worrisome levels of global warming became generally known in responsibility-generating ways around 1990 (see Singer 2002, 34; see also Page 2007; Caney 2010a), then all those old enough to address climate change responsibly (e.g., those who were of voting age at that time) belong to a generation that has intergenerational climate-related obligations. On the third definition, the addressee of these obligations comprises more than one generation, but among these there would also be meaningful distinctions. For example, if thirty years is the average time period demanded by definition 3, then those who are sixty and older (G1 at p3 in the table above, with p3 beginning around 1990) have intergenerational responsibilities to G2 and G3 as well as to subsequent generations, but part of their responsibilities to G4 and up (the "unborn" at that time, with whom G1 will not overlap) are mediated by G2 and G3. While one may thus plausibly argue that G1, G2, and G3 should reduce their emissions, prepare for adaptation, and pay compensation (especially to those more strongly affected but generally less causally responsible—largely, those in the Global South; see Gardiner 2013), I would argue that G1 should also seek to address its responsibility to G4+ (whom they may causally affect in significant ways despite the absence of overlap) by putting G2 and G3 in a better position to act responsibly toward G4+ (with whom G2 and G3 will partially overlap). These commonalities and distinctions should be captured by one's definition of a generation. Definition 3, supplemented in the ways I have indicated, seems to do this best.

However, before I argue for such a differentiated chain-of-concern model and its attendant conceptions of intergenerational reciprocities and taking turns (in Chapters 3–5), I would like to take the prior but related step of arguing for the importance of generational overlap and for taking seriously the relation between sociality and what I will call "natal mortality": the human condition that includes birth and death as crucial dimensions. Indeed, overlap is inseparable from natal mortality, and focusing on this connection foregrounds, as we will see in this chapter and the next, the relation between justice and time, what I call the "time of birth and death." I will seek to do this by reviewing the special and ontological problems that have been identified in the extant literature on IGJ.

II. Special and "Ontological Problems"

In this section, I will review the growing literature on IGJ with respect to the reasons why relations with future people are taken to present general difficulties, in particular so-called ontological problems (Becker 1986, 232). It will be good to keep in mind that not all existing intuitions or IGJ theories are affected by each one of these problems. In addition, I do not suggest that these problems could not be solved by the theories discussed if suitably amended, though I do believe that some of these problems tend to be quite profound and that solutions are not easily had. Nor do I suggest that my approach, as briefly outlined in this chapter and elaborated in those to follow, satisfactorily addresses *all* of the challenges. Rather, here I merely wish to motivate an "ontological" approach to "ontological problems," even if this approach, while reorienting our thinking about many of these issues in general ways (see section VI, below), will not offer solutions to all the problems, taken individually. If I then still include problems in the overview (in section II) that I will not solve or even come back to, it is because I believe that the specific motivation for the ontological approach stems precisely from the extent of the problems in their entirety (as well as from broader considerations, as indicated in the Introduction). Further, isolating a particular problem may recommend a non-ontological, normative solution, but at the cost of avoiding other problems or engendering new ones (some examples will be discussed below).

As indicated, then, my claim is not that these problems, to the extent they can be elaborated as counterarguments to intergenerational obligations, are irrefutable, let alone that each on its own would defeat obligations to future people. On the basis of consulting a wide variety of the extant literature, my intention is first of all to provide an overview, so as to get a better understanding as to why one may think such obligations are nonexistent or a very special case, or demand extensions of (or even extensive revisions to) existing moral concepts and intuitions.[5] My further, and more substantive, goal is to point, through this overview, to the way in which ontological considerations are called for by these ontological problems. The upshot of this is, I suggest, that a theory of justice—especially of justice between generations—should be both normatively and ontologically appropriate.

For the sake of clarity, I have divided the problems, or countervailing arguments, into four large categories: (1) the nonexistence challenge; (2) epistemic problems having to do with lack or poverty of knowledge about the future; (3) interaction problems; and (4) issues arising from world-constitution.

1. The nonexistence challenge: Since future people do not exist (or not yet), they cannot be treated as moral claimants—at least not in the usual way. As Becker put it succinctly, "Nonexistent 'people' do not have either rights or interests, and cannot make agreements" (Becker 1986, 229).

1.1. With respect to rights in general—and despite the existence of the 1994 UNESCO Declaration of the Human Rights of Future Generations—a recent commentator put it this way: "The fact that future individuals do not yet exist seems to entail that they could not have rights; rights need to be ascribed to someone (as opposed to 'floating in the air')"

(Gosseries 2010, 108).⁶ Subjective rights presuppose individual subjects, not a nebulous mass of potential existences. In this sense, Beckerman and Pasek argue that "whatever rights future generations may have in the future, they have none now" (Beckerman and Pasek 2001, 18). Steiner claims that coexistence at the same time of rights-bearer and duty-bearer would be required (Steiner 1983, 154–156, 259–261).

1.2 This affects, for example, the so-called choice theory (or will theory) of rights, according to which rights-holders must in principle be able to activate and defend their rights, to seek or waive enforcement (Pogge 1995; Feinberg 1970; Steiner and Vallentyne 2009, Steiner 1983). To speak of subjective rights is to imply a choice on the part of the rights-holder when to activate it. If the putative holder—the standard example concerns animals—is not able to make this choice, the right cannot be said to apply to her or him. As Jonas puts it in his groundbreaking *The Imperative of Responsibility* (1979): "[O]nly that *has* a claim that *makes* a claim—for which it must first of all exist" (Jonas 1984, 38).

1.3 The interest theory of rights, however, would also be affected by the nonexistence challenge. The interest theory, the alternative to the choice theory, holds that rights protect supremely significant interests and so need not require choices with respect to enforcement by their bearer. Nonetheless, interests may not be assumed to be abstract, ahistorical, or timeless entities. As Gosseries puts it, "Holding a right presupposes the existence of an underlying interest. Having an interest presupposes that its holder can be harmed. Arguably, only people who exist today can be harmed today. Therefore, future people cannot be said to have an interest today, and even less so a right" (Gosseries 2010, 112).

1.4 Many ethical theories, especially contractual and procedural ones, make morally acceptable treatment dependent on the consent of the affected. Such consent cannot be obtained from overlapping minors or non-overlapping adults living in the future. Jonas once more: "The statesman, in making his fateful decision, can ideally assume the consent of those for whom, as their agent, he is making it. No consent to their nonexistence or dehumanization is obtainable from the humanity of the future, nor can it be assumed" (Jonas 1984, 37). Many discursive or deliberative forms of ethics, which seek to spell out the conditions under which consent could be obtained in a morally and politically acceptable manner, face this problem with respect to any moral norm (not just nonexistence or dehumanization), for they make its obligatoriness depend on agreement. While discourse ethics and deliberative democracy are for this reason often accused of a presentist bias that favors the currently living (Markovits 2009; Unnerstall 2009), others argue that the frequently cited "all affected principle"—according to which only those norms are just to which all affected can rationally consent (see, e.g., Habermas 1998, 42)—may be profitably extended to cover future people (Dobson 1996; Shrader-Frechette 2002; Goodin 2003; Eckersley 2004; Johnson 2007; Heyward 2008). But this strategy is unattractive as a sole remedy because it means we will have to render agreement hypothetical (based on some sense of what all rational agents would consent to) and discursive participation virtual.[7] While stipulating a baseline to which all affected would consent could be acceptable in general (though not without its own problems), it would lose the active participation that is distinctive of discursive ethics and deliberative politics.

1.5 The nonexistence challenge may also be said to be behind the argument from political legitimacy. The argument claims that political legitimacy derives from those presently living—those who participated in elections, for example—so that it would be illegitimate for current democratic governments to constrain the interests of its electorate in favor of the interests of future generations (P. Wood 2008).

2. Now we move to problems that don't focus on nonexistence but on lack of knowledge about future people, or about the agents allegedly affecting them.

2.1 The incommensurability argument suggests that the notion of justice itself may undergo possibly radical change, so that our current concept is not applicable to future people (Ball 1985). The lack of knowledge here would pertain to the notion of justice that future people entertain.

2.2 The unknown and indefinite number of future people can be a challenge for accounts of justice and their application in the intergenerational situation. This indefiniteness, on some accounts even amounting to infinity, poses great challenges for all aggregative theories of distributive justice. Such theories typically focus on a given resource (a cake is an often-used example) and then seek to determine how to divide it fairly or equally according to some feature (equality, merit, and so on). Such division, however, is difficult to determine if one variable is missing, namely, the number of parties among whom the cake is to be divided (Lenman 2000).

2.3 For an agent to be blameworthy for an action, she must have a reasonably certain understanding of its effects upon possible victims. The uncertainty argument, however, claims that we do not know enough about the effects of our actions on future generations, in particular, distant ones (Garvey 2008, 90ff.; Routley and Routley 1979).

2.4 Lack of knowledge may pertain to effects but also to interests or needs. The argument from the unidentifiability of interests generally states that we do not know enough about the interests or the needs of future people, which may be radically altered by unforeseen circumstances or as yet unknown technologies (Garvey 2008, 90ff.; Routley and Routley 1979). For example, it has been argued that there can be no individual (at most, collective or generational) rights where they are not backed by identifiable interests (Weiss 1989). Notice that this time it is the interest theory of rights that is affected, not the choice theory of rights. According to the former, rights express (objectively identifiable) interests of individuals.

2.5 More than interests of individuals, it may be difficult to identify the agents (and the victims) of those interests. Many impacts across generations are such that they occur, at least above a determinable threshold, only if several individuals act in a certain way, often over long periods of time. Climate impacts are of this sort: an individual's emissions don't trigger the harmful impacts on their own. In such cases not only is the causal link hard to identify (see 2.6 below), but the acting and suffering individuals are as well. Hence, we have an argument from temporal complexity, according to which duties to the future are hampered by the fact that causal responsibility both for harm and for the effects of present actions stretch across generations in such a way that the agents bearing the duties are difficult to identify (Garvey 2008, 59ff.).

Jamieson attributes this problem to our reliance on "commonsense morality," which focuses on a few central concepts, such as fault, reciprocity, and harm. He defines a "paradigm of an act that is morally suspect" as follows: "An individual acting intentionally harms another individual; both the individual and the harm are identifiable; and the individuals and the harm are closely related in time and space" (Jamieson 2014, 148). Our moral alarm bells, according to Jamieson, don't go off when future people are affected. And even if they do, they become progressively quieter the less these conditions (identification of individual agent, intentional action and knowledge of harm, identification of victim of harm, temporal and spatial proximity) are met. It is then hard to say that future people are "harmed" or that we are "at fault."

2.6 A further area of difficulty stems from the lack of direct, identifiable, or certain causal links between present agents and future victims. The focus here is not on agents but on causal links. For it is one thing to say that future people are negatively affected only if many in the past pushed certain effects beyond a certain threshold. It's another to say that the causal chains are (i) temporally and spatially distant; (ii) uncertain, difficult to trace, and difficult to establish with certainty; (iii) nonlinear, not simply cumulative; and so on. A linear causality would permit us to say that action-event *1* at *t1* causes effect-event *2* at *t2*. But in the intergenerational case, where the causal link passes through (long-term) cultural and environmental systems with their own dynamics and complexities, causes can display different temporal patterns, for example, not show up for several generations and then suddenly erupt.[8]

3. So far these problems, (1) and (2), have to do with the remoteness in time and the absence of overlap, which result, among other things, in lack of knowledge (with respect to effects and interests) and resulting difficulties in tracing causal links. Now we move to *interaction problems*, which similarly rely on the difficulties that result from remoteness and lack of overlap.

3.1 Present and future people are said to be caught in a particularly vicious collective action problem: a type of prisoner's dilemma or tragedy of the commons (Hardin 1968) that pits individual rationality against collective interests (Gardiner 2006, 2011a). Specifically in the context of climate change, which he aptly titles the "perfect moral storm" in his eponymous book, Gardiner analyzes presentism as the intergenerational intensification of the type of collective action problems known as the "tragedy of the commons": what is rational from an individual's point of view (an individual consumer, say, or an individual state) is irrational, perhaps even catastrophic, for the collective. In the intergenerational case of such a tragedy, a present generation bent on utility maximization exploits

its asymmetrical power over the future. While intragenerational collective action problems may be addressed by enforcing rules that benefit the collective, such enforcement depends on shared governance that is much weaker in the intergenerational case, where we face a "problem of interaction" (Gardiner 2011a, 37, 143ff.). Supposing we accept this bleak picture—one that assumes largely self-interested agents—part of the conclusion is that we need powerful democratic institutions with sanctioning power to counter the presentist effects.

3.2 Another interaction problem results from the *nonreciprocity argument*, which holds that because there can be no mutually advantageous interaction between present and future generations, the present has no obligations to the future (Beckman and Page 2008; Page 2006). The problem is exacerbated if one believes that much of our common and theoretical accounts of justice draw on reciprocity as a fundamental moral-political building block of society (Bowles and Gintis 2013; see also Nowak and Highfield 2011, cited in Jamieson 2014, 253).[9]

Despite the large role reciprocity plays in his *intra*generational account, Rawls is a prominent proponent of the nonreciprocity view. Similar to Kant in his philosophy of history (see the third thesis to the "Idea of Universal History with Cosmopolitical Intent"), Rawls argues that it would seem unfair to expect the present generation to work for the benefits of future people, given that these latter cannot reciprocate to the advantage of the present. Rawls complains of what he calls a "chronological unfairness, since those who live later profit from the labor of their predecessors without paying the same price. . . . We can do something for posterity but it can do nothing for us" (Rawls 1971, 291). Just as in Kant's view, this complaint seems in part based on an optimistic view of progress in general and of capital accumulation in particular, a view that has become questionable today, especially due to environmental problems such as climate change, resource depletion, and loss of biodiversity.

3.3 The problem of the initial generation arises from Rawls's contractualist solution to the nonreciprocity problems, according to which the veil of ignorance requires that the contracting parties do not know in which generation they will end up. The hope is that, thus epistemically restricted, they will choose a just savings principle to the benefit of subsequent generations. But some, such as Gardiner, have argued that this in turn neglects the problem of the initial generation: the parties could not adopt a just savings principle because, putting themselves in the shoes of the first generation, they will see that it is unjust for them, as the first generation never benefits from just savings (Gardiner 2009). The problem here is in part derived from contractualism itself, but also from construing the intergenerational context as closed.[10]

3.4 Many accounts of interaction assume that the interacting parties are in a situation of symmetry in power, and often also of responsibility (my obligations correspond to your rights to the extent your obligations correspond to my rights). In the intergenerational case, however, we have a *power asymmetry* between the present and the future (Barry 1989b, 189, 246), which challenges the standard assumption in most theories of justice that the parties are "roughly equal" (see Kittay 1999; Nussbaum 2001, 2006; Brumlik 2004).

4. We now move to problems that have to do with *world constitution*. IGJ has to contend with the fact that in the case of relations between generations, at stake may be the very makeup of the world and lifeworld, insofar as it is understood in terms of institutional and social-economic infrastructure, traditions and customs, familial and societal background, and horizon of actionable possibilities. Further at stake is the identity and number of people who are understood to live in the world. (Defining "generation" in section I, I suggested that it is important to understand generational relations as taking place against the background of a culture and a lifeworld, including an ecological context.) The typical assumption is that moral relations take place in a world that is, *grosso modo*, given and constant, but in IGJ the world's constitution (gradually) moves into the arena of moral scrutiny. Let us look at the issues arising in this situation in greater detail.

4.1 As a problem of decision-making about the world of the future, one might ask whether humanity should continue to exist. A present generation could decide not to reproduce, for example, because it is expected that future conditions will not provide for lives worth living. (For example, some historians have speculated that such a decision on the part of woman slaves was a major reason behind the decline in fertility in the British Caribbean after the empire ended the Atlantic slave trade in 1807; see, e.g., Morgan, K. 2008). In fact, a generation could avoid preventing such an impoverished future with the justification that there will not be any human beings to suffer from it. From similar considerations, Jonas concludes that the first problem of an ethics for the future consists in establishing "an unconditional duty for mankind to exist" (1984, 37). If his argument is accepted—something I will not discuss here—then the future world must include future people, and some procreation is a duty, not for all individually but for a generation collectively. As David Heyd puts it, "Problems of procreation are unique among moral problems because they involve the creation or 'genesis' of moral subjects rather than the treatment of actual ones" (Heyd 1988, 153).

4.2 A full theory of IGJ should include discussion of problems of *optimal population size* and demographic planning. Ideas about the "right number of people in the world" are prevalent in the literature, so that IGJ is sometimes classified as "population ethics" (see, e.g., Fishkin and Goodin 2010, which largely discusses justice for future people; see also Mulgan 2015). Determining the optimal size of future populations is of course beset by a number of difficulties, such as (i) calculability, for many factors come into play (expectation of food and other resources, habitat sustainability over short and/or long term, etc.). Acting on such calculations might (ii) require forcibly constraining procreation in the present, when many regard having children as a right (see the recent emergence of "procreation ethics": Archand and Benatar 2010; Heyd 1988). And (iii) the danger of self-serving strategies also looms large: the present living population may justify its depletion of resources by creating fewer future people (Zwartheod 2015; Bykvist 2009).

4.3 Jonas continues his line of thinking with the problem of adaptive preferences. He argues not just *that* there ought to be human beings in the world "we" the presently living bring about, but presents an argument as to *what it is* to be a human being that we ought to bring about, namely, beings capable of appreciating value and taking responsibility for "the good" on their own accord. Without stipulating this "idea of the human being," Jonas argues, a generation might seek to mold and adapt the preferences of future people to fit an otherwise impoverished world. Jonas refers in this context to Aldous Huxley's dystopian novel *Brave New World* (Jonas 1984, 30; 1996, 106). Hence, the well-known problem of adaptive preferences or problem of cheap desires leads in intergenerational ethics to discussions about what kind of future person we are to educate. (For a recent discussion of this problem, see Zwartheod 2015.) If we assume that the well-being of a person crucially depends on how well her preferences are satisfied, then desire-based or welfarist theories of well-being would have to include discussion not only of which persons to create, but which desires to create (see Bykvist 2009). As with 4.1 and 4.2, perverse incentives may be generated by this problem.

4.4 There are also questions regarding which future persons to create resulting from the existence of possibilities of genetic manipulation (bioethics). The identity of future people is controllable by the timing of conception as well as by more artificial genetic manipulation; even if we decide against any form of genetic engineering, the very possibility of manipulation makes this decision an ethical one.

4.5 There are further problems for views based on domination. One may argue that environmental degradation, including climate change, represents an instance not of violating human rights or other problem-ridden current definitions of justice but of domination. A generation dominates a successor if it wields superior power in a harmful way, without cost-free exit on the part of the succeeding generation (Nolt 2011). Jamieson responds by arguing that it is "strange" to say generations dominate each other, for it belongs to temporal precedence and asymmetry that previous ones co-determine the very lifeworld conditions of the existence of later generations (see VI.4, below).

4.6 We now come to the nonidentity problem (Kavka 1981; Parfit 1984, 351ff.; Woodward 1986; Page 2006, 132ff.), which it is generally agreed is the persistent shadow out of which all work on future duties struggles to emerge (Humphrey 2009; Page 2007). This argument suggests that because the existence and identity of future individuals is contingent upon the actions and decisions of the currently living, even actions that arguably harm them, such as increases in CO_2 emissions, contribute to their very existence. As a result, future people are not in a position to complain of these actions. Recent literature shows that most existing ethical theories, inasmuch as they subscribe to the person-affecting view that what is morally wrong must be wrong for an identifiable someone, cannot solve the problem of nonidentity in particular (Page 2006; Roberts and Wasserman 2010).

The nonidentity problem results from the fact that the existence of future individuals, with the (partly genetic) identity they happen to have, contingently depends upon the actions and decisions of the currently living. Even actions and policies that arguably harm them, such as environmental degradation or the depletion of nonrenewable resources, contribute (even if only very indirectly and unintentionally, by affecting the time of conception) to their very existence. As a result, it is hard to see how contingent future people could be in a position to complain of these actions without which they would not exist. It is not so much that these future people should be grateful to the currently living for their lives even if these future lives should turn out to be no more than barely worth living. Rather, the problem is that morally relevant harm, on many accounts, presupposes an individual, a preexisting potential victim, who has been harmed as a result of some action. However, in many cases concerning future individuals, those who will exist are not identical to those who would have existed had the seemingly reprehensible action not occurred. Thus, what seems like a moral harm cannot be attached to a victim; we could not have chosen an alternative course of action to make things turn out better for the same individuals.

The problem arises for many existing ethical theories (as well as for most legal systems; see Peters in Roberts and Wasserman 2009) inasmuch as they subscribe to what Parfit termed the "person-affecting view": the view that what is morally wrong must be wrong for an identifiable someone (Parfit 1984; Page 2006). For example, so-called "contractualist" as well as discourse-ethical theories, from Scanlon to Habermas, ground moral evaluation on an examination of whether affected parties could (autonomously and reasonably) accept a proposed course of action or policy. Rejection would typically be based on reasons claiming that the action would harm these individuals and their interests, where harm is determined by how the individuals would have fared had another policy been chosen. However, this determination is not possible in the case of contingent future individuals, for if another policy had been chosen, the alleged victims would not exist at all. Perhaps we may already intimate here that such identity-dependent theories have a hard time reconciling the assumption of an individual's (supposedly given) autonomy or agency with the contingent dependency on pre-conception events and the choices of preexisting people. For basing moral evaluation on the capacity of an individual to reasonably accept or reject a proposal, and treating this capacity as making up that which in a person deserves moral standing and equal respect, neglects that this capacity does not simply come into the world as a "self-justifying" reason, or a "reason that grounds itself." The nonidentity problem shows that such a concept of autonomy or personhood, however well suited in other contexts, cannot without further ado be rendered serviceable in the context of intergenerational justice.

Most responses to this problem fall into four types. The first type ignores it as a merely technical or philosophical problem so as not to hinder the development of intergenerational moral theories that then often treat future people as if they existed now by erasing the difference that birth and death make. The second response foregrounds the problem, seeking to solve it or mitigate it, even at the risk of exposing themselves to the charge that they never quite get to the substantive issues of intergenerational justice (Gosseries 2009b). The third not so much solves the nonidentity problem as leaps over it by dismissing the person-affecting view in an impersonal consequentialist turn, according to which only the maximization of future utility counts, regardless of the identity of the utility bearers (Birnbacher 1988)—a view that Parfit famously showed leads to the "repugnant" conclusion that the present ought to maximize the number of future people even if their lives are barely worth living (Parfit 1984, 381ff.). A fourth response seeks to deflate the problem (Tremmel and Chambers 2010; Gosseries 2010).

Before moving on, however, let me justify why I classify this problem as an ontological one of world constitution when it seems to concern only a common definition of harm. In general, what is at issue in the nonidentity problem is the fact that due to the special relation between present and future people—not-yet-existence and power asymmetry come into play here—the actions of the living affect who will be born. Our actions co-constitute and repopulate the world that begins now, and this becomes more pronounced the further we go into the future. This feature becomes more noticeable when one looks at attempts to downplay or outmaneuver the problem. As mentioned, one intuitively appealing way in which some have responded to the nonidentity problem consists in deflating its significance, by which I mean questioning why we should give so much consideration to one causal factor, one that we single out for moral consideration when in fact there are innumerable other causes. (In Parfit's famous example, this would be the "depletion policy" of which we ask whether it can be said to have harmed the future people it was also causally involved in bringing about; Parfit 1984, 361ff.) This defence of IGJ thus bears on the arbitrariness of singling out the action in question—pollution, for example—among all the millions of factors that contributed to time of conception and thus identity. Though this may not amount to accusing the nonidentity problem of a categorically mistaken view of causality, as Tremmel and Chambers have recently suggested, their comments, drawing on those of Gosseries, point in this direction (Tremmel and Chambers 2010). Jamieson responded, convincingly in my view, by conceding the point for ordinary actions but not for climate change and, presumably, similar large-scale cultural and environmental effects on conception and future people. Climate change, Jamieson argues, is truly "world-constituting": it will "radically repopulate and remake the entire world" (2014, 166).

In section VI, I will not so much align myself with any one of these groups of responses to the nonidentity problem, let alone seek to solve it. Rather, I will attempt to uncover some of its problematic assumptions in order to motivate further emphasis on the time of life. Dismissing the problem as merely technical, one misses the opportunity to reveal a tendency to stress the living over the future, identity over change, symmetry over asymmetry, and autonomy over heteronomy.

4.7 Last but not least, there is one ethical theory that, as Rawls famously argued of utilitarianism, disregards the distinct identity of individuals (Rawls 1971), and thus may be (though often is not) cast in impersonal consequentialist terms that evaluate action outcomes without reference to how they affect identifiable persons. As indicated, this theory fails on another score: it leads to an implausible view, which Parfit calls *the repugnant conclusion*. The idea is that, to increase overall (i.e., non-person-specific) utility (e.g., happiness), it would be morally advisable to generate as many future individuals as we can, provided their lives would still be worth living, even if barely (Parfit 1984, 381ff.; see also the Mere Addition Paradox, Parfit 1984, 419ff.). This problem, then, also has to do with world constitution and population ethics in asking how many people to leave behind (see above, 4.2).

In concluding section (4), we can say that, by thus constituting a new and different world in which future people will live, many of the large-scale actions that present generations engage in, it seems, are beyond inherited moral notions. Typically, moral evaluation takes place within a world whose structures and possibilities for being are given; IGJ in general and climate change in particular ask us moral questions about possible worlds: Is it better that a world with fossil-fuel-driven infrastructure (and the affluence it affords to some) come about, even with the deleterious environmental consequences? As Dale Jamieson puts it, "Commonsense morality operates within a horizon of possibility. It is not well-equipped to make judgments about the conditions that fix these possibilities" (Jamieson 2014, 167).

In ending this overview of the "ontological" or "special" problems affecting IGJ, we may already underline how much we rely on temporal and ontological terms in formulating the challenges, such as the notions of existence and nonexistence, not-yet-existence, absence, presence, shared and divided time and space, identity or nonidentity of agents and their agency, world and lifeworld, and so on. Regarding existence versus nonexistence, for instance, we may ask the following questions: What is it for a moral claimant to exist? Many jurisdictions respect the wills of the deceased—if the dead can exist as claimants, why not future people? Is "not-yet existence" not more appropriate than nonexistence when it comes to future people, indicating that existence is a temporal concept? Is the ideal of reciprocity (that stands behind the diagnosis of the nonreciprocity problem) of an exchange that takes no time? Does reciprocity not usually involve a temporal-futural moment, as when A gives to B who *will* return the gift or benefit to A? As concerns absence and presence, we should ask: Is there a relevant difference between spatial and temporal absence? Can we say the dead and the unborn are simply absent, while living contemporaries are simply present?

In relation to the identity or nonidentity of agents and their agency, we may ask what role identity over time plays in constituting moral status. And finally, regarding the issue of what I called world constitution, we should ask: What do we mean by "world"? What is it to share a world across time (and space)? How thickly or constitutively are humans situated in worlds?

As I will argue, we would do well to reflect on these temporal-ontological notions in seeking to render a theory of justice between generations ontologically appropriate. Before I argue that ontological problems call for ontological approaches, and go on to propose an approach that takes generational relations to be constitutive of human agency, allow me to briefly present common approaches to IGJ to see to what extent they address or avoid these ontological challenges or introduce new ones.

III. Intergenerational Ethics as Extension or a Special Case

In this section, I briefly review some of the (in English-speaking philosophy, dominant) ways in which theorists have sought to understand and model IGJ. At times, the approaches are put forward as explicit responses to the special and ontological problems encountered by IGJ. At other times, the method suggests itself either by the assumption that temporal-historical location should morally matter as little as geographical location, or by virtue of existing theories of intragenerational justice; in yet other cases, the overarching goal is to distill the intergenerational justice relation in its purity. My goal is not to review, at least not in any detail, responses to individual problems (of which there are many, and certainly some convincing ones). My overall point is simply that some typical ways of addressing these problems, and of approaching IGJ in general, do not address these problems as ontological problems. Specifically, they do not consider how we as human beings are constituted in time, in a world that we inherit and that we therefore have to leave for others.

1. Extensionism: By "extensionism," I mean an approach to IGJ that begins with extant theories of justice, or intuitions regarding justice, and then seeks to extend them to cover relations with future people. Extensionism could be said to operate on "commonsense morality" or on existing theories of (intragenerational) justice, and of course the latter could be taken to build on or revise commonsense morality by, for example, drawing on it for the elaboration of a theory of justice, or by testing such theories against commonsense intuitions (see, e.g., Rawls's "reflective equilibrium"; Rawls 1996, 385ff.).

A paradigm case of treating IGJ in this way is Rawls, who explicitly calls justice between generations a "problem of extension" along with relations to other nations, to the disabled, and to animals and the rest of nature (Rawls 1996, 20ff.). Future people thus do not belong to the core problem of justice, a core obtained by "simplifications" for theory construction (Rawls 1971, 45–46), even if Rawls allows that insights gained from extensions may alter the core. Other IGJ theorists have also suggested, largely for reasons of expediency, that IGJ is generally best treated if we rely on existing well-worked-out theories of justice that we seek to amend to cover or include future people (Gosseries and Meyer 2009).

It's probably fair to say that extensionism was a more natural or widespread approach when future people were indeed more of an afterthought, triggered, for example, by nuclear-waste issues in the 1970s. Today, there is a lot more work on IGJ specifically (see Mulgan 2015), which of course need not mean that extensionism recedes. On this extensionist assumption, the primary and paradigmatic subjects of justice are living contemporaries, sharing time more or less unproblematically. Generational relations—to parents, grandparents, and ancestors as well as to children, grandchildren, and future generations more generally—would be seen as contingent features of subjects. Time and agency are not intrinsically linked, for the extensionist assumes that time and generational relations can legitimately be brought in at a later stage of theory development, when we seek to "extend" a model of justice developed for living contemporaries to future generations.[11]

2. Abstraction from Overlap: As I indicated in defining generations, many theorists suggest that, to understand the problem of why and what we owe future people in its pure form, we should model the relation such that generations come on–stage all at once, *en bloc* (Gosseries 2009b; Gardiner 2011). In fact, at times it is argued that IGJ should be modeled on the "time bomb": what would be wrong with planting a bomb that explodes only after all those currently living have died? (Gosseries 2001; Gosseries and Meyer 2009). In response, one may argue that if we model the relation to the future in such a way that there is no overlap among generations, the distance or gap between generations appears artificially inflated, inheritance of a lifeworld is not taken into account, and care for infants and elders is avoided.

3. The Two-Theory Approach: Some argue that the ontological problems besetting IGJ (especially the nonidentity problem and the choice theory of rights) force us to have two theories of justice, one for contemporaries (usually more generous) and one for future people (usually more sufficientarian) (e.g., Meyer and Roser 2009). The implication is that justice is either purely nongenerational or intergenerational. As in extensionism or the abstraction from overlap, then, generational relations (having predecessors and successors) are not seen as a defining feature of human beings as the subjects of justice.

4. The Dehistoricizing Approach: Several IGJ theories propose that, to achieve moral objectivity and model IGJ appropriately and fairly, we must imagine a legislative meeting of generations outside of history (Rawls 1971; Birnbacher 1977; Partridge 1978; Barry 1991; Beckermann 1999; Tremmel 2013). On this account, those who devise principles for intergenerational justice are not generational beings themselves; they are, in theory, abstracted from time.[12]

5. Generic Universalism. One way in which we may include future people in our moral-political universe is by construing the latter by way of a generic category. If we owe moral respect to all members of the genus "human," without regard to time, actual existence, and so on, then future people are owed duties as well. No matter what their specific identities or interests, future people will belong to the genus "human" and so deserve the same moral treatment as living representatives (e.g., Weiss 1989; Caney 2010b).

IV. Ontological Problems Call for Ontological Approaches

IV.1. Abstracting from the Time of Birth and Death

Most of the problems and arguments discussed in section II involve temporal distance to some extent: the lesser the perceived gap in time, the smaller the problem. In what follows, I will not deny the obvious: temporal distance and poor knowledge constitute a problem for any theory of justice as well as for moral motivation. If we don't know very much about a person's needs and interests, and are not in direct, unmediated position to address them, it will be difficult to ascertain our duties and to act on them. And if we hold that "ought implies can," our responsibilities will be diminished. Still, the fact that these challenges have to do with time and the alterity, asymmetry, and distance it introduces into human relations may also suggest that we consider the role of time for agents and for social relations.

However, as we've seen, most of the approaches we just reviewed downplay time and its role for justice. Extensionism takes the parties to the core of justice to be contemporaries. As a result, generational temporality is not seen as central to its account of the person, and the alterity that time introduces into human relations (separation, but also relation, by birth and death) does not affect the relations among the parties to justice. As discussed in the definitions of generations in section I, abstraction from generational overlap (the first definition of generation as comprising all those living at any one time) comes with consequences: it appears to inflate the distance between generations; inheritance is hard to explain if there is no generationally shared time during which gifts are passed on (both material and symbolic goods; e.g., how could a language be learned from a previous generation?); and the asymmetries (in power and in responsibilities) that go along with care for infants and elders are avoided.

Perhaps even more visibly, the neglect of generational overlap, as well as the generic and dehistoricizing approaches, *abstracts* from the role of time in social relations. This is because the time that separates and links generations is first and foremost seen as a problem for morality. For example, in the nonreciprocity and nonidentity problems, distance and change over time hinder normal interaction and application of terms. Time may also be taken not to matter morally at all (as when we abstract from different temporal instantiations, arguing that future humans equally belong to the conceptually atemporal genus "humanity"). Further, time may be viewed as a gulf by assuming the living to be separated from the dead and the unborn rather than also being linked to them by birth and death, as when theories propose different principles in the intra- and intergenerational cases owing to the special challenges of the latter.

Abstraction from, or neglect of, certain features of persons and relations for moral purposes is of course legitimate in many respects. In determining which values, norms, rights, and entitlements apply to a person and her relations, we must distinguish between morally relevant and irrevelant features of individuals. Put this way, the fact that people are born of and in different generations, and die by leaving the world to others, is highly relevant. Birth and death may be constitutive of moral agents, and social relations may thus always be temporal and generational as well. Further, perhaps we should not assume too readily that contemporaries share a time that divides them, as if by a great gulf, from the dead and the unborn. Time may not be shared among the living, or not in any simple way, and if it is not, perhaps the gulf separating us from the other generations is not as big as we think.[13]

IV.2. Ontological and Normative Demands on a Theory of Justice

It seems advisable, then, to look for conceptions of intergenerational justice that are both ontologically and normatively attuned. Indeed, I believe (though will not argue in detail here) that theories of justice in general must satisfy both ontological and normative demands, despite the widespread tendency to regard one as primary. The tendency in stressing normative adequacy is to smuggle in an often inadequate ontology; the tendency in stressing ontological considerations is to smuggle in normative assumptions, or not to help us think about the extent and content of normative obligations at all (Floyd 2016). Normative adequacy is often defined as agreement between intuitions regarding justice, abstract principles, and inherited theories (think, for instance, of Rawlsian "wide reflective equilibrium"; Rawls 1971; Nielsen 1993; Fritsch 2007). Theories that focus on normative adequacy tend to emphasize justifying norms, ideal theory, and answering the calculative question as to how much parties owe to each other. By contrast, ontological considerations insist that moral theorizing first and foremost consider not why and how much we owe according to some principle, but how human beings are constituted in relation to each other and situated in the contexts in which moral life is said to occur.

IGJ theory, then, needs to have its debate around social ontology. In Western debates (largely English-speaking) of IGJ, normative considerations dominate, but it is also widely recognized, as we have seen, that normative theory—ideal theory in particular—runs into formidable ontological problems if applied to noncontemporaries. In relating to the dead and future individuals, relational-ontological issues stand out in a particularly pressing way. There is, then, a certain desirability of rendering social ontology sensitive to normative ideas and vice versa. As I hope will become clear, my argument will be that an ontological account, if sensitive to normative principles from the beginning, suggests better models of IGJ (e.g., what I develop in subsequent chapters as "asymmetrical reciprocity" and "taking turns," notions I wish to be understood as both social-ontological in characterizing the being of social groups and individuals, and normative in implying ideas as to what groups and individuals should do).

But the relation of the social ontology to normativity must be made more precise still. In response to this demand, I argue that generational relations are necessary for moral and political agency. The time of birth and death, in the form of what I will call natality and mortality, makes human subjectivity, as both vulnerable and liable to normative demands, possible. Not only do we need both ontological and normative considerations, but we need a social ontology of the ineluctability and origin of normativity, or justice.

V. The Generational Self and the Time of Birth and Death

In response to the ontological problems, then, we should deal directly with the relations among subjectivity, time, and generations. As indicated in the Introduction and elaborated throughout this book, I argue that the time of birth and death is constitutive of human subjects in their interrelations with each other. Humans are normative beings—agents liable to moral concerns, but also themselves vulnerable—to the extent that they are temporal beings, which is to say, nonpresentist generational beings: born mortals who can only emerge from a previous generation and who are dying to give way to future people. But birth and death, and the intergenerational linkages they entail, are not contingent facts of who we are. By contrast, natality and mortality should be seen as constitutive of moral subjectivity, which I take to comprise both moral status (being a legitimate object of moral concern) and moral agency (being capable of freely choosing from among available courses of action).

In making this point, I draw more and more throughout this book on phenomenology and deconstruction. The phenomena of birth and death have received much-needed attention in these strands of philosophy, especially in connection with accounts of human subjectivity and sociality, even if these accounts are rarely related to intergenerational ethics and moral relations with future people. In this chapter, I will only offer a brief sketch of arguments that will be more fully developed in subsequent chapters, in particular Chapter 2. The sketch is intended to indicate how one might reframe the discussion around ontological problems and philosophical methods in IGJ. In this light, let us begin to examine the relation between the time of birth and death, on the one hand, and agency and its relations to others, on the other. As we go along, I will discuss this account's normative implications.

V.1. Mortality

I begin by suggesting briefly why one may think mortality is not accidental to agency. As we will see in greater detail in Chapter 2, Heidegger argued that to be an agent means to grasp one's present time not as "is" but as "to be," full of (inherited) potential to be actualized (in the future). Such realization of possibilities, however, demands understanding my life as mortal, for otherwise no choice would really rule out another. Deciding to become a carpenter, for instance, would not exclude my becoming a philosopher if an infinite time remains available to me, and devoting my time to this loved one would not distinguish her or him over others. Without grasping choices as finite and my life as mortal, the very notion of "my time" would disintegrate. Along similar lines, Simone de Beauvoir (1946) has suggested—in part in fascinating novelistic form[14]—that immortality would bring about inevitable boredom and apathy. As Bernard Williams puts it succinctly: "[D]eath gives the meaning to life" (Williams 1973, 82).[15] Discussing Lucretius, and acknowledging that death robs agents of meaningful pursuits, Martha Nussbaum writes that "the structure of human experience, and therefore of the empirical human sense of value, is inseparable from the finite temporal structure within which human life is actually lived. . . . the removal of all finitude in general, and mortality in particular, would not so much enable these values [love, friendship, justice, and the various forms of virtuous action] to survive eternally as bring about the death of value as we know it" (Nussbaum 1994, 225–226).[16] It is mortality that makes life, values, action, and virtues matter in the first place. If I do not have to fear that death will take my loved ones from me, and if no one can sacrifice her life for others, all social relations take on the lax, merely optional, and playful character they indeed have in the ancient Greek depictions of the Olympian gods. Things and people matter to us against a background of mortality: only knowing they and we are vulnerable and mortal inspires a sense of beauty and the good. Without this sense, there could be no dignity and feeling of self-worth, a necessary ingredient in a meaningful life (see Kass 2002, 2003). Similarly, as immortal, my existence would hardly be the object of care that Heidegger argues in *Being and Time* to be our fundamental being, and whose temporality he outlines so carefully as a finite and historical temporality (GA 2).

What is important to grasp here is first of all the indispensability of death to the disclosure of a world, not in the sense of a collection of objects but as a horizon of intelligibility that permits meaning to arise. But of great significance here is also the understanding of death as not primarily the endpoint of life, an understanding Heidegger attributes to most people in everyday life: the sense that "one" dies, but not I, not yet (GA 2, §51, 297/336). By contrast, human life is, as Heidegger's expression has it, a "being-toward-death" (GA 2, 296/335) at each of its moments because the enabling as well as disabling effects of finite time are operative at every turn of life. Grasping something in this or that way, or choosing a course of action, are meaningful, and appropriable by me and imputable to me, because they rule out other understandings and other actions, and this ruling out and concomitant reopening of possibilities is inseparable from the mortally limited time available. In this sense, death temporalizes life as finite throughout.

But as we can also see here, the relation to death not only temporalizes life's moments as "to be," but renders actions imputable to an individual whose singularity is thus formed only in conjunction with this imputability or responsibility. To grasp the present moment not as a predetermined moment coinciding with itself but as full of actualizable, futural potentialities, I have to understand that this actualization depends on me. Mortal time is not indifferent to me and my being, but addresses me, as it were, as the one who has to take over her or his life. However one may feel about the existentialist pathos in Heidegger's descriptions of the "call of conscience" (GA 2, §§56–57) and "authentic resoluteness" (GA 2, §61) in the face of one's "being-toward-death," the connection between death and individuation, between time and imputability or responsibility, appears convincing (for a detailed treatment, see Raffoul 2010). On this view, self-imputable choices depend on individuation and thus confrontation with a dying that no one can take over for the agent. In confronting death as a possibility (a possibility that ends all possibilities), a meaningful world comes to be disclosed in which I can see choices as mine. In this sense, a certain normativity and responsibility emerges with finite temporality. The "ultimate demand" for human existence, says Heidegger, is that it "takes upon itself again, expressly and explicitly, its own being-there and to be responsible for it" (GA 29/30, 171/254). In this taking up, not only does the gift or event of being precede the self, but the self in fact comes about only in such a responding or corresponding. As Heidegger writes, "Only in responsibility [*Verantwortung*] does the self first reveal itself" (GA 24, 137/194).

In his response to Heidegger, which I discuss in detail in Chapter 2, Levinas agrees with the finitude of time, but argues that death is not accessible "as such." Rather, it can be accessed only indirectly, by way of other people—or, on a weaker reading of his claim, at least not without them. "Death," writes Levinas, refers "to an interpersonal order whose signification it does not annihilate" (TI 234/261). Death is inseparable from vulnerability to others: it generates both the fear of the murderer and the call for the doctor. It subjects me to a mortal time that opens up possibilities to me, but also renders me vulnerable to unforeseen changes, including those caused by other, "alien wills" (TI 236/262). In this sense, death cannot be separated from others who have power over me. Sociality reaches deep into the very constitution of agency. In confronting the death that is co-disclosive of my finite world of action and comprehension, I necessarily encounter mortal, vulnerable others. From these others, mortality issues both the threat of murder and the imperative to let the other live, such that moral normativity in general begins with the birth of a mortal. On this view, subjectivity is co-constituted by a futural demand to let others have possibilities for life beyond my death. Agents must have a relation to future people for access to their own world of action and meaning: to being. Hence, against Heidegger's "being-toward-death," Levinas speaks of human existence as a "being-against-death" (TI 224/247, TI 235/261) and a "being-for-beyond-my-death" (CPP 93/45; see also TI 236/263, TI 253/284, TI 301/336). It is also what leads him to characterize freedom and responsibility as "fecundity" (TI 267/299) and, no doubt problematically (see Chanter 2001; Gürtler 2001), as a "paternity" without which, Levinas writes (referring implicitly to Plato's *Timaeus* 37c–e), "time would be but an image of eternity" (TI 247/277). (For some empirical evidence of the pro-social intergenerational effects that can emerge with heightened death awareness, see Feiler and Wade-Benzoni 2009.)

Perhaps the Levinasian claim that the link between death and meaningfulness is pulled into a time beyond death is supported by Aristotle's insight that the value of our lives can be affected by what happens to us (or our plans and interests) after our death (*Nicomachean Ethics* 1.10–11; see also Pitcher 1984; Nussbaum 2013, 33–34). And indeed, in her discussion of the immortal Greek gods, Nussbaum rightly points out that intergenerational relations depend on the meaningfulness mortality both enables and threatens to undermine (1994, 228). If adults do not have to care for children to survive and grow (and perhaps not even to give birth to them), and no one needs to care for the old, then it is hard to imagine that generations even remain. While justice is hardly needed among gods, as Aristotle said (*Nicomachean Ethics* 1178b, 10–16), intergenerational justice would make even less sense among immortals.

If a meaningful world is disclosed only in the confrontation with a death that also commands to let the other live, then to give the gift of life beyond my own, meaning must be constitutively referred to and depend on the relation of the present to a future time belonging to others, including overlapping and non-overlapping future people. In this sense, mortality is inseparable from human relations as we know them. But birth, too, connects humans intergenerationally.

V.2. Natality

In his account of the finite temporality of human agency, Heidegger did not forget birth. He argued that in grasping the present as to be, in care, "birth and death are "connected" in a manner characteristic of Dasein" (GA 2, 426–427/495). Thus birth is ongoingly present in each caring, handing down of possibilities in the course of being-toward-death: "Factical Dasein exists as born [*gebürtig*: not born in the sense of *geboren*, a mere fact in the past, but ongoingly born-birthing]"[17] (GA 2, 442–443/516). And despite using the word "generation" sparingly, later in *Being and Time* Heidegger stresses that his account of human agency places *Dasein* into inextricable generational relations.[18] The world into which one is thrown has been handed down from previous generations, and its appropriation, however much Heidegger stresses its singular "authenticity," takes place in the context of one's "own" generation. Two of the most well-known criticisms of Heidegger's "being-toward-death" both extend and deepen this intergenerationality. First, as we've already noted, Levinas claims that Heidegger's death privileges solitude over interpersonality, in particular the relation to future people opened up by the constitutive relation to mortal time. Second, Hannah Arendt argues that Heidegger's account of the finite temporality of agency illegitimately privileges death over birth. Obviously, I cannot go into detail here, but allow me to expand just a bit more.

Arendt argues that *natality*, the fact of being born, is not just an accident from which an account of moral personhood may abstract, but central to human agency (Arendt 1958). Birth indicates that humans are both of this world, empirically and corporeally belonging to its facticity and history, and yet never coincide with it on account of birth's resistance to conscious grasp and causal explanation. If my birth was just another effect in a series, I could not grasp my being as capable of free action. Natality means that a human being is not one with its birth or its natural kind, for as creative, free beings that give rise to something new against the background of inherited circumstances, we are not born once and for all but rather remain in the process of being born. Agency (parsed by Arendt as labor, work, and action) is thus intrinsically connected to biological natality, the fact of being born:

Labor and work, as well as action, are also rooted in natality in so far as they have the task to provide and preserve the world for, to foresee and reckon with, the constant influx of newcomers who are born into the world as strangers. However, of the three, action has the closest connection with the human condition of natality; the new beginning inherent in birth can make itself felt in the world only because the newcomer possesses the capacity of beginning something anew, that is, of acting. In this sense of initiative, an element of action, and therefore of natality, is inherent in all human activities. Moreover, since action is the political activity par excellence, natality, and not mortality, may be the central category of political, as distinguished from metaphysical, thought. (Arendt 1958, 9)

Birth is the appearance of the new to the extent the newcomer can initiate something new in history by her speech and action. In this sense, the political arena must welcome children not only as potentially disruptive strangers needed to maintain its "relative durability and permanence" (1958, 96), but to maintain alive its own sense of political action and human plurality.

Human natality, then, comprises both being born as a body into unchosen circumstances, and the demand to appropriate them to the point of giving birth to something new, the hallmark of human action (Arendt 1958, 8–12, 246–247). If birth is a constitutive feature of agency, then agency is intrinsically referred to others. With respect to this reference to others, however, recent scholars have argued that Arendt privileges the political sociality established by the second, nonbiological sense of natality over the biological meaning: that of agents giving rise to something new, in action and speech, in the context of a political community. Along with the privilege granted to action over labor and work, the public over the private, and human action over the allegedly cyclical time of nature and reproduction (1958, 246), the relation natality establishes with birth-giving mothers above all is secondarized (Durst 2004; Diprose 2009). If we do not stress the biological relation of reproduction in natality, however, it is much harder, Diprose and Ziarek argue, to grasp today's biopolitical subordination of women's capacity to give birth (Diprose and Ziarek 2013, 112ff.). Further, Adriana Cavarero has argued that deemphasizing the maternal in the natal, and thus only offering what she calls an "erect" natality, misconstrues sociality in general, and the political realm in particular, as one of a symmetrical "scene of mutual apparition" (Cavarero 2014, 14). On this scene, and once the mother has been pushed off-stage to let the baby come forth "from nothingness," we no longer understand that sociality is "marked by a deep asymmetry and originary dependency" that begins with the relation between (maternal) caregiver and infant and goes on to characterize human relations more generally (Cavarero 2014, 22; see Cavarero 2000). To stress this asymmetry in the birth of agency, Cavarero concludes, would help us to better appreciate Judith Butler's Levinasian stress on vulnerability, feminist care ethics, and indeed the legacy of Arendt's natality in the much more asymmetrical (though overly deontological) ethics of Hans Jonas (Cavarero 2014, 27), whose overall intergenerational intent, however, should here be stressed beyond Cavarero's more immediate interests (Jonas 1984).

By contrast, if we reinsert the mother—as well as the parents, the caregivers, the educators, most of them women—back into the nativity scene, the normative ontology of the subject paradigmatically highlights the asymmetrical dependency on previous generations. Human existence is, then, as Lisa Guenther argues in her rereading of Heidegger's "being-toward-death" after Cavarero, a "being-from-others" (Guenther 2008). The relation to previous generations is not just mediated by inheritance in the form of language, culture, norms, habits, and institutions, but also necessitates asymmetrical, corporeal, intimate relations, care for material and symbolic needs, and so on. Agency comes with asymmetrical intergenerational relations of ontological and normative import.

However, as the references to dependency and vulnerability indicate, the embodied nature of agency demands that we allow for not only its giving birth to the new, but also its subjection to the threat of violence, its passive exposure to forces beyond human freedom, including death and other people. And if the conversion of Heidegger's "being-toward-death" into natality foregrounded the parent generation ("being-from-others"), vulnerability, as we noted, transforms mortality into generativity and highlights future generations in what Levinas calls "being-for-beyond-my-death."

Moral normativity, then, in general begins with the birth of a mortal. On the view defended here, natal and mortal time is not accidental to moral subjectivity and human sociality. If birth relates us to previous generations, and death to future generations, then we are "generational beings" (in Anne O'Byrne's felicitous formulation; O'Byrne 2010, 6, 41). Thick embeddedness in backward- and forward-looking historical chains and social-cultural milieus is a feature of our existence both social-ontologically (it is constitutive of our being) and normatively (we owe backward and forward, and indeed in such a way that the two are hard to distinguish). The next chapter seeks to deepen and more carefully justify this view (chiefly with respect to Levinas), while subsequent chapters propose ways of better capturing this constitutive normativity. They will address the question as to how we may think this co-implication of the past and the future in the present, and how we should flesh out and operationalize the normativity implied in this mortal natality.

For now, however, let us see how this sketch of what I call "natal mortality" may help us to reorient our responses to the ontological problems often said to affect IGJ.

VI. Natal Mortality and the Ontological Problems

If death gives meaning to life, opens a world, and permits agency in it—even as it also aborts projects and exposes subjects to the actions and demands of others—then it is not just the end of life, at its outer limit. Death is in the midst of life, every moment of meaning drawing on a death that we do not fully understand. The unknown future is already here, and indeed in making sociality possible or structuring it meaningfully. If we see mortality in this way, and with Levinas and others see responsibility among human beings emerging with it, then even relations to contemporaries are separated as if by a gulf of death from us. Temporal alterity structures our relations even to the living. Future people, then, are no longer in such a different category. The demand from actual future people on the living would thus not be anomalous but exemplary of moral normativity.

I will now come back to the special and ontological challenges the extant literature on IGJ has made out, seeking to sketch, in broad outlines, how the time of birth and death may help us to think differently about them, even as it does not "solve" them in a normative "ideal theory" that offers a moral axiomatics.

VI.1. The Nonexistence Challenge

Although I cannot argue this in detail here, I think we can see the outline of a response to some of the ontological problems of IGJ. If nongenerational contemporaries (individuals whose generational relations are seen as inessential for the purposes of a theory of justice) are tacitly assumed as the model for entities with moral status, to the point of abstracting from or neglecting their natal mortality, then attributing moral status to (for instance) the unborn confronts ontological problems of attributing moral standing to non-existent entities, and neglects the certainly morally relevant dependence of future people on the presently living. But if we recognize that the assumption of co-presence among the living is problematic (as discussed, we should not assume a common time without further ado)—if we take note of the temporal alterity (natal mortality) in the now-living other, an alterity that both connects and divides individuals—then correspondingly, the temporal distance of future people may no longer appear as anomalous as it often does.

In response to the challenge of nonexistence, then, natal mortality makes two corresponding moves. First, it makes contemporaries less present to one another, for each agent lives her finite time "stretched out" between always singular birth and death. On this view, we recognize the temporal alterity in the now-living other, and see this alterity as involved in the very reason why others make demands on us. Vulnerability means being subject to mortal time. One is born before the other, and one will die before the other. This is why the idealizations of the third (the idealized familial) definition of "generation," while necessary, must also come undone. One may thus argue, for example, that social relations among the living are structured by an anticipatory mourning, by the sense that one will die before the other, having to interiorize and bury her or him.[19]

Correspondingly, the temporal distance of nonpresent generations (including the dead) is no longer so anomalous. Most IGJ already realize that nonexistence is not the same as not-yet-existence, to the point where they tend to obliterate even this difference (e.g., extending human rights to future people). Without denying alterity, we can see specifically future people as (borrowing a word from Derrida's *Specters of Marx*) "spectrally" present, for example in the following ways.

(i) First, we should stress, rather than abstract from, overlap among generations, in the sense captured by both the familial and idealized familial sense of generation (see section I). On these definitions, different generations exist in a present time that is then no longer simply shared, as the same time, by the living. We then understand better that those living at the same time still live in different generations and birth cohorts, which are further differentiated by the singularities of lives stretched out between singular births and deaths.

(ii) Further, to do justice to the spectral presence of future people, we can see many of our projects as depending upon being taken up by future people, including non-overlapping future generations. We draw on future people to allow meaning in the here and now, according to Levinas (see Chapter 2); without them, if death was nothingness, life was "desperate blows of a head struck against the wall" (TI 236/263). Similarly, Janna Thompson has argued that what she calls "lifetime-transcending interests" are essential for a meaningful life, and required for making a rational plan for one's life (Thompson 2009). As I will stress in the next chapter, by contrast to *interests* in the lives of future people, Levinas underlines the connection to meaning that comes from a futural *responsibility*, although he tends to downplay the (also asymmetrical) reciprocity in this between present and future generations. The latter, then, are spectrally present in our feeling already addressed, in our very agency, by the demands future people make on us in the here and now. In fact, for Levinas futural duties transcending one's lifetime are the very hallmark of normativity, even the signature of our age: "Our age is . . . defined by . . . an action for a world to come, a going beyond one's epoch" (CPP 93/46).

(iii) Levinas also recognizes that, beyond the always singular and personal "face-to-face" named in fecundity, future people are spectrally present in the *institutions* we share with at least some of them (see also Carr 2014; Wade-Benzoni 2009; de-Shalit 1995). If my agency is, as we've seen, referenced in its very constitution to a world beyond its time, to a time beyond its world, then a mortal being "has its time at its disposal precisely because it postpones violence, that is, because a meaningful order subsists beyond death" so that it can seize "the other chance" in the time it has left "by its being against death: the founding of institutions in which the will ensures a meaningful but impersonal world beyond death" (TI 236/263). (I will say more about the intergenerational sharing of specifically democratic institutions in Chapter 4.)

Of course, it is not just political institutions that are common to us and future people. Despite all discontinuity and alterity, we share a "world" with future people, from traditions and languages to habitats, climates, and the earth (see also below, on world constitution). As I will elaborate, given the noncoincidence of time that disallows a group, a tradition, or an institution to simply be present to itself, affirming a group or institutional identity is to promise its future survival, in many cases beyond one's death. For example, a commitment to democracy is what it is only by promising the future survival of democratic institutions. Accepting an inheritance means promising to reinstate it in a different context, to remain faithful to it in such a way as to inevitably recontextualize and "iterate" it.

In this sense, one may claim that individuals recognize the spectral presence of future people by seeing themselves *as members of communities* (from families and clans to nation-states and perhaps even humanity at large) that they take to persist beyond them. (Imagine a world in which there are no more future generations, as in P. D. James's *The Children of Men* and its filmic adaption by Alfonso Cuarón.) This much, we may say, is true about "communitarian" approaches to IGJ (de-Shalit 1995; Thompson 2009; see also Wade-Benzoni 2009, who discusses studies that show such group-belonging, in addition to long-term goals or lifetime-transcending interests, as one of the factors that can undo the presentist favoring of the position of the living in the present[20]). We should recall, however, that lifetime-transcending groups are not simply identical to themselves over historical time, but internally, as well as externally differentiated and constituted by the temporal asymmetries discussed above.

(iv) There is a sense, however, in which these asymmetries and alterities also bring to the fore another spectral presence of nonliving generations. If to live with the mortal other is to live with her dying—that is, her mortal time—and in mourning for her dying or her death, one also mourns for "her" dead that die with her a second time (i.e., the dead that contextualized her life), then the dead are "with us" not only in our memory, but in this indirect way, that is, by way of relating to the mortality of living-dying and already deceased others.[21] Arguably, there is a similarly transitive, capillary relation to the unborn and their spectral presence among the living. For if we take asymmetrical responsibility for living minors, we must seek to enable their future responsibilities as adults: G_2 owes G_3 the means to support G_4, and G_4 to G_5, etc. To relate to your generative possibilities, to your births, is to relate to your children, biological or not, and thus to future people. This is one of the reasons why Levinas speaks of the "infinity" of the obligation that emerges with natal mortality. The demand to let others live may be called "infinite" not only because the presently living cannot fully acquit themselves of a demand that is co-constitutive of their subjectivity, but because, in taking asymmetrical responsibility for overlapping future generations, the demand transitively extends to children's children, their children, and so on. To take responsibility for those who are to outlive me in the present is thus to equip even more distant future people to address their future-related obligations.

Let us now turn to the second cluster of special and ontological problems.

VI.2. Problems of Epistemic Access

This second cluster gathers problems of epistemic access. As we've seen, one may argue that uncertainty about the effects of our actions on future people and about their interests and needs, as well as uncertainty about causal links and the number of future people, will decrease or even obviate obligations we may have to them, especially if one accepts the claim that "ought implies can": if we cannot act in moral ways toward the distant future, then it's hard to see how we could have duties to do so. As already said, these are serious issues that will plague any account of future justice, including the account of generational relations sketched here. Nonetheless, on the basis of natal mortality we can make two general observations.

(i) The first concerns a reiteration of the point that we should not abstract from overlap, and in particular we should not neglect the fact that our relation to distant future generations is relayed by intermediate generations. While G_3 might face many and extensive uncertainties with respect to, say, G_{10}, G_3 has a much better grasp with respect to G_4 and G_5. Its primary task is thus to act on its obligations to these more proximate generations while keeping in mind not only their needs and interests but also the needs and interests of more distant people. This is why it is important in my view to stress not only the generational relation of responsibilities to needs (or duties to rights), but of responsibilities to responsibilities. As stated above, Levinas speaks in this context of "infinity," but also of "fecundity engendering fecundity" (TI, 269/302), that is, a responsibility that, in being taken up, grows rather than diminishes. G3 must keep in view G4's responsibilities to G5, and G5's responsibilities to G6's responsibilities to G7, and so on. On this basis, for example, long-term environmental responsibilities may be justified not only because we may assume that future people will need a livable planet, but also to enable more proximate and intermediate generations to care for their overlapping and more proximate generations, whose number, needs, and interests it will be in a better position to specify. In this sense, the epistemic problems highlight the need for intergenerational cooperation among overlapping and more proximate generations, and point away from modeling IGJ all too purely or abstractly.

(ii) The second point natal mortality can make with respect to epistemic issues is a bit more challenging, and its relevant consequences may not be immediately obvious. Stated in a general way, the point is just that we should not see lack of knowledge with respect to the future other as only a problem for obligations. For one problem with many approaches to ethics in general, and thus with its extension to intergenerational justice, is that the unpredictability of the future is seen merely as a challenge to accounting for obligation. Of course, as indicated, the unforeseeability of the (e.g., long-term) effects of an action may decrease the blameworthiness of the action's initiator. However, on the account presented here, unpredictability also plays a role in obligations and responsibilities in general, for an entity that was not exposed to an erratic future, including unknowable death, could not suffer or be vulnerable. In this basic sense, moral relations are also triggered by the failure of epistemic comprehension, that is, by the alterity of the other.

This point may be furthered by saying that the possibilities for life given to another by responding to what Levinas figures as the fundamental injunction—namely, not to kill—by letting her live must also, precisely by being given to the other, be uncontrollable and thus unpredictable by any moral agent. It is not only identity and knowledge, then, but also alterity that plays a role in the generation of obligation. One of the central difficulties of intergenerational ethics, already in the relation between overlapping generations, lies in negotiating this twilight zone between granting autonomy and charging with responsibilities, in predetermining by bequest and one's own choices the context of future others while allowing them the freedom and responsibility to appropriate it for themselves in view of their needs and responsibilities.

VI.3. Interaction Problems

In section II above, we also discussed so-called interaction problems, in particular an intergenerational version of collective action problems, nonreciprocity, and asymmetries in power and responsibility.

(i) With respect to the latter, it should be clear that natal mortality does not recommend taking symmetry and equality as the right social-ontological model for ethics, even if equality is a central moral, legal, and political norm. As Hans Jonas and Micha Brumlik have argued, and feminists like Martha Nussbaum and Eva Kittay agree, the starting point for ethical reflection should not be "rough equality" but asymmetry, especially if the latter is temporally inflected (Jonas 1984, 39, 130ff.; see Brumlik 2004; Nussbaum 2001, 2006; Kittay 1999). As Jonas puts it, "[A]nd *indeed*, it is in this one-way relationship to dependent *progeny*, given with the biological facts of procreation, and *not* in the mutual relationship between independent adults (from which, rather, springs the idea of reciprocal rights and duties) that one should look for the origin of the idea of (basically one-sided) responsibility in general" (Jonas 1984, 39; emphasis in original).

(ii) As for the problem of nonreciprocity, stressing overlap among generations on the familial and idealized familial definitions means that at least overlapping generations can (and in fact usually do) reciprocate (McCormick 2009 uses overlap to argue against the nonreciprocity thesis in some detail; see also Gauthier 1986; Heath 1997). If we take three generations to overlap at any one time, and take these to cooperate in some form of direct reciprocity (care in old age for infant care, and so on), then all generations are linked to each other as if in a chain (G_1-G_2-G_3, G_2-G_3-G_4, G_3-G_4-G_5, etc.).

(iii) There is, however, another form of reciprocity that on my view should be understood to underlie this direct reciprocity and to take the asymmetry and temporal dislocation among generations more centrally into view. What I call "asymmetrical reciprocity" (as developed in Chapter 3) tries to flesh out and operationalize the normativity entailed by mortal natality: a moral subject first of all receives from the past and (partly) for that reason owes forward. The extant literature on intergenerational transfers speaks in this context of "indirect reciprocity," discussed more often by economists (Kolm 2006; Arrondel and Masson 2006) and only at times by moral philosophers (Gosseries 2009b). As opposed to the two-party relation of direct reciprocity, indirect reciprocity means that B receives from A but gives "back" to C. Asymmetrical reciprocity insists that future people are not only owed duties indirectly, as a result of the living having accepted benefits from the past; rather, I argue, the source of morality in temporal alterity implies that we cannot, in the end, locate the generational origin of obligations so precisely as to neatly distinguish between the dead and the unborn, or overlapping previous and future generations.

To go very quickly here, on the basis of mortal natality and with the help of Derrida in particular, I want to rethink (in Chapter 3) indirect reciprocity as asymmetrical reciprocity. While retaining the three-party relation, asymmetrical reciprocity makes the gift from A to B not just an empirical fact but an indispensable aspect of B's being. What B receives (from the past) is co-constitutive of her very subjectivity, and that means of her capacity for giving itself. (Chapter 3 draws on Mauss's *Essai sur le don* and its long history of appropriation in economics, sociology, and philosophy.) So the gift is not something from which she could be fully acquitted, no matter how well or much B gives to A and to C. The debt to the past is then not just a debt to be repaid; it cannot be repaid, for it also includes an excess that B cannot make her own. This inappropriable excess to debt is one of the reasons I speak of asymmetry, for B cannot be equal to and measure up to the gift.

The past from which a generation necessarily receives is not only the past of empirically identifiable generations (parents, caregivers, teachers, role models, forebears, ancestors, and so on), but (in both Levinas's and Derrida's terms) an "immemorial past" excessive to all economizing and bookkeeping. Because it cannot be appropriated and repaid, the excess looks at us and implores us generational beings from the future.

What this means, I argue, is that the usual (economistic) way of distinguishing past and future people in determining debt and repayment obligations in accounts of indirect reciprocity, as practiced by economists and philosophers, is insufficient: every obligation and transfer to future generations involves repaying a debt to the past, but a debt from which agents can only break free in opening themselves to a future. Speaking of asymmetry in intergenerational reciprocity is meant also to capture this ultimate impossibility of clearly assigning intergenerational obligation to either the past or the future. Asymmetrical reciprocity is thus not as vulnerable as indirect reciprocity to the objection that it cannot account for (the much stronger) direct obligations to future people.

In fact, in insisting that in every relation to future generations there is an element of past debt, asymmetrical reciprocity opens the door to further specifications of owing forward, but now specifications that take our Janus-faced generational entanglements seriously. Taking them seriously is also to recognize that, if the futural excess in every gift is co-constitutive of agency, then there is also a reciprocity relation, however qualified, between present and future people, overlapping and non-overlapping. For the excess involved in natal mortality means that contemporaries cannot but draw an advance credit on the future, a future that they invest with a meaning and a hope that contributes to the present. The claim that there is no reciprocity with future generations is thus shown to be mistaken once we take this social-ontological level into account, beyond mere material transfers. However, it remains the case on this account that responsibility is profoundly asymmetrical in relation to the future in particular.

VI.4. World Constitution

We've said that the difference between intra- and intergenerational justice is also one of world constitution. Normally, we take world in the sense of background (horizons of intelligibility, infrastructure, how many will live, their desires, etc.) for granted, but in IGJ, this world itself becomes subject to moral concerns. In morally relating to future others, we must also consider the world we will leave them (showing that there's also a problem of asymmetrical power). In section II, we mentioned many problems under the heading of "world constitution" (from the question of whether future humans should exist, and how many, to the nonidentity problem and the repugnant conclusion), and we cannot treat them all here. But I do want to point to the general need to consider the relation between time, world, and generations in a more basic way in the context of IGJ.

In defining generations in section I, I stressed that generational relations are best understood as taking place in the context of a culture, a lifeworld that consists of inherited assumptions and a nexus of significance, but also of socioeconomic infrastructure and political and social institutions. With Heidegger's account of finite existence as "being-in-the-world" (GA 2, §§12–38), we have now indicated an ontological elaboration of this claim. To specify the reason why it is important to explore the idea of a world that is shared, but also altered and recontextualized, by generations, let me return briefly to one of the ontological problems affecting world constitution: the problem for views based on domination. One may argue that a generation dominates its successors if it abuses its power asymmetry in a harmful way, without cost-free exit on the part of the succeeding generation (Nolt 2011). We registered Jamieson's response that it is "strange" to say generations dominate each other, for it belongs to temporal precedence and asymmetry that previous ones co-determine the very lifeworld conditions of later generations. For instance, the present generation has no choice but to accept that Manhattan is no longer an island full of birds and nature but a concrete island full of houses and interesting but nonnatural experiences (Jamieson 2014, 159). If those who remade Manhattan could have but did not consult the contemporary residents who have to live with all the concrete, we might say an injustice took place; we typically don't say so in the case of generations.

While I agree with Jamieson on this point, I find his own cutoff for intergenerational domination—that domination occurs only when the content, not the circumstances, of choices have been predetermined by previous generations (Jamieson 2014, 159)—arbitrary and unconvincing. Inherited circumstances provide the content of action alternatives. New Yorkers can no longer choose to live in wild Manhattan, at least not at significant cost to themselves and others. If a previous generation allowed a species to go extinct, we can no longer choose to live in the ecological web of which it was a part. If corporate-driven monoculture farming eliminates ancient grains for short-term profit, we can no longer choose to make our bread with it even if we are not told which of the remaining alternatives to use.

There are several preliminary conclusions to draw from this. First, especially when it comes to IGJ, the cut between normative and nonnormative realms, the cut between what a theory of IGJ can cover and what it must accept as factual, is itself a decision that is to be scrutinized. Indeed, facts and values intermingle here in a way that calls for reflection on the source of this intermingling in the very constitution of our terrestrial lifeworlds. Further, this discussion shows us that, when considering the relation between present and future, we must also look at the relation of the present to the past, that is, inheritance, for the present generation was and still is in a similar position with respect to its predecessors as the future generation is to the presently living. Generations should be understood to be placed in a chain of generations, in which a preceding and exceeding world is passed along, enveloping, preceding, and exceeding each link in the chain even as it is altered by each generation. A theory should not just restrict itself to that for which it thinks would-be agents can take free responsibility, but should reflect on the emergence of agency in history against the background of a world in which there are dimensions that are involuntary, inherited, and yet binding.

These considerations demonstrate that it makes sense for IGJ theories to consider the role of inheritance in the constitution of agency and moral relations. Even if it is difficult to say something general about which circumstances were inherited in a way that could not be altered, it is important to be able to say that inheritance and historical immersion belong to the very being, the ontological constitution, of human agents. This motivates further exploration of what a world or lifeworld is, how the commonality of world across individuals—intragenerationally as well as intergenerationally—is established, and what role nonhuman elements, like the terrestrial biosphere, play in world constitution.

The basic point here, then, is not to solve the issues of world constitution in one fell swoop (from the question of whether future humans should exist and if so, how many, to the nonidentity problem and the repugnant conclusion), but to point to the need to examine the relations among time, world, and generations in a more basic, ontological way. The question of world constitution could thus be taken to show that what comes into play, what is at stake in IGJ, is (i) the ontology of world formation, including (ii) the divisibility of worlds (do worlds coincide with generations? what if the latter do not come on-stage *en bloc*?) and (iii) the ethics of building a world for others. Here too I will argue that the usual division between intra- and intergenerational settings is overblown.

For Levinas, ethics at its most basic consists always in letting others have their worlds, a letting that hovers between activity and passivity. What we should not do is suppose that the world-as-background-to-interaction is firmly given, and that subjects remain distinct from these interactions and from each other, at bottom unchangeable in their internal, self-referential identity. In fact, relying on the concept of "world" found in Heidegger, Levinas, and Derrida, I will argue that the identity of individuals always—of course to varying degrees—depends on these circumstantial, worldly factors as well as on other identities in the context. Largely for pragmatic reasons, we often, though by no means always, abstract from these constitutive world-relations when making normative judgments. The light that IGJ casts back upon intragenerational questions undoes these abstractions; this light reveals that, at its most basic, ethics does consist in "the gift of the world to the other," as Derrida put it early in his career in discussing the relation between Heidegger and Levinas (WD 148/185).

Further, in Chapter 3 I will argue that the necessary precedence and excess of lifeworlds to the generations they envelop and co-relate to each other plays a crucial role in obligating generations. For this excess is incalculably "unpossessable," and thus always futural for each generation. Thereby, it puts generational relations in touch with a spectral future that has not yet arrived, and will in fact never materialize as such, not even for future generations. For what cannot be appropriated in the world of inheritance by each generation is not only its immensity and its ultimate untraceability as to its origin, but the fact that it is not totalizable: it is the necessary background to all things and significances that move into the foreground. Taken in the basic, ontological sense of a horizon of intelligibility, a nexus of significance, world itself, as worldliness or contextuality, never appears as such.

Despite this nontotalizability, however, worldliness is not independent of particular lifeworlds, but on the contrary names their hold on being-in-the-world. Owing to their worldliness, human beings always find themselves in a world that therefore exceeds them. In this sense, if we recognize natal mortality as giving rise to agents, then we also multiply worlds. In Chapter 5, we will reflect more on this plurality, in particular by distinguishing individual worlds (each agent inherits and projects her own; the world as island), collective-cultural worlds (e.g., national), the common world (presumed to be objectively the same for everyone), and "earth" as the history and habitat of mortal life, as well as the spatiotemporal difference that first of all prompts individual worlds to project their own but also to project a common one. Properly understood, then, the problem of different worlds already affects contemporaries, and to deny this, to assume a common world simply shared, was always already morally and ontologically problematic.

To be sure, it remains the case that giving the other a world to live in, where world in particular involves socioeconomic and political infrastructure, the number of people and their desires and worldviews, and so on, remains more of a moral-political issue in the intergenerational case. But we should not divide this problem into two worlds, the world of contemporaries and the world of future people. Disaggregating the former also leads us to differentiate the worlds of future people.

Conclusion

While the sketch of natal mortality did not address all ontological problems at times said to affect future people, I hope it has motivated the basic idea that taking the time of birth and death into account affords a better general starting point for responding to many of the special challenges of IGJ. In addition, natal mortality may suggest certain IGJ models, such as asymmetrical reciprocity and taking turns among generations, that respond to the social-ontological co-implication of the past and future in the present. While the next chapter will discuss Levinas in greater detail, Chapters 3 and 4 will elaborate these models.

2

Levinas's "Being-for-Beyond-My-Death"

The previous chapter began to argue that the ontological problems besetting many approaches to intergenerational justice call for ontological investigations into the links among time, sociality, and normativity. In this chapter, we will go beyond a sketch of these links by discussing the constitutive role of natality and mortality in greater detail through a sympathetic yet critical reading of Levinas on time and responsibility. The goal is not to show that Levinas offers a full-blown theory of intergenerational justice, but that discussions around his work on "ethics as first philosophy"—a discussion that includes his predecessors and the reception of his work by his successors—helps us to reconceive justice in general as intergenerational from the beginning. Levinas challenges the presentist assumption, as it were, head-on, by rethinking and explicating the very ground of responsibility in general, beyond a narrower focus on obligations to unborn claimants. While relations between presently living individuals remain Levinas's focus—and indeed relations to the unborn are thought to be inseparable from these—all moral relations are conceptualized as intrinsically characterized by a future-directed aspect that points beyond the life of the presently living.

Once we have better understood this future directedness in the present, we can deal more specifically with "nonpresent" future people as the subjects of justice. This discussion of Levinas, and particularly the concluding discussion of deconstructive and feminist responses to him, will prepare us for the more extensive development (in Chapter 3) of the model of intergenerational justice that I call asymmetrical reciprocity. As we will also see, however, given its source in responsibility and justice in general, the model does not divide justice by theoretical fiat into intra- and intergenerational issues, but maintains the moral and political contestability of that division.

I. Why Levinas for Future Justice?

Since the publication of his first magnum opus, *Totality and Infinity* (1961), Levinas has enjoyed a strong and widespread reception, with particular intensity in the last twenty-five years (for an overview, see Morgan 2007; Mensch 2015; Davidson and Perpich 2012). Levinas's work has had significant impact not only on philosophical ethics, religion, and theology, but also in the study of literature, culture, history, and postcolonial studies (Drabinski 2011). However, despite the obvious relevance of his work to intergenerational justice, and despite the increasing importance, in academia as well as in global civil society, of sustainability and long-term, future-oriented responsibilities, few attempts have been made to reread Levinas with these concerns in mind (but see Waldenfels 2017; Liebsch 2017; Severson 2017; Fritsch and Menga 2017).

And yet some scholars have recently devoted book-length studies on the centrality of time to Levinasian ethics, subjectivity, and sociality (Severson 2013; Lin 2013). While these studies do not consider future people specifically, they do point in the right direction and may be used as helpful springboards. In particular, what this recent body of work has made increasingly clear is that time, for Levinas, is a fundamental way to think the conundrum of the emergence of normativity as he sees it. For Levinas, socialization and responsibilization are constitutive of human subjectivity. An agent does not become an agent in a value-free way, only acquiring obligations later, for instance, when she recognizes the validity of the moral law or commits to a social contract or accepts the demands of particular others. On his view, obligation is not generated in an agent's being confronted by the universalizable interest of an obligating party (e.g., avoiding pain, having her rights respected, and so on). Rather, obligation is also, and indispensably, generated by what we *cannot* know of a concrete singular other, by her or his very otherness and the fact that they cannot be absolutely subsumed under a general category (e.g., nationality, humanity, vulnerability, etc.). Alterity here means, therefore, "singularity" (Perpich 2008, 18), but also the "ultimate unidentifiability" of that which obligates me. My obligation is always incompletely justified. This is reminiscent of Kant, who, even if he stressed the universality of the law and the autonomy of the rational agent, knew well that the moral law is a command beyond reason of which we must be content to "comprehend its incomprehensibility."[1]

The source of moral obligation is thus never wholly accessible to the responsible subject. It appears not in a concept such as humanity or vulnerability, but only on the (for Levinas, primarily or even exclusively human) face. Levinas does more than just stress the singularity of the other in his ethics. He also challenges the basis of any ethic that abandons, or fails to account for, what he takes to be the factual starting point of moral responsibility in a first-person perspective. This failure affects all forms of ethics that begin with a third-person standpoint, for instance, by grounding themselves on a general law or on previously identified and universally shared traits under which all entities with moral status have been subsumed. This subsumption could be by reference to sentiment ("they can suffer, too"), reason ("they, too, are rational and hence autonomous"), or in some other way, and it misses what is crucial to Levinas, namely, the first-person perspective from which an agent finds herself obligated by the needs of a concrete other who is never just the exemplar of a concept (Levinas 2001, 114; see Fritsch 2013).

But in the ultimate inaccessibility of the singular other's alterity, we find the basic conundrum that his phenomenological accounts keep circling around, knowing full well that they cannot reach the center: that which must appear to an agent cannot appear as such without betraying the singular and concrete alterity, and the only ever incomplete justifiability, of the moral source as it addresses the singular subject in its inescapably first-person standpoint.

Paying attention to time is one way, though arguably a privileged one, of attempting to describe the paradoxical source of responsibility without straightaway betraying it: hence the proliferation of temporal notions in Levinas's oeuvre, such as patience (TI 236/263ff.), diachrony (TO 105/*d* ff., OB 7–20/20–39), hope without awaiting (GDT 67/80), fecundity (TI

240/268ff.), infinity (TI), the immemorial past (GDT 162/186, 177/204; TO 111/*d* ff.), the pure future (TO 89/83, 90/85, 114/*d* ff.), and so on. The basic idea is to understand the agent as always already obligated by the other, who, however, cannot ever be fully grasped by the agent and so remains outstanding, obligating the agent from a futural excess that will not appear fully in the present. The moral source comes from an "immemorial past" whose unrepresentability by memory turns it toward a future said to be "pure" on account of its unpredictability. Normative socialization and subjectivization occur in the "posteriority of the anterior" (TI 54/47; see Ciaramelli 1998; Wenzler 1984²). Alter and ego are related to each other in a time they do not simply and wholly share and in which they thus cannot engage in reciprocal and symmetrical exchange of benefits and debts, or rights and duties (i.e., in exchanges in which my right or duty straightforwardly entails your duty or right, etc.).

We can begin to see here why one might think Levinas's work is particularly helpful for intergenerational justice. Levinas conceives of subjectivity as inherently, and interrelatedly, temporal, social, and responsible. That is to say, human beings are understood, on the basis of a phenomenological social ontology, as constitutively related to others in normatively binding ways that point beyond the lifetime of individuals. Normative sociality is characterized by an "infinite time" that is situated "across the discontinuity of generations" (TI 268/301). Despite the seeming presentism of Levinas's emphasis on the "face-to-face" relation as central to social ontology and ethics, and despite conceiving the other's face as living, the alterity of the face is elaborated as addressing an ego, in constitutive ways, from a futurity that that ego cannot share, appropriate, or render commensurable with the time of its life. Far from being presentist, nongenerational, or otherwise cut off from future people, the very being of the human subject is conceived as a "being-for-beyond-my-death" [*l'être-pour-au-delà-de-ma-mort*], a fecund or generative being "for a time that would be without me" (CPP 93/*h* 45). This generativity promises to render the moral status of future people, born and unborn, less problematic and anomalous.

What is more, this mortal futurity of our being is recognized by Levinas not just as an ahistorical thesis, but as the very signature of our age, a signature pitted against technology and modern nihilism:

Our age is not defined by the triumph of technology for the sake of technology, as it is not defined by art for the sake of art, and as it is not defined by nihilism. It is an action for a world to come, a going beyond one's epoch.... There is a vulgarity and a baseness in an action that is conceived only for the immediate, that is, in the last analysis, for our life. And there is a very great nobility in the energy liberated from the hold of the present. (CPP 93/*h* 46)

Two questions need careful consideration here: How does Levinas arrive at the conception of moral subjectivity as "for" the time of the other? And why would that time refer to a time beyond my death? As in the previous chapter, I will briefly return to Heidegger, whose early work on being and time Levinas considers an "obligatory passage" (GDT 22/32ff.). In *Being and Time*, Heidegger famously argued that a world, understood as the context within which entities and possibilities for action appear meaningful, arises for an agent in her or his confrontation with death: only "being-for-death" permits the authentic temporalizing from out of the future that allows entities and the agent herself to appear in a meaning-conferring context of reference (GA 2). As we already discussed in the previous chapter, the basic claim is that there could be no agency and no meaning without relation to death, a claim that I will not unfold and defend in great detail here (but see, e.g., Dahlstrom 2001; Gethmann 1993; Caputo 1988), although I will now seek to motivate it again in this context.

If facing death is necessary for the authentic temporalizing that discloses a world of meaningful possibilities to me *qua* agent, one may think that death is, at least initially if not essentially, encountered in or by way of another person: I encounter death through the death of another. But for Heidegger, while it may be that I first learn of death by way of the other's, this knowledge is still too "objective" (GA 2, §47, 281/316): "We do not experience the dying of others in a genuine way but are at most always next to it [*immer nur "dabei"*]" (GA 2, 282/318). A "genuine" relation would be one in which an agent relates to her own death in "anticipatory resoluteness" *as* her ownmost possibility. Seeing as the Heideggerian agent must grasp the present moment not as an "is" but as a "to be," that is, ripe with futural possibilities to be actualized by the agent herself against the background she has inherited alongside others, this way of relating to death is necessary. The present must be seized by the agent as coming toward her from a future in which no one can replace her, a future in which she exists as an absolute singularity. The agent's future has to be wrested away from "the masses" (the "they," *das Man*) and their "fallen," "inauthentic" (*uneigentliche*) self-understanding so as to allow the agent to take responsibility for her own choices. Because death—and Heidegger argues, controversially, death alone (for doubts about this, see Hügli and Han 2001)—is that futural possibility which no one can assume in place of the agent, anticipating one's own death temporalizes the present in such a way that an agent can present choices for action to himself or herself in a meaningful way. The meaningfulness of these possibilities depends on its limited, finite character, for if I were immortal, as we suggested in Chapter 1, no choice or action of mine, nor social relations, would have meaning to me. Choosing to do A now would not mean sacrificing my chance to do B; I would have time enough to do everything I want—and perhaps more. As Levinas puts it, glossing Heidegger, "An immortal person is a contradiction in terms" (GDT 45/56).³ This finite, ownmost, and possibilizing effect can thus only be had by anticipating one's death as one's proper possibility: "Death is the possibility of the absolute impossibility of Dasein. Thus death reveals itself as one's *ownmost, non-relational, unsurpassable possibility* [eigenste, unbezügliche, unüberholbare Möglichkeit]" (GA 2, 294/333; emphasis in original).

In response to Heidegger, Levinas agrees with the dependence of meaning and agency on death, but he emphasizes the inaccessibility and utter alterity of my own death to me. While it remains true for Levinas as well that "human freedom" demands that the "present moment does not coincide with itself" but is "dispersed in the inexhaustible multiplicity of the possible" (TI 238/265), death is not a possibility of the agent but the very impossibility of agency, the point at which all activity ceases and a fundamental passivity reveals itself. Levinas is fond of making this point by saying, with and against Heidegger's words, that death is not the "possibility of impossibility," but the "impossibility of possibility" (TO 70/*t* 57, 114/*d*; Levinas 2001, 122; TI 235/262) because it signifies the end and limit of the autonomous "I can." And yet, to have access to her agency and a meaningful world, a human being must know of death, must develop a relation to it and come to understand it as a threat to her projects and her interest in survival. The agent is caught between the need for a relation to death and its inaccessibility.

While Heidegger attempts to solve this conundrum by turning away from "the masses" and toward the "mineness" and "non-relationality" of death, Levinas develops an intersubjective (if we may use this otherwise problematic word for the moment) solution: the experience of mortality, the encounter with death, cannot bypass other people and their mortality. As noted very early by Heidegger's students Dolf Sternberger and Eugen Fink, in his account of mortality Heidegger does not fully pursue the ontological significance of "being-with" (*Mitsein*) and its existential care for the other and the other's mortality.[4] Heidegger does not press the question of how we can think together individualization and being-with in relation to death, even if in the infamous §74 of *Being and Time* he does allow a co-historizing of *Dasein* with others in a "generation" and, notoriously, in "the people" (GA 2, 436/385).

By contrast, Levinas zeros in on the question of individuation and relation to others in the face of dying. Space does not permit me to go into the details of Levinas's argument in this context, an argument well investigated in the secondary literature (Beardsworth 1996; Rolland 1998; Chanter 2001; Köveker 2004; Klun 2007). We could say that Levinas here extends and intersubjectivizes the long philosophical tradition that associates time with sensibility, receptivity, and mutability.[5] For Levinas, to be enabled by, but also subject to, mortal time implies a relation and exposure to others: "The solitude of death does not make the Other vanish" (TI 234/260). Sociality is based on the fact that we are temporal and vulnerable. To be temporal is to not be one with oneself, to be constantly changing, and thus to be subject to change by the other. While this connection between temporality and receptivity, and thus also between finitude and sociality, is a fundamental insight of much recent philosophy, Levinas makes it more precise, and radicalizes it, by carrying the other right into the heart of agency.

Death threatens to reduce a free being to a mere thing, to something that lacks inner distance, that merely coincides with itself. Temporal distance defines what Levinas calls the will or freedom, and what we have called agency, to the extent that only this distance, this noncoincidence with itself, allows a self to experience itself as being-possible. "Human freedom" demands that the "identity of the present splits up into an inexhaustible multiplicity of possibles that suspend the instant. And this gives meaning to initiative, which nothing definitive paralyses" (TI 238/265). "To be conscious is . . . to have a distance with regard to the present: to relate oneself to being as being to come, to maintain a distance with regard to being even while already coming under its grip. To be free is to have time to forestall one's own abdication under the threat of violence" (TI 237/265). As a result of this temporalizing anachronism, the human being never coincides with its birth, its natural kind, or its definition: it is never completely born but remains in the process of being born. As Hannah Arendt argues in *The Human Condition*, human natality comprises both the aspect of being thrown as a mere thing or body into unchosen circumstances and of appropriating them to the point of giving birth to something new, the hallmark of human action (Arendt 1958, 8–12, 246–247).[6]

Owing to this inseparability of death from an interpersonal order, there is also a point "where death no longer touches" the will (TI 240/268), for the inseparability permits it to shift the center of gravity away from egoism. The violence of vulnerability, pain, and death—all those things that reveal agents as also passive objects by means of their bodies, as potentially things exposed to the actions of the world—this violence "occurs in a world in which I can die *as a result of someone* and *for someone*" (TI 239/267; emphasis in original). The interpersonality of death, then, "changes its concept: it is emptied of its pathos that comes to it from the fact of it being my death." It is this re-centering of the ego in the other, in the beyond-egoism, that Levinas says he analyzes as "fecundity," from which the "time of patience" flows (TI 240/267). (We will come back to fecundity shortly.)

If the fact that death is inseparably connected to an interpersonal realm allows a mortal being freedom to re-center itself toward the other, then this possibility is not first and foremost its own. It is a possibility that responds to the death of another, the death that articulates the basic demand "Do not kill." For the other's mortality, a dying and a vulnerability that an agent cannot bypass lest it miss its own agency is never free from a claim upon the concern the agent has for the other—a care (*Fürsorge*) that Heidegger already grounded in Dasein's ontologico-existential "being-with-others," despite determining Dasein's being as care (*Sorge*) for its own being, and without conceiving of this care for the other as responding to the other's claim. On a certain reading of

Heidegger, he too recognizes that death first of all allows the recognition that the other's possibilities call for surpassing my own death. For Heidegger, the singularizing assumption of one's mortality first of all permits one to recognize that time, the temporality of existence not thought on the basis of the revolution of celestial bodies, is not shared, for singularizing death is not shareable and death is what gives access to time. Only resolute running ahead toward death permits the recognition of this nonsharing of time, thus of the other's alterity, of her own time. In encountering being as being-toward-death and thereby understanding one's own possibilities as finite, Heidegger writes: "Dasein dispels the danger that it may, by its own finite understanding of existence, fail to recognize that it is getting *outstripped* by the existence-possibilities of Others [*die es* überholenden *Existenzmöglichkeiten der Anderen*], or rather that it may interpret these possibilities wrongly and force them back on its own" (GA 2, 308–309/264; translation modified). Hence, while death singularizes, it also "makes Dasein, as Being-with [*Mitsein*], have some understanding of the potentiality-for-being of Others" (GA 2, 309/264, §53). This understanding makes it possible for Dasein "to let the others who are with it [*die mitseienden Anderen*] 'be' in their ownmost potentiality-for-being" (Heidegger 1962, 344/298, §60). To understand the alterity of others, then, means to understand that letting them be in their being implies giving them possibilities for existence that surpass, or pass beyond (*überholen*), me in ways unassumable by me. Already in Heidegger, recognizing the connection between agency and mortality, between freedom and the noncoincidence of time with itself, leads to an account of social relations as never just restricted to the ontological assumption, so frequent in approaches to intergenerational justice (see Chapter 1), of sharing life in the sense of belonging to the same generation—even if what we mean by "world" will also have to include the shared structures of meaning and public norms of our being-in-the-world (see McMullin 2013, 122ff.). But in Heidegger, the mineness of death calls me to responsibility for my being, while in Levinas the interpersonal order from which death comes calls on me to take responsibility for the other above all.[7] Further, Heidegger's existential analytic does not stress the fact that Dasein is embodied, hungry (TI 134/142), sexed, that it ages, has sex and perhaps children (see Mensch 2015, 148).

The differences between Heidegger and Levinas come to a head in the latter's claim that death is not nothingness but rather belongs to an interpersonal realm that is already in the process of outliving the individual. Let us look at this more closely.

II. Death Is Not Nothing

The way we approach death is thus the key to grasping the relation to others, including future others. As indicated, this issue concerns the heart of Levinas's philosophy: if the alterity of death cannot, *pace* Heidegger, be appropriated for an authentic temporalizing, then how can it appear at all? Death is that which an agent must access for her very ability, but it is defined by its coming to me rather than my going to it. I run to death, and death toward me, but the encounter seems impossible: as Levinas references Lucretius, when I am, death is not, and when death is, I am not (TO 78/*t* 66; cf. TI 235/261–263; Cohen 2006). For Levinas, the problem is precisely not that death is nothing; on the contrary, this conundrum can be approached only by understanding that death appears with others, in an interpersonal world.

To the Levinas of *Time and the Other*, the alterity of death, its inaccessibility "as such," seems to be incapable of being solved conceptually; only in the "concrete situation" of the encounter with another person can we approach death. The other person can fulfill this mediating role because, in everyday life, she is both knowable as another "me," another species of the same genus, constituted by the activity of the subject—and refractory to the genus, different from me, utterly incomprehensible in her own mortality and vulnerable exposure to an unknown future (TO 83/*t* 75). Hence, "[d]eath, source of all myths, is *present* only in the Other, and only in him does it summon me urgently to my final essence, to my responsibility" (TI 179/195, Levinas's emphasis).

It is not so much that Levinas wants to show that death comes from the other first, and only then, by an analogical transfer, can be experienced by the self as also applying to it. Particularly in physical pain, there is, he says, what naturalism calls an "instinctive knowledge" of death: pain points to a beyond that appears to threaten with something worse (TI 233/259). Despite this knowledge, however, the point is to show that death is inextricable from an interpersonal order without which it could not be experienced as death, in its imminence, its threat, and its approach from the outside without my knowledge or control. In *Totality and Infinity*, Levinas adds to the sketch of an argument in *Time and the Other* the idea that to be meaning-giving, death must be understood as a threat to my projects, and this requires that death be personified. To grasp death as possibly interrupting my projects, I must model it on the experience of other people, as we do when we anthropomorphize it, as in fact many cultures do (e.g., Thanatos, the Grim Reaper, the Hooded One, King Yama, Enma, Shinigami, etc.). But agents can personify death and see it as the activity of a foreign power only if they already have the experience of an alien will, that is, another person. Both the other and death reveal the agent as utterly passive, exposed to a violence that does not originate with the agent.

In his phenomenological analyses, Levinas adds a few other indices to the fundamental inseparability of mortal temporalization and ongoing socialization, analyses that come to a head in the claim that death is not nothingess but rather the ethical relation to futural others whose life and world is not, or not totally, appropriable by me. As one of these indices, Levinas argues that fear of death is not fear of nothingness, as perhaps in Heidegger's account of anxiety (TI 236/262–263), but of violence and pain. As such, it extends to the other person, who can inflict or alleviate the pain. In death, the other is present both as potential murderer and as caregiver: "The doctor is an a priori principle of human mortality. Death approaches in the fear of someone and hopes in someone" (TI 234/260).

But Levinas warns that we should not (as Heidegger does on Levinas's view) reduce the affects before death to either flight (as in the case of "the masses," the quotidian others) or existential anxiety (as in the case of authentic resoluteness), for it is possible that fear of the other's death may affect me more than fear of my own (GDT 93/109, 105; LR 82/93–94e). On this view, humans have "the capacity to fear injustice more than death [*sa possibilité de redouter l'injustice plus que la mort*]" (LR 85/106e), as testified to in the "banal fact—which is no mere banal fact—that one can die for someone" (Levinas 2001, 127). This possibility shows that death, while never accessible as such, is not nothingness; it is, in fact, inseparable from a life beyond it: I can die in order to let someone else *live*.

In his discussion of Ernst Bloch on hope, Levinas argues for this nonequivalence of death and nothingness from the perspective of agential projects. In general, my projects depend on others providing me with the world of alternatives on which my free choices depend, and making possible my self-separation and temporal noncoincidence central to freedom (see Mensch 2015, 126). For this reason, my work and my projects are also always aimed at others. If, then, part of the fear of death is the fear to leave my work unfinished, this fear cannot but also reference others who may abort, forget, or carry on my work. In this sense, my death is always premature (LR 82/e), characterized by fear of abandoning my projects and by hope that others will carry them on. To Heidegger's anxiety before death, then, Levinas pits Bloch's "melancholy of fulfilment" (Bloch 1985, 343):

For Bloch, the anxiety of death comes from the fact of dying without finishing one's work [*oeuvre*], one's being. It is in an unfinished world that we have the impression of not finishing our work. . . . There is failure in every life, and the melancholy of this failure is its way of abiding in unfinished being. This is a melancholy that does not derive from anxiety; on the contrary, the anxiety of death would be a mode of this melancholy of the unfulfilled (which is not a wounding of one's pride). The fear of dying is the fear of leaving a work unfinished, and thus of not having lived. (GDT 99–100/115–116)

What Bloch calls the "darkness of the lived moment" (Bloch 1985, 341), and what I have called the noncoincidence of the present, makes freedom possible but also renders each moment incomplete and thus referenced to a future of hoped-for completion: "The subject, in the darkness of the pure fact of being, works for a world to come and for a better world" (GDT 101/117).

This temporal structure of agency is what Levinas has in mind when he characterizes our being as a being-for-beyond-death. If my agency depends on "my" time not coinciding with itself, and this noncoincidence is the entry point for an ongoing socialization that has always already opened "my" time for the other and her moral demands, then "my" time is structurally stretched out toward the future of others. This structure would hold even if I were the last person on earth, as in Routley's famous thought experiment (see Routley 1973 for the "last-man argument"). The meaningfulness of my acts would still depend on my being in a world that is fundamentally social and futural. If, in that extreme situation which we should beware of turning into a revealing model, my acts were not just "desperate blows of a head struck against the wall," it is because "a meaningful order subsists beyond death," a death that is never calculable and thus remains "a death ever future" (TI 236/263; see also GDT 183/211–212). This meaningful order is that of the untraversable interval between me and my death: there would still be the time that is not for me but for the other to come.

That death is not mere nothingness for the ego is confirmed by the fact that, on this view, the other cannot be morally (though can, of course, be physically) annihilated. Murder is, in Levinas's words, physically possible but ethically impossible (TI 199/218, 232/258). The force with which the other confronts the murderer is not just a measurable, physical force but also something other than force; otherwise, the murder victim would be a mere thing, and a thing can be destroyed but not murdered. What is other than force in the other is her very alterity, which Levinas here begins to describe as the "unforeseeableness of his reaction," the transcendence to calculations and totalizing comprehension, the unpredictability of the other's future. Even in murder, the other retains an immeasurable alterity or infinity and thus an "ethical resistance," a remnant of agency condensed into the moral command not to kill (TI 199/218). This agential remnant derives from the incalculability of death for both victim and killer, and thus from an unpredictable future. Death is separated by a "leap" from the consciousness of our lives (TI 235/261), granting still some postponement of death and possibility for unpredictable actions to the victim. Death is not presentable or presentifiable: it is not a calculable moment in time that agential powers can produce, neither in oneself nor in others, but rather an anachronistic event.

Crucially, this noncoincidence of the present with itself (and thus of the murderer's calculations with themselves) implies that there is an infinity in the present, a futurity that extends beyond physical death and that renders impossible the sending of the victim to nothingness. If agency (including that of the murder victim) depends on the anachrony of time, and this anachrony entails (in the way discussed above) a constitutive being-with-others, then even a socially isolated murder victim, in principle, "lives on" in these others as a constitutive aspect of *their* time. Ethical resistance in the present communicates with the memory of survivors.

Cain may have wanted to consign Abel to nothingness, but we, Abel's future people, remember him (TI 232/258). A murder victim survives in the conscience of the killer and in the memory of relatives and society. That is why Macbeth, in the defeat that follows his murder of King Duncan, can only *wish* for the destruction of the entire universe, for death to be a total void (TI 231/256, 146/155).

For Levinas, then, the finite time that permits agency by opening up the present as "to be" is inseparable both from a futurity unmasterable by the living and from the demand to let the other live, to let her have her time, a time inappropriable by me and in the end incommensurable with mine. As we will see in Chapter 5, in volume 2 of *The Beast and the Sovereign*, Derrida condenses this constellation of mortality, alterity, vulnerability, and futurity—that is, my inextricable relatedness to others who may or will survive me—by focusing on the corpse: the alterity of the other could be defined, Derrida says, by the fact that she will have to bury me (BS2 126–128/188–190). The others are those before whom I am not just another living being with whom they share time, but are also those who are already in the process of surviving me, and who will come to treat me as the passive thing that I, in my embodied vulnerability, already also am. There will be others after my death who encounter my corporeal passivity in purer form, as it were. As I will argue in the last chapter, however, these others are not just my "neighbors" (loved ones, family and friends), but also always political powers who co-decide the fate of the corpse, and the earth that lays claim to the body.

If agency, then, can come about only with the demand to let the other live in a time that cannot be appropriated by me, then we can say the demand has always already been expressed to me. As the "always already" indicates, the demand precedes the agent in an unpresentable, unmasterable time Levinas calls the "immemorial past"; this past, however, is also ahead of us as the "pure future" in that it remains outstanding (TO 111/*d*, 114/*d*). Thus, the demand, and the mortal face that bears it, is in "diachrony," not synchronous with my time (TO 97ff./*d*; OB 7–20/19–39 et passim). Given its futurity, the demand is not from the beginning limited by the autonomous capacities of the agent, that is, by the dictum, at times attributed to Kant, that "ought implies can."[8] Rather, the demand to let the other live, to let her have her time, is for Levinas unpredictable in what it will require, and is in this way infinite. It is this infinity of the heteronomous demand that leads Levinas to further characterize obligation in general as always displaying a relation to the future time of others.

Accordingly, our being is, as we have seen for Levinas, a "being-for-beyond-my-death" (CPP 93/*h* 46; see TI 236/263, 253/284, 301/336–337), and this futural structure holds even if the other in question is born before me: if, say, I take care of a parent generation, or someone my own age, I give possibilities for life to a time that is not synchronous with mine, and whose possibilities thus always outlive me, even if the other were to die before me. But of course, the futurity of being-for-the-other is even more pronounced in relation to those born after me, to today's children and their children after them. In addition to this literal coming-after, members of future generations in this specific sense are characterized by the fact that I, or others in my generation, give birth to them. To stress this biological, ontological, and ethical relation to the future, Levinas also characterizes responsibility in general as "fecundity" (TO 90–95/*t* 85–89; TI 267/299). Fecundity is "an ontological category" (TI 277/310)—of which biological fecundity is one noncontingent form (TI 247/277)—that takes note of the fact that human beings exist generationally (see Mensch 2015, 156).

Let us look at this more closely.

III. Fecundity and Future Generations

If "my" time (the time in which I realize my projects) is only given to me by the relation to death and the way in which it discloses possibilities to me and postpones its violence, but death comes to me only by way of (or at least not without) another person's pleading face, then "my" time has always already been claimed by another and for the time of another. This time of the other is not contemporaneous with mine, not already part of a common time that we share, such as the universal time of history or of nature (TI 55/48ff.); this is what Levinas means when he says that ethics takes us "beyond being," or at least toward a being that is plural (TI 301/336–337). The noncontemporaneity is most clearly revealed when the other's death precedes mine or when other people persist beyond my death. By postponing its violence, death both gives time (and hence a world of possibilities) to the agent and threatens to take it away. This "threat" is inseparable from the demand to give my time to another, without its returning to the self.[9] This nonreturn or lack of reciprocity is part of the Levinasian "infinity" just mentioned, which he contrasts with "totality" in the title of his first major book (we will come back to the notion of totality below). The infinity of obligation calls on the agent to give possibilities not assumable by the agent herself, to let the other have her time, his potential, her future.

Now this giving of my time to and for the other happens willy-nilly, but always also as demanded by the other. The description of the happening and the prescription of the demand are, for Levinas, joined in a "morality" that "is not a branch of philosophy, but first philosophy" (TI 304/340). Further, the giving of my time—what we will call the gift—happens when I give to another living person, and thus another person already marked by her mortality and the futurity of her responsibilities that reach beyond the present. Indeed, I always give to a world potentially beyond my appropriation, and thus I give to infinity: I never share the other's time completely, as we've seen, so my gift could never return full circle, not only if, as remains a possibility, I died in the meantime, making of the gift one more conventionally thought to be for members of a future generation. The infinity of the demand, the way Levinas understands it, calls on us to expressly give altruistically, that is, without calculating a return to the self. For if letting the other live *as* other is to be obligated (in part) by her alterity to give, then I am giving to an alterity, in an inappropriable way, without calculating, or properly being able to calculate, any self-regarding return of my gift. And if, as we have seen, the alterity of the other consists chiefly in the other's exposure to an unknowable future that does not belong to her, then to give to the other is to give to an absolutely other time. The basic demand not to kill, far from a mere negative duty, calls on us to give to the future, for the ego cannot reappropriate what it gives beyond its death.

This is what Levinas calls "being-for-beyond-my-death." Only an open future coming to me from the other human being, thus beyond me, allows the disclosure of a meaningful world in which my agency can come to birth. My agency is thus referenced in its very constitution to a world beyond its time, to a time beyond its world. A mortal being, Levinas writes, "has its time at its disposal," that is, can appropriate and impute the time of its life to itself, because it "postpones" death, and that means "because a meaningful order subsists beyond death." And it is on this basis that it can seize "the other chance" in the time it has left "by its being against death: the founding of institutions in which the will ensures a meaningful but impersonal world beyond death" (TI 236/263). More personally, this "other chance" is seized by the rebirth of subjectivity in the child, that is, in the relation Levinas calls fecundity.

In a moment, we will look more closely at fecundity and discuss the contrast between the personal and the impersonal, what in Levinas is also discussed as the family and the State, and what has been taken up in the burgeoning literature on Levinas as the relation between ethics and politics (e.g., Bergo 2003; Morgan 2016). First, however, let us deal with a possible criticism. At this point, one may object that although Levinasian ethics may be futural in the sense described, it does not offer an account of obligations to future people specifically. Further, one may object that future people are here addressed only indirectly, by way of the infinite responsibilities the presently living have for each other. While the present may be de-presentified by Heidegger's being-toward-death, Arendt's natality, and Levinas's being-for-beyond-my-life, the present of the living still appears to be given some privilege here. But do not future people have a more direct, less mediated claim on us?

In response, we should first recall the strategy we are pursuing here, in line with Chapter 1. The ontological and motivational problems affecting duties to future people urge a reconsideration of morality and sociality more broadly, especially in relation to time. Above all, it is critical to overcome a presentist, nongenerational conception of the self and its time, one that views the present as cut off from the absent past and the absent future. This view of time, we've seen, makes responsibility to future people seem anomalous and problematic from the beginning, for such responsibility would have to cross the abyss between presence and absence. What we achieved here with Levinas is the de-presentification of the present by constitutively linking agency, responsibility, and sociality to the future. To be sure, this de-presentification should not fail to do justice to what we may call the presentness of the present, which Levinas does by starting from the face-to-face relation. Bringing out the futurity in that relation (that is, its infinity, alterity, and asymmetry) does not undo the difference between the present and the future, as if faces were without historically situated bodies. But with the help of Levinas, we can avoid a presentist starting point that places "us" the living on one side, and non-overlapping future people on the other, to then ask why and what "we" should owe to "them."

Second, Chapter 1 concluded (section VI) by discussing some advantages of conceiving agency as natal-mortal and responsibility as futural from the beginning. Stretching the living out toward the future pulls future people into the presence of the living, whose contemporaneity is thus put into question. Undoing the assumption of co-presence among the living by recognizing the temporal alterity (and natal mortality) in the now-living other renders the temporal distance to future people less anomalous. It thus leads us to stress, among other things, (asymmetrical) overlap among generations, intergenerational communities, and institutions, the dependence of many of our current projects on future people, and so on.

On the basis of the more detailed account of being-for-beyond-my-death, we can here add another dimension to this spectral presence of future people. As we've seen, the meaningfulness of a world of action and comprehension, as accounted for in Heidegger, comes for Levinas at the price of the infinity of responsibility. For not only are the other's needs, always futural, unpredictable to some extent and thus infinite in this sense of immeasurable. And not only is the basic demand to let the other live infinite in the sense of not returnable to my time. Rather, "infinity" takes on another, concrete meaning here, one often missed. The responsibility for another person whose possibilities outlive mine—most obviously, those of the "child"—includes the responsibility for the "child's" responsibilities for its "children" and their responsibilities, opening up to an infinity of generations. Responsibility is infinite because by its very exercise, it produces more responsibilities: "The summons exalts the singularity precisely because it is addressed to an infinite responsibility. The infinity of responsibility denotes not its actual immensity but a responsibility increasing in the measure that it is assumed; duties become greater in the measure that they are accomplished" (TI 244/273–274). The intergenerational justice indicated in this "infinity" is contrary to the view that each generation is only responsible for the next, as in what we might call a "strict" view of the generational chain, but also contrary to the view that each generation is equally and indiscriminately responsible for all the following. Rather, on this view responsibility passes by way of each generation, indeed by way of each generation's individual members, but includes responsibility for the responsibilities of the following. Thus, emphasis is placed on enabling the next generation or generations to address their obligations, intra- and intergenerationally. (See Chapter 3, section IV in particular, for more on how what I will call "asymmetrical reciprocity" underwrites and transforms kindred chain-related accounts of intergenerational justice.) Key to this understanding is an account of the object of responsibility. The relation between the presently living and future people should not just, or predominantly, be construed as the relation of the duties of the one to the rights of the other, or of obligations to needs, but also of responsibilities to responsibilities.

In this way (and as we will explore further in later chapters), the infinity of intergenerational responsibility has implications for such burning issues as climate change, among others. If the presently living have the possibility of severely hampering, perhaps irretrievably, the means of future life to respond to its obligations to the next generation, then mitigation as well as adaptation may be mandated not so much by future generations or future people as a collective (and distant) entity, but by the responsibility to enable future others to handle their duties to others and their right to life. While one may criticize Levinas for privileging relations among the living, we should note that by paying attention to temporal alterity in these relations, he discovers a relation to future others in it: in the responsibility for the overlapping but singular other who will have to face her own responsibilities, including environmental and intergenerational ones (see also recent work on Levinas and environmental philosophy in Edelglass and Diehm 2012; also Lewellyn 1991; Smith 2011).

From here, one may return to the objection that the relation responsibility-responsibilities renders the relation to non-overlapping future people merely indirect. Does the face-to-face not deprivilege the demands of the unborn, when the task in fact should be precisely to put them on an equal (moral, if not ontological) footing with those of contemporaries? Do we not need, then, to resort to universal norms of equality, or to more generic categories, such as co-nationals or fellow humans, norms and genera that abstract from temporal location?

To respond to this reemergence of the objection, we should refer, even if briefly, to Levinas's account of the third party (*le tiers*). I already alluded to Levinas's discussion of the futural world beyond the mortal face in terms of both personal fecundity and the more impersonal State; the third party mediates between these two. It can be seen as an account of how egalitarian norms respond to the shortcomings of the face-to-face. For the incalculable responsibility of the latter does not account for the calculation needed when an agent is confronted by not only the face of an other, but also a second face, the third party. Having to compare and weigh different demands, the obligated parties devise principles and norms (in Levinas's terms, "justice"; TI 213/234) to adjudicate between them. These norms will also come to cover the singularized I (the obligated agent), thus permitting a "we," and the norms can come to be formulated as laws to be administered by an arbiter, here simply called the State:

> In the measure that the face of the Other relates us with the third party, the metaphysical relation of the I with the Other moves into the form of the We, aspires to a State, institutions, laws, which are the source of universality. But politics left to itself bears a tyranny within itself; it deforms the I and the other who have given rise to it, judges them according to universal rules, and thus as *in absentia*. . . . The irreplaceable unicity of the I which is maintained against the State is accomplished by fecundity. (TI 300/335)

Thus, the third party can be understood as an account of the normative universalization of the living face beyond its singularity, a universality Levinas at times simply (perhaps too simply, too immediately, and too humanistically) calls "the whole of humanity which looks at us" in the presence of the face (TI 213/234), and other times (more carefully, I think) calls "all the others than the other" (OB 158/246). This universalization can be understood to include future people in a more generic and impersonal way than that addressed in the singular and personal relation Levinas here calls fecundity and pits against the "tyranny of the State" (see TI 46/37, 176/191, 252/282).

At this critical juncture, it is important to maintain the tension between universalization and singularization in the right way. Otherwise, as Michael Fagenblat puts it, "[Levinasian] ethics risks becoming a political safe haven for the very individualism it set out to overturn" (Fagenblat 2010, 179). The singular other (to whom I stand in fecund responsibility, a responsibility that first of all makes "unicity" and selfhood possible) is not an object of moral concern merely on account of representing the universal or of being covered by universal norms (hence, the claim that the face-to-face "gave rise" to the movement of abstraction). Nor is the other ever accessed without what Levinas calls "language" or "discourse" (TI 213/234). This means that the other is always encountered within the context of cultural-historical notions that will have begun to abstract from the singularity of the other. These notions, however, lack ethical or political import without their constitutive relation to the singular individuals who alone can be mortal and vulnerable, and who stand in significant relations to others, including members of future generations. Levinas tries to account for these relations by way of many terms that seek to outflank both individualism and egalitarian universalism, from being-for-beyond-my-death and fecundity to responsibility, fraternity, paternity, and maternity. (We will come back to them in a moment.)

Here I cannot treat in any detail the many issues raised by this tension between "ethics" and "politics" (see Critchley 1992, 2009; Drabinski 2000; Bedorf 2003; Bergo 2003; Bensussan 2008; Morgan 2016), and by the relation between the various terms and accounts. But we can see that, for all his emphasis on the singularity of living faces, Levinas allows that the living other (or even others) for whom I am responsible, futurally but in the here and now, is or are not alone. Both by way of discursive-cultural notions and by way of significant personal relationships, the living other reaches beyond present space and time, and may come to be treated as part of a larger group, beyond even the *group* of living others. If I focus, for instance, on my responsibility to a child in my proximity, I should also understand that the child will have responsibilities to his or her children and his or her children's children. Further, I must also see that it is unique only in relation to other children of its generation; fecundity, paternity, and maternity, are inseparable from what Levinas—albeit seemingly excluding the daughter and the sister—calls "fraternity" (TI 278/310). In brief, fraternity (the multiplicity of children) means that the child can carry the hope of the parents for a renewal of time only if she or he is not alone, so that the future is opened up in contestation among siblings, and a single child's time is not a mere continuation of the time of the parents (see Mensch 2015, 168; for a productive development of fraternity as permitting a Levinasian politics beyond individualism and universalism, see Fagenblat 2010, ch. 6).

The next generation must thus be thought both as plural ("fraternity") and in singular relations with its parents (what Levinas calls "election"; TI 279/312). Hence, the focus on the living singular other merges with obligations to future generations, differentiated along singular and generational lines (see Chapter 1 on defining "generation"). Future people, then, can be thought of as situated between the singular other and the third. For Levinas, the important point, however, would be not to dissolve the singularities and singular links of responsibility in such broader categories of generations, nations, or humanity, or in political institutions. As he sees it, "the state, society, law and power" do not exist because "man is a beast to his neighbor (*homo homini lupus*)" but "because I am responsible for my fellow" (LR 247–248). On this view, political and legal institutions do not in the first instance protect individuals and their property from one another, but serve the amplification of care and responsibility (see Drabinski 2000; Morgan 2016), including (as I am arguing here) for future individuals.

Further, just as a concern for universal human rights should not lead us to overlook singular others (see "The Rights of Man and the Rights of the Other" in Levinas 1995), so the interest in justice for future people should not lead us to forget the abstractness of this notion ("future people," "future generations") and the "spectral presences" and transitive mediations by way of which we are already responsible for those who come after us, overlapping and unborn. That is why, as we already hinted, being-for-beyond-my-life can take the more impersonal form of contributing to institutions and communities (TI 236/263) as well as the more personal one of fecundity, which Levinas takes to be "more true than [the dimension and perspective of the political], because in it the apology of the ipseity does not disappear" (TI 301/335). By "apology," Levinas means the personal appeal to the moral judgment of another that is not sanctioned by political institutions and preserved in objective history, including the reason someone might have for dying for another (TI 240/268). At times, Levinas refers to the paradigmatic example of members of the French Resistance who even under Nazi torture did not reveal the names of their collaborators (see the discussion in Mensch 2015, 141–145). Converting fear of pain and death into the fear of committing murder, they "gave birth" to a future for others whose judgment upon this singular act of fecundity will not fully merge with that of "visible history," political institutions, and their universal norms (TI 243–244/272). As Levinas argues in the passage cited above (TI 300/335), responsible subjectivity is only born of a "personal" exposure to others beyond my time, that is, in the "fecundity" that is "maintained against the State" (TI 300/335). Only in the natal-mortal exposure to an other beyond my time can responsible subjectivity emerge, a singular agency whose "apology" and "invisible" response is, for Levinas, effaced and forgotten by anonymous institutions and the "cruel" judgment of history (TI 243/272).

Lastly, we can respond to the objection above—according to which Levinasian fecundity is either not specific to future people, or treats them only indirectly—by pointing to the next two chapters and their elaboration of two models of intergenerational justice, namely, "asymmetrical reciprocity" and "taking turns." For now, I want to prepare the way for the former by critically discussing the relation between Levinasian fecundity and previous others in history, from mothers to ancestors.

IV. Precautions Regarding Fecundity, Paternity, and Maternity

As discussed above, Levinas explores infinite responsibility further by introducing the notion of fecundity, which is largely elaborated as paternity in *Totality and Infinity* (TI 247/276, 267/299ff. [with a passing mention of maternity that we will look at shortly]) and re-elaborated as maternity in *Otherwise than Being* (OB 67–79/109–127, 104–108/165–170; for an overview, see Sandford 2001, 2002).[10] Before rendering these notions fruitful in the context of intergenerational justice, let us take some precautions. Levinas introduces fecundity in *Time and the Other* and *Totality and Infinity* in order to rethink the temporality of the ethical relation in general in such a way that its affective, always particular or singular side is revealed. (We could also say that here the enabling role of the other's mortal alterity in the constitution of subjectivity is to show its *quasi*-transcendental side, that is, the aspect of ineluctably biological and "empirical" forces that must come to play a role in forming subjectivity.) This approach lends itself to misunderstandings because Levinas seems to position parental generativity as both biological (and thus particular to biological procreators) and as the model for all moral relations.

But Levinas in fact uses *fecondité* to combine biological and nonbiological (if you wish, cultural or spiritual) generativity without illicitly universalizing the desire or responsibility to have children. Levinas does not mean to claim that without children, life lacks generative transcendence toward ethical alterity. Nor does he intend to elevate or distinguish parenthood above other roles, familial or otherwise, one might play in one's life. To say that maternity and paternity can serve as models for ethical responsibility is not to say all should become biological mothers or fathers—indeed, one may argue that in the context of rapid population increase and global poverty, procreative rights, however central to human life one may take them to be, have come under moral pressures in perhaps unprecedented ways.

And yet there is also no ethical life without biological fecundity. If fecundity is elevated to an "ontological category" (TI 277/310), then biology—provided we take our philosophy of biology "beyond mechanism . . . , finalism and a dialectic of the whole and the part" (TI 276/309)—is more than a merely regional ontology, Levinas argues (once more, though this time implicitly, against Heidegger's project, in *Being and Time*, of a "fundamental ontology"):

> If biology furnishes us the prototypes of all these relations, this proves, to be sure, that biology does not represent a purely contingent order of being, unrelated to its essential production. But these relations free themselves from their biological limitation. (TI 279/312)

Similarly, biological paternity is but one way to live ethical "paternity," or moral subjectivity in general:

> Biological fecundity is but one of the forms of paternity. Paternity, as a primordial effectuation of time, can, among men, be borne by the biological life [*s'appuyer sur la vie biologique*], but be lived beyond that life. (TI 247/276)

In *Time and the Other*, Levinas, seemingly more strongly, insists that fecundity is a "nonbiological notion" (TO 37/*t* 15). We can understand biological generativity, then, as both a prototype, a model for all moral relations of responsibility—letting the other live is always a kind of giving birth—and as a part of the noncontingent order of being itself.

There are several important ways to explain the both particular and universal significance of fecundity. First, as discussed above, we are situated here between two extremes, neither of which is taken as a model: on one side, the extreme of the last human being in complete absence of overlapping or non-overlapping future people, and on the other, the universality of procreation in which every person would at some point have children. While he often reasons from limit situations, in this case Levinas places us, with good justification, between these extreme points. The existential analytic of human existence and its necessary embodiment should neither treat us as sexless, nonreproducing beings for whom death would be nothingness, nor assume the universality of parenthood. Hence, if the temporality of human life points to the necessary reference to another being between me and the death that I will never experience as such (as argued above), then it is reasonable to let this other not just be figured by the doctor or the murderer (as above), but by the "child." Our lives take place in the midst of children, whether our own or those of others, and some of these children, we should presume, will have children of their own. Given the futurity of subjectivity and the asymmetry of the relation to the vulnerable other, fecundity is then a legitimate model for responsibility in general—although it must seek to avoid centering ethical life exclusively around children, in particular in a way that privileges heteronormativity (see Edelman 2004; for a response to these legitimate concerns, see Fritsch 2017a). For our purposes, fecundity makes manifest that relations with future people are not an afterthought but exemplary of ethics in general.

The second point that justifies the exemplariness of fecundity is the fact—one that relates futural fecundity to the past in a way we will explore further below—that all human beings owe themselves to it. Even nonprocreators are implicated in fecundity. This point can be further elaborated as the insight that nonbiological relations between human beings are to be understood against the background of biological dependencies. Feminist ethics and nonindividualist political and social theory have long argued for the shortcomings of the idea of a society emerging with equality among its members (Gilligan 1982; Ruddick 1989; Nussbaum 1999; Noddings 2002; Held 2006). It is in this way that we may understand, for example, Eva Kittay's claim that the interdependence of adult human beings, as articulated in the division of societal labor, emerges from and in some way continues asymmetrical dependencies among different overlapping generations, paradigmatically the dependence of infants (Kittay 1999). Certainly Levinas would agree with Kittay that social cooperation is misconstrued if theorized as resulting from a contract among equal independent beings (see Nussbaum 2006).

Third, conceiving, bearing, giving birth to, and raising children stand in an ethical context, a wider sociality without which they would not be possible. As the well-known saying has it, it takes a village to raise a child. If biological fecundity gives rise to the complicated density and conflictual intricacy of wider social relations, then the latter in turn form the noncontingent context in which the former can succeed.[11]

Fourth—and here a certain reciprocity with the future emerges—Levinas argues that it follows from his account of the interpersonal region from which death comes that the meaningfulness of at least much of our action depends on a social world assumed as continuing beyond the death of the individual. "The being thus defined has its time at its disposal precisely because it postpones violence, that is, because a meaningful order subsists beyond death." Hence, without the transcendence represented by a new generation, actions would appear to be, as already said, "desperate blows of a head struck against the wall" (TI 236/263). However autonomous and discontinuous with respect to the previous generation, children inevitably carry a promise, a faith or a hope, that all was not in vain. On this point, Hannah Arendt's reinterpretation of Heidegger's "mortality" in terms of "natality" concurs with Levinas's once more:

The miracle that saves the world, the realm of human affairs, from its normal, "natural" ruin is ultimately the fact of natality, in which the faculty of action is ontologically rooted. It is, in other words, the birth of new men and the new beginning, the action they are capable of by virtue of being born. Only the full experience of this capacity can bestow upon human affairs faith and hope, those two essential characteristics of human existence which Greek antiquity ignored altogether. (Arendt 1958, 246)

Both Arendt and Levinas discuss the need of the living for a renewal of time by the future in terms of forgiveness: forgiveness signals the possibility of beginning again without being tied to the consequences of one's actions. As beginning anew depends on one's being born without belonging to a determined causal sequence or to a biological species that reproduces only ever the same copies, forgiveness is rooted in natality as well as in human plurality. These two factors, Arendt argues, combine to imply the dependence of my renewed capacity for renewed action on others, "for no one can forgive himself" (Arendt 1958, 237). Similarly, Levinas argues that the past of one's actions tends to become determinative of one's horizon of future possibilities, one's "fate," as a result of habituation, promises made, and the inertia of history (TI 281/314). To overcome this fate, members of a new generation can, owing to their "freedom," offer to fecundity their "pardon," that is, a recommencement of time beyond the alternative of continuity or discontinuity: "This recommencement of the instant, this triumph of the time of fecundity over the becoming of mortal and aging being, is a pardon, the very work of time" (TI 282/315). As Lisa Guenther puts the point, "[M]y promise *to* the child is bound to the promise *of* the child: the promise of a new and undisclosed future. In his newness, the child is unlike anyone who came before, and so this child—any child—brings with him the promise that the future may be otherwise than the past" (Guenther 2006a, 79; emphasis in original).

This connection between fecundity and forgiveness suggests, as we will pursue shortly, a reciprocity whose specific intrigue lies in the fact that it is premised not on sharing time and the annulment of owing such contemporaneity seems to make possible, but on a rupture in time, a discontinuity that renews the past without repeating it. Levinas discusses it as the "paradox of pardon," which makes of time the "non-definitiveness of the definitive [*non-définitif du définitif*], an ever-recommencing alterity of the accomplished" in which future instants do not come at me indifferently, but "extend from the Other unto me" [*s'étalent d'Autrui à Moi*] (TI 283/316).

To take one more precaution regarding fecundity, we should underline its difference from Plato's claim that through offspring, mortal subjects participate in eternal life (*Laws* 721b–c). For Levinas, by contrast, offspring mean, not only for the parent but for all moral agents, an infinite, discontinuous time that requires an abdication of control over the life of the other, a renunciation of my survival and indeed an affirmation of my mortality: "Infinite time does not bring an eternal life to an aging subject. The infinite time that passes through the discontinuity of generations is *better*; it receives its rhythm from the inexhaustible youths of the child" (TI 268/301; emphasis in original). Fecundity, the relation to the child, "articulates the time of the wholly other," so that "being is society and thereby time" (TI 269/301).

V. Intergenerational Reciprocities

While Levinas's ethical ontology thus ties human subjectivity, morally and socially, to a future beyond that subjectivity, the relation to the past receives a less sanguine treatment. This shows itself, as we will explore in the next section in greater detail, in the way that Levinas both figures the "mother" and views history. In this section, however, we will first seek to elaborate the reciprocity between present and future people that we have already discovered, and argue that it must include a reference to the past. For once we stress that the relation between fecundity and forgiveness involves a kind of reciprocity, however temporally displaced and without singular, identifiable origin, we are bound to ask about the place of forebears. If the child is addressed not only as in need of fecund care but as herself able to give at some point, then the one who is called upon to give is viewed as also a recipient, that is, as someone who, in relevant ways, appropriated from predecessors and/or received pertinent assistance from contemporaries.[12] The father's relation to the son cannot be understood without the mother, and both paternity and maternity are enabled by inheriting from their forebears in history.

In this section, then, the goal will be to reconstitute the role of the past in the ongoing formation of social subjectivity such that responsibility relates, at the same time, to past and future. If subjectivity can give birth to a fecund future only by owing to preceding others, then its moral-ontological historicity can be captured by a Janus-faced form of reciprocity that refers both backward and forward. The forward-looking (and already in some sense asymmetrical) reciprocity we discussed briefly as holding between fecundity and forgiveness will then be complemented, and complicated, by a third party to the otherwise dualistic relation between, in the patrilineal language of *Totality and Infinity*, "father" and "son."

Levinas himself, as I have indicated in passing, rejects the idea of (direct) reciprocity in favor of an altruism of giving to the other without expectation of return: "[T]he I is without reciprocity" (Levinas 2001, 133). Nonetheless, "asymmetrical reciprocity" has been introduced by commentators on Levinas (Young 1997; Paradiso-Michau 2007; Tatransky 2008),[13] largely in order to stress, often against Levinas, that there is some reciprocity or search for mutual recognition in the moral relations among contemporaries, even if, with Levinas, such relations start in asymmetry or their perspectives remain not fully reversible. For instance, Tatransky's notion of asymmetrical reciprocity credits Derrida and Ricoeur with having pointed out, apparently against Levinas, that I can recognize the other as my neighbor only if I see myself as the other of the other (Tatransky 2008, 299ff., referencing Derrida's discussion of "transcendental symmetry" at WD 157/185; and Ricoeur's *Oneself as Another*, Ricoeur 1992).[14] In her excellent work on Levinas, Judith Butler, too, has reworked, in ways that are helpful here, Levinas's strong negative stance on reciprocity. She argues that the distinction between my life and the life or lives of others is too strong, and thus so is the distinction between egoism-based reciprocity and other-regarding asymmetrical ethics. Working toward a theory of "cohabitation," Butler wants

> to insist upon a certain intertwinement between that other life, all those other lives, and my own—one that is irreducible to national belonging or communitarian affiliation. In my view (which is surely not mine alone) the life of the other, the life that is not our own, is also our life, since whatever sense "our" life has is derived precisely from this sociality, this being already, and from the start, dependent on a world of others, constituted in and by a social world. (Butler 2012, 140–141)

While this dependence points to a generational aspect, the notion of indirect or asymmetrical reciprocity that we will introduce in a moment as a relation between *three* parties does not seem to have been considered by Levinas commentators, and in particular not in an intergenerational context, as we do here. But the two-party relation between present and future, it seems, must be seen to be in fact a three-party relation. In the relation between fecundity and forgiveness, we noted that Levinas's diachronic temporality would appear to allow that future people are in a position to give back, to reciprocate even before their time, and to do so without slipping into the circularity of exchange. I stress "before their time" in order to highlight that the kind of reciprocity at issue does not assume that the donor gives only to receive something back. Nor does reciprocity here suppose a common, objective time in which a third party, with access to a metalanguage, measures equivalences of desert and benefits. Before its time, then, the future gives "back" to the present an infinite time without which the present would lose its possibility for recommencement. But to the extent that we, the presently living, are the future of "our" past, we could say that the past, in a not necessarily voluntary sense, has "intended" or, in the famous words of Walter Benjamin's "Theses on the Concept of History," "expected" us. The content of this expectation may take many forms, but invariably includes the "claim" (what Benjamin calls an *Anspruch* in Thesis II) to assume a legacy and continue it in some way (Benjamin 1968, 250).[15] It is this address from the past that I now want to rediscover in Levinasian fecundity.

Levinas does not overlook that the living have appropriated from the past. If the future can give possibilities for action and meaning to the present even before it comes on the scene, then this is a kind of reciprocation, a response to a benefit insofar as the present gives (more or less ethically, more or less willingly) to the future in the form of a bequest or inheritance. In Levinas's account, this finds its reason in the fact that death, as we've seen, robs agency of its "totality" or total activity, its control and simple self-identity, installing instead a fundamental and yet enabling passivity in the heart of agency. The intergenerational significance of this passivity is not restricted to the claim, as discussed, of future others on the present, but also ties the present to the past: the "primary self-alienation" that exposes every agent's work to "alien *Sinngebung* [conferral of sense]" also exposes it to "appropriation by the survivors" (TI 227/251). In fact, just as an agent has to leave much to others through her death, so an agent cannot come about without inheriting the work of others—from material goods to symbolic ones like language and the "tradition" that already opens up a meaningful world. An agent will have profited from the passing of preceding others. Agents depend on others, in particular preceding others, for their birth as well as their material well-being and their symbolic recognition. No one can give to others without herself having received and appropriated intentional and nonintentional benefits. In Levinas's words, the presently living are "survivors" who "appropriate the works of dead wills to themselves" (TI 228/252). It is this appropriation that, in Levinas's terms, is recounted as "universal history" (TI 55/47ff.) or "historiography" (TI 228/252).

If this is so, then the fecund relation to the future, which for Levinas escapes history and the State (see again TI 300/335), cannot be understood without taking this past donation into account. The relation to the future is also a relation with the past. As indicated in Chapter 1 and to be elaborated in Chapter 3, being-for-beyond-my-death is also a being-*from*-others. This is the sense that I would now like to give to the term "asymmetrical reciprocity": a form of reciprocity, not only without the uncritical assumption of a time shared between the parties or full reversibility of perspectives, but also with at least three parties, in which the gift received is given "back" not to the same other, but to other others. The return is "indirect" in that what I owe is not exclusively to the person from whom I initially received, but to other others. That is why we can say that there is a kind of reciprocation here that never slips into the circularity of exchange, a tenuous but still crucially operative connection that respects the alterity of a time that is never simply shared. The past will have given to another from whom it cannot get back in the time of the recipient, and the future reciprocates even before its time.

It would thus seem that the elementary ethical command to let the other live, if read against the background of a social time that is always already intergenerational, yields a thickly historical sense of an ethical connectedness across generations in both directions. The present, Levinas argues, depends on the future to continue its projects, but it also depends on inherited frames of meaning and resources that the living must inherit and appropriate from the past. Such a heritage is never free from "intentions," "expectations," and "claims" on the part of predecessors, just as its appropriation for the sake of the present's responsibilities claims the future to continue its projects. We thus obtain a kind of alternating asymmetry between the generations, an indirect reciprocity in which the living are morally "de-presentified" in a double way: by the claim of the past to pass on its legacy to another future, and by the claim of the future to inherit its "own" possibilities for life.

Perhaps the futural asymmetry involved here is in fact most obvious in biological fecundity. One cannot "return" the gift of birth to one's parents, only to a third party, a future generation. And yet one can only give birth because one has been born of others. But this does not make giving birth a mere species reproduction, a handing down of the "same" gift one received; then there would be no freedom and no natal giving birth to novelty. As we've seen, natality entails independence from natural reproduction as part of a causal chain; one can be free to the extent one's being is not reducible to having been born to a natural species and its species behavior. In fecundity as tripartite reciprocity, this means that in giving the gift of life, procreators draw on a power to which they owe themselves and which thus refers them to their parents, but which they nonetheless cannot wholly appropriate as their own nor pass on (see Gürtler 2001, 362). My use of "asymmetrical" as qualifying "reciprocity" is also meant to capture this inappropriability of the gift of giving. This aspect of the gift comes from beyond historical generations, and remains asymmetrical with respect to human intelligibility.

And yet the gift of fecundity, biological and nonbiological, can only appear with and in history. The fecund relation to the future cannot be reduced to what Levinas calls the "totalization [that] is accomplished only in history . . . analogous to nature" (TI 55/47), but fecundity can also not be understood without taking past donation and appropriation into account. As I will argue in some detail in what follows, on my view Levinas fails to think fecundity not only as reciprocity but as a three-party relation, owing to his tendency to oppose totality to infinity in a way that is too binary and too unproductive. For him, no singularities and singular relations of responsibility "appear" in "universal history," but "only totalities" (TI 58/51). This leads him to see the works of the dead as belonging to the totality of "the same"—that is, to a finite, already played-out and decided history whose judgments, as already indicated, is made in absentia and thus impersonally "cruel" (TI 243/272). On this view, the works and the faces of the dead no longer exert a moral claim on the present. However, once we rethink the opposition between finite totality and positive infinity in terms of an infinite totality—in Derrida's words, history as the unfolding of the difference between totality and infinity (WD 191–2/227; see also 180/213, 177/208, 166/195)—then the asymmetrical reciprocity that, in my view, constitutes human life between birth and death will stand out.

For the dualistic relation between totality and infinity does not allow the call to responsibility to be borne along by the dead, but instead emerges from a past that is, precisely, wholly "immemorial" (TO 111). For Levinas, on this reading, the dead are reabsorbed into the totality of history as the totality of the same, at the disposal of the appropriating subject: "The being that thinks at first seems to present itself, to a gaze that conceives it, as integrated into a whole. In reality it is so integrated only once it is dead" (TI 55/47). But of course, this totalizing perspective of the historian and the survivor cannot be the whole story—otherwise, history could not be produced out of singularities and their relations before becoming totalized at the hands of the survivors. As discussed, this requires that death be not nothing, that "death which for the survivor is an end be not only this end," so that "universal history" does not subsume singularities but permits another time, another reality (TI 55/48). It is this other reality, the direction that death takes other than wholesale integration into the objectivizing perspective of the historian, that we are pursuing here in the interest of exploring the normativity inherent in the very ontological connectedness of the generations, an ontology marked by the time of birth and death beyond universal history.

In Levinas's text, however, there is a tendency to oppose to the time of what he calls universal history and the time of nature only "immemorial time." Although Levinas acknowledges that the dead leave claims of a sort, they are now, in their particularity, without expressiveness: The dying face, says Levinas, loses its expressivity and becomes a mere mask (GDT 12/21). In dying, we become part of mere totality. The contrast between totality and infinity is then also an opposition between history and ethics, between the visible face and its mortality, between life and death. Despite the many complexities of Levinas's phenomenological descriptions of sensibility and vulnerability as "alterity in the same [*altérité-dans-le-même*]" (OB 67/109), in this form the dualisms cannot fully explain how the alterity of death can appear for a subject on the living face to issue its commanding plea. Similarly, the actual or "empirical" debt to ancestors that Levinas suggests both by insisting on fecundity as the generative beginning of each and by casting the ego in the role of a survivor appropriating from forebears, is difficult to link to the "metaphysical" (or ethical, or religious) guilt that simply is the fundamental obligation to asymmetrically take responsibility for the other by giving to a world beyond my life or my death. On Levinas's account, the absolute past (or the pure future) appear not to be traced in, and co-articulated with, history (see Fritsch 2000).

Because he thinks "visible history" in this way—such that ethical subjectivity, responsive to the other, can only appear beyond it—Levinas had to introduce paternity. The role of paternity is to show that there is a time beyond the common time of history, the time that subsumes the ethical relation to alterity under the same. That is why Levinas concludes the section on the ethical will and time in *Totality and Infinity* (III.C: "The Ethical Relation and Time"), which concentrates on the notion of visible history, with a reference to the paternity that will be the chief subject of the next part (part IV: "Beyond the Face"): "It is necessary to go back to paternity, without which time is but the image of eternity. Without it the time necessary for the manifestation of truth behind visible history . . . would be impossible" (TI 247/277). However, as we will see, the father-son relation can in its turn link up with history only by way of what Levinas calls "the feminine" and (in a rare appearance in TI) "maternity." Paternity is possible as fecundity only in relation to a woman who, as beloved, does not seem to reach transcendence beyond history (TI 256/286ff.), and as homemaker and mother effaces herself or is effaced to become what we will treat below as the "matrix" of the relation between father and son.

In discussing the connection between "the feminine" and history, several absences are thus noteworthy in Levinas's work: first, at the time of *Totality and Infinity*, the massive patrilineage that seems to deny mothers at an least equal share in the generation of moral competencies and daughters an equal place among the brothers on the receiving end; second, the absence of what we might call a backward infinity that comes into view when we see the "father", too, as being able to elect his "son" only when he has himself been elected (by a previous "father"); third, the absence of a connection between the "immemorial past" from which the other's appeal reaches us with the past that we can and do remember and by which we might feel obligated; fourth and finally, the connection of the futural infinity with this backward infinity, that is, what I would like to introduce here as the asymmetrical reciprocity that views the "infinite" obligation to the child, the gift of the power of giving, as complemented by the recognition that those who take on such responsibilities for the future do so in (an albeit paradoxical) gratitude for being the recipient of such a gift.

VI. The Feminine, History, and the Elemental Earth

To further motivate and elaborate asymmetrical reciprocity, we therefore turn to what Levinas says about "the feminine" and about history. These two themes are connected (see Guenther 2012), for Levinas recognizes that the fecund, responsible relation of paternity or filiality, as relations of natal-mortal bodies, cannot be thought in a merely transcendent realm, but require a connection with embodiment, history, habitation, and the "elemental" earth from which food and shelter are derived (TI 142/151, 147/157, 158/169ff., 175/190). The feminine in general and the mother in particular establish this connection in his account:

> The notion of maternity must be introduced here to account for this recourse [to the thread of history]. But this recourse to the past, with which the son has nonetheless in his ipseity broken, defines a notion distinct from continuity, a way of resuming the thread of history—concrete in a family and in a nation. (TI 278/311)

To situate the son in a discontinuous history, in a family and a nation to which he belongs but with which his freedom breaks, thus requires a mother, who, for this very reason, must efface her face, in the sense of the Levinasian ethical call, and demand no reciprocation. If she expressed her face, then the relation of the son to the mother would also be one of fecund, infinite responsibility, which as this infinite and transcendent relation would not, in Levinas's conceptuality, be connected to history and to nature. Fecundity, as infinite responsibility, must take place in a material medium, a history and an earth, that allows their connection without undermining the free transcendence and the infinity. The feminine and what Levinas calls the elemental earth (TI 156/167), as Eric Severson has argued, thus play the role of a matrix similar to the *khōra* as maternal receptacle in Plato's *Timaeus* (see Severson 2013, 269–286).

In Plato's cosmological dialogue, for eternal and unchanging forms (the models or "father") to give rise to particulars (the "offspring"), a third, middle term is required which permits contact between these otherwise distinct realms. With its common Greek meaning of "receptacle," *khōra* is introduced as this third element, a matrix that serves as "nurse of all generation" or "maternal receptacle" in which father and offspring can meet (*Timaeus* 50c7–d4). The maternal element can receive all forms only because it is itself devoid of form (see Sallis 1999, 109ff.; Margel 1995). If we just pay attention to the distribution of gender among these three elements, the father is the active form-giving power, while the mother remains formless in permitting contact between father and offspring. Similarly, Levinas's "feminine" withdraws to give rise to paternity and a fecund subjectivity, threatening to reduce, in the words of Irigaray, ethics to a "culture of men-amongst-themselves" (Irigaray 1991, 178). If these patriarchal consequences are unacceptable, even offensive, but seem to result from the basic conceptual setup of Levinas's moral ontology, we have good reason to reconsider the very opposition between totality and infinity, immanence and transcendence, and history and the future of the other.

While the feminine appears as the paradigmatically other in *Time and the Other* (1947), in *Totality and Infinity* it appears as either beloved, the object of male desire (as Irigaray argues; Irigaray 1991, 1993a), or as the feminine abode, the home in which a self can first of all emerge. Levinas argues that a subject can evolve its capacity to experience itself as constant and to disclose the world only by way of an originary familiarity with an abode. A self does not originally coincide with itself, neither temporally nor spatially, and so has to constantly work at making of "itself" a self at home in the world. Human beings confront the "strangeness of the earth [*l'étrangeté même de la terre*]" in its "elemental" character that is extended in the existential dread of the *il y a*, the anonymous and ungraspable "there is" (TI 142/151). The subject has to live from the earth in its strangeness, but so as to acquire some constancy and security, it has to create a habitation for itself. A dwelling (*la demeure*) is not so much a tool for human activity as its condition of possibility, its starting point (TI 152/162). A self cannot be thought without a home, a *chez soi* (*casa* is the root of *chez*), from which the self goes out into the world and to which it returns. Levinas understands subjectivity as "separation" from the world in which the self finds itself—a separation he takes to be "non-contingent and non-provisional" (TI 48/40). Separation designates the becoming-individual of individuality, an "interiority" irreducible to totality, to the totalizing time of history and of nature into which, as I have stressed, Levinas thinks that the self is integrated only "once it is dead" (TI 55/47). It is from the home base that subjectivity reacts to the world in view of its projects, enjoyments, and work.

Projects, work and enjoyment thus entail an affirmation of the appropriation from the earth and from history in view of rebuilding and returning to a home. Even in the smallest of a subject's pleasures, there is an agreeableness and an agreement with the elements, for without them no such pleasure was possible. The emergence of subjectivity requires, in Levinas's phrase, a "primary agreeableness/agreement" (*un agrément préalable, l'agrément premier*; TI 143/152), a sense of an agreeable home to return to, an originary consent to the things from which life lives. Only this affirmation or "love" of life as dependent in its joy—the section of *Totality and Infinity* discussed here is called "The I and Its Dependence"—then permits denial, making it impossible even for suicide, Levinas argues against "the philosophers of existence," to refuse being in its totality (TI 145–146/119). The world can appear as hostile only on the basis of this "*agrément de la vie*" (TI 149/123). (We will shortly come back to this prevoluntary, presubjective affirmation of our dependency on the elemental character of the earth.)

Levinas further discusses this originary agreement by splitting it up into two aspects. First, there is an anonymous moment that consists in the accord of human needs with nature (as indicated, we will come back to this in later chapters: Chapters 3 and 5 will develop the self-other affirmation of life as the gift of nature and the claim of the earth upon the living). Second, the agreement includes a personal moment that consists in the "primordial phenomenon of gentleness [*douceur*]" or in "the warmth of intimacy" (TI 150/161). The latter is provided by what Levinas calls "the feminine," which is always already at "home," its "warmth" signaling a "peaceable welcome" that explains why peace is prior to war for Levinas.[16] As it is only this primordial "hospitality" (TI 156/166) that permits the self to form, prior to welcoming another, a welcoming face must have been welcomed:

> The Other precisely *reveals* himself in his alterity not in a shock negating the I, but as the primordial phenomenon of gentleness. . . . The welcoming of the face is peaceable from the first, for it answers to the unquenchable Desire for Infinity. War itself is but a possibility and nowise a condition for it. This peaceable welcome is produced primordially in the gentleness of the feminine face, in which the separated being can recollect itself, because of which it *inhabits* and in its dwelling accomplishes separation. (TI 150–151/161; emphasis in original)

In other words, agential competencies can develop only in response to being cared for by another. Without care during infancy, and without the continuing recognition by others of the ego as agent, no subjectivity could form and be maintained.[17] "Recollection [the return of the ego to itself as ego] refers to a welcome" (TI 155/165). In this sense, Levinas himself appears to argue, every gift depends on, and requires a prior affirmation of, the heteronomous but agency-enabling acceptance of a prior gift, the "gift of the power of giving," as Levinas will say later of fecundity (TI 269/302). It is not only that altruistic giving is enabled, transcendentally, by another prior gift, but that the donor must have affirmed or accepted the gift as a gift owed to another, as a debt. And this prior gift must have been given to her alone, a singling out that is here not called, as in the case of the father-son relation, the "election" of the unique (though among equals, as we've seen), but rather "a gentleness coming from a friendship [*amitié*] for that I" (TI 155/165).

While recognizing the dependence of agency, and thus of future-oriented responsibilities, on a prior gift, Levinas will, however, subtract any debt to this gift. While the relation to history and to the earth is necessary, and affirmed as such by the subject, for him no moral relation is thereby set up. This is because the woman of the house effaces herself, and withdraws in favor of the subject and its relation to other subjects. As feminist criticism has elaborated above all (Irigaray 1986; Chanter 1988, 2001; Gürtler 2001; Guenther 2006a), Levinas does not, or not consistently, position "the feminine" as a donor, a subject to whom one could owe. As Tina Chanter puts it, woman is "ontologized"—she loses her singularity—in the blurring of the distinction between nature and culture, between the abode in being and the home prepared by a woman in the house—as if food did not have to be cooked (Chanter 1988, 35–36). While the woman who prepares the house is called a face and an "Other" in Levinas's text (TI 150/161) and retains "all the possibilities of the transcendent relationship with the Other" (TI 155/166), she does not reach the height of what it is to be a face in the Levinasian sense. This is because, says Levinas, the "intimacy of recollection" can occur only if the face of the other is "revealed, simultaneously with [its] presence, in its withdrawal and in its absence" (TI 155/166). Intimacy requires discretion: the feminine, domesticated womanhood, must efface herself and so deny that the child owes her. It is as if the "son" could become a subject only by facing someone who does not demand that he acknowledge his dependence, together with the debt he incurs in his formation. Despite Levinas's critique of the virile, heroic agent, in favor of the responsible self, a subject (figured as "son") seems to emerge only by denying a primordial debt—a denial that consists not so much in the faceless as in the self-effacing withdrawal of the caregiver, a self-effacement we must, it seems, expect of women rather than men.

To build on the feminist critique of Levinas for intergenerational concerns is to recognize that Levinas misses the ethical debt to preceding others—women in particular—despite his recognition that there can be *no* subject without those others who bring the child into being and nurture it, biologically and socially. (Nor can subjectivity be maintained even "after" its formative years without the continuing support of a "home" whose constitution and support remains intersubjective. Responsibility remains, for Levinas, dependent on a preceding and unmasterable otherness even after its empirical formation during infancy, although the latter remains a particularly striking phenomenon of dependence.) Ambiguously denying woman (as biological/nonbiological mother) transcendence belongs here, on my reading, to the same overall setup that denies the dead posthumous claims on the living, an "empirical" debt to the past. In assimilating the woman to an abode in being, to the "strangeness of the earth" from which life must draw and which it must affirm, concrete predecessors become something like the ancestor as such, a generalized other time that Levinas calls the "immemorial" source of the call to responsibility:

> The home that founds possession is not a possession in the same sense as the movable goods it can collect and keep. It is possessed because it already and henceforth is hospitable for its proprietor. This refers us to its essential interiority, and to the inhabitant that inhabits it before every inhabitant, the welcoming one par excellence, welcome in itself [*l'accueillant en soi*]—the feminine being. (TI 157/168–169)

The concrete debt to the mother is here assimilated to a "welcome in itself," a "human welcome [*un accueil humain*]" (TI 156/166) that cannot be ascribed to any one prior inhabitant (alone), and so calls for the thought of an inhabitant before all inhabitants. But if we were to recognize that the prior inhabitant owes the house to yet another prior one, does this backward infinity, the ultimate untraceability of the human genealogy, license the supposition of a "welcome in itself"? (It would be odd if Levinas's infinite ethics felt it had to stop an infinite regress here.) In ascribing the presupposed welcome to an "inhabitant before every inhabitant," do we not risk "ontologizing" it once more along with the feminine?

The point here is to read "visible history" not as existing prior to the generative relation, but as discontinuously regenerated by fecundity, in just the way "fraternity" is unthinkable without relation to the father and the mother, and thus also to the daughter. Conversely, fecundity can exist only by presupposing and drawing from an earth and a history of inheritance that it at the same time interrupts and resumes. The interruption, however, does not cancel the owing. Rather, we can think the owing as both specifically traceable and ultimately untraceable, as both concrete and infinite, in the way that Levinas attempts to think the relation to the face: as concretely singular and yet carrying a call from all other others whose lines of interconnection are untraceable in the end.

This is where a reading of Derrida can help us. I alluded to what I see as the weakness in Levinas's argument, namely, the dualistic relation between totality and infinity, between history and the ethical relation, between the visible face and its mortality, between life and death. It is this duality, I have suggested, that calls for the feminine to serve as the self-effacing matrix permitting contact between paternity and history. But these dualisms still cannot satisfactorily explain how the alterity of death can appear on the living face that "expresses" itself or that "faces up" (in the sense that a "face" demands such taking of responsibility by "looking up" or making a demand) for an agent: we must think a "totality" (a field of intelligibility or being as the process of coming to presence) that allows alterity to appear in it while still preserving its incomprehensibility (see Bernasconi 1988, 1997, 1998; Beardsworth 1996; Osborne 1995, 117ff.; Fritsch 2000, 2011a; Hägglund 2004; Marrati 2005; Hanson 2010; Kleinberg 2012). In other words, we must think the way in which death (as well as birth) can appear in, and structure, permeate, and co-constitute life, without being reducible to history and an objective, totalizing perspective.

While this is not the place to discuss this rich text and its expansive history of reception in detail, this is precisely what Derrida's "Violence and Metaphysics" attempts. While supportive of Levinas's notion of the "trace" as a way of thinking alterity in history as "a past that has never been present" ("Within these limits, and from this point of view at least, the thought of *différance* implies the entire critique of classical ontology undertaken by Levinas"; MP 21/22), in this text Derrida questions what he sees as Levinas's "silent axiom": the axiom according to which totality is finite (WD 133/154) and so does not admit of infinity. Meanwhile, infinity is thought, by Levinas, to be a positivity beyond history (WD 142/68), as in Descartes's idea of an infinite God (TI 48/40, 84/82, 196/214, 210/231–232) or Plato's "good beyond being" (TI 218/241, 293/326), Levinas's favorite examples of the absolute alterity he seeks on the expressively mortal face beyond history. In response to this, Derrida suggests that this silent axiom be replaced by a thinking of history as the open-ended differentiation process between life and death (WD 144/70): precisely, that is, as an infinite totality (WD 153/80). The field of intelligibility against whose background a subject can alone encounter the other, while not without violence, is not absolutely totalizing but made possible by the infinity of differentiation Derrida calls *différance* (WD 161/190). The latter, as the quasi-transcendental horizon of meaning and agency, reconstitutes Levinas's ethical-metaphysical relation: *différance* requires that a living entity can be itself only by ongoingly relating itself to others in its context.

On this view, the self, as what Levinas calls the same, has to be understood as emerging by separating itself (or being separated) from the other and the others. But given the need for differentiation, it must also "welcome" the other (SM 177/224) in an ongoing process. This requirement of a differential context of separation and belonging means that some others must have preceded the self. And what's more, the relation between self and others, as a differentially productive or futurally deferring relation, is nontotalizable and enveloping: it is inseparable from a larger shifting context that Levinas tends to cast to the outside, as the elemental earth or the nourishing feminine matrix (see Derrida's own reading of Plato's *khōra* in Derrida 1995 and in AV).

Différance, then, offers a thought of a self-other relation that is each time singular, a relation that is nothing without the relata it reconstitutes each time anew. The difference is thus beyond the opposition between "totality" and "infinity," for it names both an "immemorial" past and a "pure future"—that is, it cannot be remembered, appropriated, or totalized, exceeding the self from an "infinite" future that will not appear as such in "history"—and yet, as a mere differential relation, having no positivity elsewhere, it can only be borne along, and reproduced, by concrete, empirical history. The relation between self and other can only take place in a preceding context of differentiation from which both appropriate but which cannot be said to remain merely external, at a distance, totalizable at the hands of the survivors. A living being cannot but appropriate from its environments and other living beings in its contexts, but such appropriation is never complete and will not return full circle to the living being, which will therefore have to leave a remainder to its successors. Life lives generationally, but also environmentally: in the history and habitat of life that in Chapter 5 we will call "earth" or "the world as world of life-death" (BS2 263–264/365).

In showing *différance* to name the "alterity in the same," the "infinity" traced in history, Derrida allows us to recognize the debt as both absolutely and concretely other, making of hospitality both an unconditional and a conditional welcome (see Derrida 2000). Levinas's "prior agreement"—as said, both hospitable agreeableness and consent—is then not a structure we can merely describe from a neutral standpoint. In describing it we must also perform it from where we are, in "our" historical context, to which we respond with a promise to renew it. The "welcome" extended to the other is necessarily a response to a prior welcome by a preceding other. As Derrida puts it in discussing Levinasian hospitality in *Adieu*: "[T]he welcoming *of* the other (objective genitive) will already be a response: the *yes to* the other will already be responding to the welcoming *of* the other (subjective genitive), to the *yes* of the other" (AEL 23/51–52; emphasis in original). In affirming itself, a "living ego" thus affirms its material and symbolic inheritance, its socioeconomic context, as well as its lifeworld, language, tradition, and environment. This "capital," productive and social, is not simply there, not receivable in a prepackaged bundle, as it were, for it can exist as "capital" only by being in the process of being repeated, appropriated in an inevitably new, indeed unpredictable, context (see Derrida 2002a, 86ff.).

Affirmation of one's preceding context, of the earth and the home, is "double": it must affirm the self along with the other, and the other along with the self. But it is also double in a temporal sense: to affirm oneself requires that one affirm one's past as promised to the future, the future as being constituted in part out of the past (Fritsch 2017b). Self-affirmation affirms the self as born a mortal: as child and parent at the same time. That is why, as Levinas has said, ethics is not just a relation between two but at least between three (OB 159/248), the third party "facing up" in the face of the one other before me (TI 213/234, cited by Derrida in AEL 149n123/190–191n2). If justice is intergenerational from the beginning, then the politics of calculation and equality is co-originary with it in a symmetry before time, a "fraternity" that, as we've seen, seeks to maintain election and maternal friendship in and through equality, thus enabling the "we" of the "strange conjuncture of the family" (TI 279/311, cited in AEL 145n69/123–124n1). The question for us is whether the family can recognize its debts beyond its home, to the other others who made it possible, from beyond its walls and its time, so that, as Derrida asks in *Adieu*, Levinasian hospitality can help along a genuine cosmopolitical hospitality beyond Levinas's at times perhaps all-too-Jewish humanism (see Bankovsky 2005).[18]

Conclusion

I've suggested that Levinas may help rethink some ontological problems and related issues often seen to beset duties to not-yet-existing people. From Levinas's point of view, the ontological problems we discussed in Chapter 1 tend to overstate the degree to which obligation derives from the presence of the identifiable other, whereas obligation arises not with identity alone but also with the otherness of the (albeit living) other. Given the relation between alterity and the future for which Levinas argues, responsibility is thus always the responsibility to give beyond my life. However, in Levinas this idea is not, or not unambiguously, connected with the fact that all moral agents are themselves survivors who appropriate from the dead and from the still-living but preceding generation. Hence, my reading of Levinas suggests developing the idea that the duty to give to a future from which I cannot benefit derives from the fact that what I have is not really or fully mine to begin with. The reason it is not fully mine is that I inherited it, and inheritance, coming from others, always also stands under a moral claim to share what I have with others. On a certain understanding of temporality, the obligation is then best discharged by giving (back) to future others. The next chapter will seek to elaborate this idea further.

3

Asymmetrical Reciprocity and the Gift in Mauss and Derrida

The current chapter will present the first model of intergenerational justice that attempts to do justice to the social-ontological-cum-normative co-implication of the past and the future in the present, as elaborated in Chapters 1 and 2. Chapter 1 sought to show that the ontological problems of most extant theories of intergenerational justice call for a rethinking of the nature of subjectivity and social relations on the basis of what I call the time of birth and death. Chapter 2 drew on Levinas to detail this rethinking in terms of a responsibility that calls on subjects to be responsible to others beyond their own time. Toward the end of the previous chapter, we saw that the mortal alterity of the other tends to be misrepresented by Levinas as being beyond empirical history. If the call to justice stems from historically concrete others, then it cannot just be futural but must also be related to gifts from predecessors. Wishing to put to work and flesh out the understanding of human time and agency developed in the first two chapters toward answering questions specifically related to intergenerational justice, I here introduce a notion of reciprocity. With the notion of reciprocity I hope to convey that indebtedness to preceding others plays a role in giving to future others, no matter how asymmetrical and altruistic the gift to future people is taken to be.

The present chapter goes on to connect Derrida's critical reading of Levinas to economic and anthropological literature on intergenerational transfers. Some of this literature draws on the premodern notion of the gift, as famously elaborated by Marcel Mauss. His work may thus provide a bridge between the extant economists' work on intergenerational reciprocity and Derrida's reading of Mauss. Mauss's famous *Essai sur le don* (in English, *The Gift*) proposed a new theory of the origin of society and normativity by addressing the question of why a gift obliges the recipient to reciprocate. Ever since Claude Lévi-Strauss's critique of the essay as too reliant on "magical" notions, however, Mauss's answer to this question has seemed either unconvincing or unclear. In response to this, and more particularly to Derrida's reading of Mauss, I will here provide a new reading of Mauss's account.

The overall goal is to suggest that the much-discussed notion of indirect reciprocity—(past) A gives to (present) B who "returns" the gift to (future) C—should be elaborated into what I call asymmetrical reciprocity. By asymmetry I mean, among other things, two aspects of intergenerational relations. First, if A's gift is co-constitutive of B (i.e., is part of what allows B to *be* B), then B cannot ever fully repay the debt; full appropriation would amount to self-annulment. Thus, the gift remains inappropriable, excessive, and asymmetrical for B, who therefore must also free herself from the debt in some way.

Second, because the excess remains outstanding, B thus has future-oriented obligations in a way that connects up once more with Levinas's "being-for-beyond-my-time." Speaking of asymmetry in intergenerational reciprocity is also meant to capture this ultimate impossibility of clearly assigning the source of intergenerational obligation to either the past or the future. I will conclude that asymmetrical reciprocity is thus not as vulnerable as indirect reciprocity to the objection that it cannot account for direct obligations to future people. In this way, Derrida's understanding of the gift as both part of (intergenerational) chains, and also futurally excessive to them, can both bolster and transform the extant philosophical and economic accounts of intergenerational justice, some of which, as indicated, draw on Mauss for the notion of indirect reciprocity.

In *The Gift*, Mauss argues that for the archaic cultures he studied, a donor is not separable from the thing given, so that the recipient also receives some of the donor's "spirit" (*hau*, *mana*) that wishes to return to its origin—that is, wishes to return to the one who gave the gift in the first place. In my reconstruction below, I stress that the donor is not separable from her gift, because she is not taken to be the *sole* owner. Rather, a gift is understood to come from her clan or tribe, its tradition and ancestors, as well as from its "native soil" and natural elements, which are taken to be unpossessable. The obligation to reciprocate then stems from the fact that in accepting the gift, recipients assimilate into themselves that which remains inassimilable and thus necessarily overflows them, so that it cannot but be passed on to others and to nature. It is this inappropriable, "natural," untraceable element in the gift that is named the "spirit" of the thing, a spirit conceived as co-constitutive of both donor and recipient.

Linking this unpossessability or alterity and its force to *différance*, Derrida turns against what he calls the "Rousseauist schema": the attempt to trace society and normativity back to an archaic origin and to a nature whose foundational status and cyclical turning ensure that the gift returns to its origin. In this vein, he criticizes Mauss as well as Lévi-Strauss for their attempt to return to the archaic and the elemental, to seek to found the intergenerational *socius* on bedrock, a firm foundation, as origin of every gift. In response, I will argue that the indeed problematic nature of this Rousseauism should not lead us to overlook the role of intergenerational gifts and the noncultural, material, or "natural" in gifts as they circulate in and between cultures. The cult of ancestors and the cult of nature, as discussed by Mauss, not only name the desire for the origin but also the unownable elemental that turns and re-turns, noncyclically, in all gifts. In conclusion, I suggest that this understanding of economic circulation—namely, as dependent on gifts from previous generations and from "nature"—confronts economy—understood as the field of the circulation of goods and the amortization of expenditures and revenues—with the gift as its enabling but never fully calculable condition, and that means to call restricted economy out on its problematic externalizations.

I. Mauss's Gift

I.1. Mauss and the Critique of Political Economy

Since its first publication in 1924, Marcel Mauss's *The Gift* has continued to attract interest among anthropologists, sociologists, economists, and philosophers, in particular those seeking to explain the origin and ongoing institution of society, and the force of normativity among social actors. As Marshall Sahlins famously wrote in his *Stone Age Economics*, the question Mauss raises in *The Gift* is that of Thomas Hobbes, though the answer is very different. That question concerns the foundation of society understood as a normative order. If Hobbes finds this foundation in the social contract that forms the state, then Mauss finds it, prior to the state, in the "gift," and more specifically, in the Maori *hau*, the spirit that demands that a gift be returned (Sahlins 1972, 149, 169). This "spirit" yields a very different account of human nature. Sahlins writes, "[I]f as Macpherson [C. B. Macpherson, the great critic of modern "possessive individualism"] argues, Hobbes' conception of human nature is just the bourgeois eternalized, then Mauss is squarely opposed to it" (174).[1]

For Mauss, the gift indeed promises "a general theory of obligation" as well as "one of the human foundations on which our societies are built" (G 16/82, 5/65–66). We must return to these foundations in order to address "certain problems posed by the crisis in our own law and economic organization" (5). As a non-Marxist socialist, Mauss saw these problems as related to the capitalist disruption of social relations, its individualism, and the prevalence of utilitarian self-interest, which Mauss thinks is in his day (the 1920s) too often taken to be natural. That individuals are more or less separate rational utility-maximizers, we might mention, is still one of the most frequent assumptions made by economists, and also by some intergenerational and climate ethicists (Gardiner 2012). For Mauss, the notion of the gift can help us see that the eminently modern alternative of self-interest or altruism is mistaken (93). The human being is no utility-calculating machine (98) whose only reason to engage in relations with others had always been to barter for his own ends. A mistaken theory of human nature, Mauss complains, cements the status quo in the form of a retrospective historical teleology. Apologetic political economists suggest that sale for money, and eventually our own more advanced economy built on credit, developed, as if by a necessary law of history, from the barter system (46). The problem with all this, Mauss counters, is the lack of historical evidence, especially in archaic societies. Instead of self-interested barter, what we in fact find is the prevalence of gift relations that already imply a complex system of credit and suggest a more complex human being than *homo economicus* (98).

This non-Marxist critique of classical political economy, social contract theory, and today's rational choice theory may explain the massive interest in Mauss's work, lasting to this day.[2] To counter the conception of human nature as basically self-interested, however, you have to be able to explain why a gift should obligate the recipient to reciprocate. If the gift did not bind the recipient to return the favor, the gift could not institute social relations. All we would have would be one-offs without actors bound to each other in a lasting way. And this would be the case even if individuals were obligated to give to others, for whatever reason; without the return obligation, gifts would remain aleatory occurrences, unable to commit actors to each other.

Hence, to help explain the origin of society and an ongoing socialization, the recipient's obligation to return the gift has to be the crux of the matter, even more so than the donor's prior reason for giving. If the recipient is obligated to return the favor, then a chain is created with the very first gift: every recipient is now obligated to give, in an open-ended manner. Once a gift has been given, there is always an unpaid debt somewhere. A social net founded upon this kind of gift relation—and, as we will see, the intergenerational chain—constantly demands reweaving at each of its knots, strengthening existing ties or opening up to new ones. This is, we may assume, Mauss's reason for privileging the recipient's duty over the donor's (G 4/64–65, 9/72, 16/82, 23/95).

Before I turn to examine the return obligation in some detail, let me note briefly that, *pace* Liebsch (2001), Mauss conceives this social net explicitly as intergenerational as well as intragenerational. The accounts of the gift in the archaic societies he studied stress the role of ancestors in particular, but also the binding of others to one's children. The chiefs who may make gifts on behalf of a tribe are often said to incarnate ancestors and gods of nature (G 49/140). Gifts deliberately destroyed at the potlatch of some northwestern American tribes are considered a gift to the clan's dead (G 142n141/136n2). With respect to Melanesia, and just before introducing the *kula* ring of gifts made famous by Bronislaw Malinowski (who today is hailed as the "father of modern anthropology"), Mauss cites the speech of a New Caledonian herald at a gift festival. The food presented at the festival is possessed by "the spirit of their ancestors who causes "to descend . . . upon these portions of food the effects of their action and strength. . . . The result of the action you have accomplished appears today. Every generation has appeared in its mouth." (G 26/100). The food in one's mouth, in this example, bespeaks the presence of ancestors. Human life cannot be thought without the inheritance of food-related benefits such as tilled land, knowledge about farming, hunting, fishing, gathering, cooking, and so on. And since gifts to the dead and to contemporaries indebt others to one's family or clan, they are often considered a means of ensuring the well-being of one's children (G 139n131/132–132n1). If gifts pervade social relations as "a system of total services" (G 7/64)—every material item or status symbol is implicated for everyone in a system of gifts given and received—then these crucially involve past and future generations: "Everything passes to and fro as if there were a constant exchange of a spiritual matter, including things and men, between clans and individuals, distributed between social ranks, the sexes, and the generations" (G 18/86). The chain of obligation I just mentioned is one that interlocks not only different clans, tribes, or peoples but also different generations—even if, as will become important later on, the isolation of the intergenerational chain from intragenerational relations, on the one hand, and from nature, on the other, should never be taken for granted and needs to be rethought at crucial junctures. Nonetheless, this intergenerational chain has been noted in particular in the use economists have made of Mauss. As economists Arrondel and Masson write, for instance:

[T]he concept [of reciprocity] must be adapted to the succession of generations, taking a particular form which has been introduced by the French anthropologist Mauss (1968): namely, indirect (serial) reciprocity, involving three successive generations at a time and leading to infinite endless chains of descending or ascending transfers between parents and children. (Arrondel and Masson 2006, 976; see also Kolm 2006, 395–396)[3]

As opposed to the two agents involved in direct reciprocity or exchange, indirect (or serial, or transitive) reciprocity names a three-party relation in which A gives to B, who "returns" the gift to C. Tracing the notion back to Mauss, Arrondel and Masson argue that intergenerational transfer motivations can be explained satisfactorily neither by direct reciprocities (such as self-interested exchange) nor by pure altruism:

[W]e shall try to convince the reader that *indirect* forms of reciprocity between generations may be viewed as appropriate dynamic syntheses of altruism and exchange allowing, with minimal deviations, the introduction of "intermediate" motivations for transfers which better fit the data. (Arrondel and Masson 2006, 976; emphasis in original)

Arrondel and Masson discuss a great range of empirically observable conduct among generations that cannot be explained by the standard alternatives, that is, self-regarding tit-for-tat or pure altruism, and that call for a "dynamic synthesis" which, for different reasons, we also encountered toward the end of the previous chapter, in discussing the feminist and Derridean objections to Levinas's fecundity. Here, too, I will present such a synthesis, again not for strictly empirical reasons, important and revealing as these are, but this time on the basis of close readings of Mauss and Derrida on the gift. As we will see, one motivation for renaming indirect reciprocity as "asymmetrical" lies in this combination of elements of reciprocity and of altruism in a way that overcomes their usual, even defining, contrast (the one is usually defined over and against the other). The altruistic aspect can be read, in a way Arrondel and Masson do not, to stress the asymmetry in power and responsibility in the typical relations between generations. However, the dynamic synthesis can succeed only if the recipient accepts a return obligation with the gift. If the recipient was not obligated, we would have a simple one-off transfer, perhaps as an altruistic act; if the only obligation he felt was to return the gift or an equivalent at the earliest opportunity, exchange, or direct reciprocity, would obtain. In both cases, there would be no chain and no "system" of services, benefits, and debts.

Once we have reviewed Mauss's and Derrida's attempts to explain the return obligation to us, I will note just how central this question is in the philosophical literature on reciprocity, specifically intergenerational reciprocity. Connecting Mauss and Derrida with this literature, from Rawls and Nozick to Barry and Page, will allow us to show its relevance and detail the notion of an asymmetrical reciprocity, one that precisely overcomes the strict oppositions between reciprocity and altruism as well as between past and future.

I.2. Mauss on the Return Obligation

So how does Mauss account for the return obligation? Here is the most relevant passage:

What imposes obligation in the present received and exchanged is the fact that the thing received is not inactive [*n'est pas inerte*]. Even when it has been abandoned by the giver, it still possesses something of him. Through it the giver has a hold over the beneficiary. . . . This is because the *taonga* [everything that may properly be termed possessions, everything that makes one rich, powerful, and influential, and everything that can be exchanged: precious articles, sometimes even traditions, cults, and magic rituals] is animated by the *hau* [the spirit of things] of its forest, its native heath and soil. It is truly "native," the *hau* follows after anyone possessing the thing. It not only follows after the first recipient, and even, if the occasion arises, a third person, but after any individual to whom the *taonga* is merely passed on. In reality, it is the *hau* that wishes to return to its birthplace [*lieu de sa naissance*], to the sanctuary of its forest and the clan, and to the owner. (G 15/80–81)

In a nutshell, which we will crack open in a moment, then, the "archaic" mindset (here, of the Maori, but Mauss is fond of generalizing on the basis of the many ethnographical sources he considers) believes, according to Mauss, that (a) the donor is not separable from the thing given, so that the recipient receives some of the donor's "spirit," and (b) this spirit wishes to return to its origin, its birthplace, which is characterized both in terms of ancestors (tradition and other forms of heritage, both symbolic and material) and nature (the forest and its animals, native heath and soil, etc.). The recipient is bound to the giver because she[4] has something in her possession that is animated by a spiritual force seeking to return to the owner, either directly or, more often, indirectly, by being passed on to a third party (G 14/79).

One can see why Lévi-Strauss would later complain, in a famous introduction to Mauss's work, that Mauss accepts a self-explanation from the peoples studied that is simply too spiritualist: to accept the *hau* or the *mana* (which Mauss translates as a kind of spiritual life force; G 11/74) as the central explanatory element is to forgo a more "rationalist" and "objective" explanation. What is called for is an explanation of the origin of normativity among human beings and the socialization of individuals and groups "without recourse to magical and affective notions" (Lévi-Strauss 1987, 49ff.). The reliance on *mana* and *hau* in Mauss's text has also been criticized for an illicit generalization, a critique that has been extended to Derrida's reading of it.[5] Above all, however, there is widespread disagreement in the extensive secondary literature on just what makes the return gift obligatory. In reviewing this literature, David Graeber cites twenty scholars who reinterpret the "*hau* of the gift" and notes that "just about none of these authors accepts Mauss's own interpretation" (Graeber 2001, 179).

I will not be able to discuss these interpretations here, many of which are based on the scholar's own, often years-long ethnographical fieldwork. Much would have to be said about the power of the gods, the divine generativity of nature (which was also called *hau*), the taboos surrounding violations of natural power or *mana*, and so on.[6] The limited goal here is not to contribute to the ethnographical efforts aimed at understanding the indigenous explanations on their own terms, but to interpret Mauss's text in view of intergenerational socialization and gift-giving. I focus on that which neither donor nor recipient can make their own, and which I take to be part of what the contested "spirit" of the thing involves, because this aspect seems not to have received due consideration in explaining the recipient's obligation.[7] Further, it is an aspect that I think plays a central role in Derrida's own, perhaps recondite reconstitution of Mauss's argument. Read in this way, Derrida's quasi-ontology supports Mauss's explanation of normative force. However, the role of "nature" in the unpossessable, I will argue, merits a closer look at Derrida's reading.

Before discussing Derrida's account of the normative force of the gift, let me try to reconstitute Mauss's reasoning. It helps to separate two key claims that appear in the passage just cited—claims I marked (a) and (b). I will begin with (a), the inseparability of donor and thing given. The archaic mentality that Mauss seeks to extract from several different sources views the donors as not separable from their gifts because they are not the sole owners; ownership is here not an exclusive, all-or-nothing relation. This is one of the places where one should keep in mind Mauss's warning of economistic "modern ideas" (G 46/133), including individualistic and developmental prejudices. In studying the gift in archaic societies, from the Pacific to the ancient Romans and Germanic tribes, Mauss believes we are tracing one of the true sources of contemporary societies, but this source should not be misunderstood on the basis of individual ownership. Rather, archaic mentality understands the gift as coming from the owners' clan or tribe, their tradition, ancestors and "native soil" (the forest and its "wild fowl," the earth and the sea; G 14/78). The donor gives something that she cannot be said to have made all by herself; previous generations and her native soil contributed to her ownership and to her ability to give it. In giving she inevitably gives something that she cannot fully claim for herself.

Further, these enabling factors of her ability to give also co-constitute her as a person. Her native habitat and her traditions, the customs and skills of her tribe, and the actual collaboration of others in the production of the thing given make the donor who she is.[8] This is particularly evident when the donor gives on behalf of a group, as was usually the case, but would hold even without such a representational element. To be sure, there is an element in the thing given that is the donor's, but the relation is not a two-factor possessive relation. Rather, it is a tripartite co-constitutive relation: both the gift and the donor owe themselves to a preceding context that makes donor and gift inseparable from each other. The preceding context or inheritance refers to the ontologically given, and giving, "world" of emergence of people and things within which relations among generations and tribes take place. The world includes natural habitat and previous generations: its precedence is, in the cultures discussed by Mauss, marked by the gods of nature and the spirits of the dead. Its precedence, its worldly givenness, is part of what the donor cannot fully claim as her own. In this way, the threefold relation explains both the inseparability of giver and gift and the fact that the gift is, but is not fully, the donor's, retaining an element of inappropriable alterity that even the donor cannot appropriate as hers alone. The *taonga*, Mauss writes, "are strongly linked to the person, the clan, and the earth," and only as such can they become "the vehicle for its *mana*, its magical, religious and spiritual force." It is this force, which as stated earlier may at times be understood as the ancestors' spirit active in the food in our mouths (G 26/100), that asserts itself over the recipient when "the obligation to reciprocate may fail to be observed" (G 13/78). This tense relation between inseparability and giving as separation, and further between appropriative ownership and inappropriability, is a decisive factor in the obligation to reciprocate.

Before moving on to consider what this tripartite relation means for the recipient, let us note that the *hau* or *mana* is not just an immaterial "spirit" of things. It may seem that in the case of the dead, these could only reappear as immaterial spirits, but in the form of inherited cultural practices, tilled land, housing and infrastructure, tool use, and so on their presence is not wholly spiritual. And yet their "presence" cannot be fully tangible, owing to the literal absence of the ancestors, the ultimate untraceability of the lineage, the difficulties of memory, and so on. Similarly, the spirit of things is also tied to the earth, the sea, the native soil and its animals. In indicating a kind of natural productivity, the *hau* is material and natural as well as "spiritual." In fact, the translation as "spirit" may have caused many misunderstandings, as it suggests, at least to Western ears, the binary divisibility between reality and magic, nature and culture, matter and mind, persons and things, individuals and groups. As opposed to this divisibility, Mauss underlines that the force of *mana* over the recipient is "moral, physical, and spiritual" (G 16/82). The force binds people to one another, within and between clans and tribes, by way of natural elements and cultural artifacts that are not simply distinct entities.

Mauss draws in part on this mélange of the immaterial and the material, this mixture of the appropriable and the inappropriable, in the thing given to explain why the donor should give in the first place. Nature, in particular, often approached by way of animistic gods, as well as that which the dead contributed to the living, cannot be exclusively owned by the donor and her clan; consequently, the recipient already had some claim, however indirect, to the thing given. "Also, one gives because one is compelled to do so, because the recipient possesses some kind of right of ownership over anything that belongs to the donor. This ownership is expressed and conceived as a spiritual bond" (G 17/84–85). This is so not because donor and recipient are co-owners, as when one says, for example, the earth is the common property of all humankind and all generations; in that case, human generations would be thought of as separable from what they own. By contrast, the idea here is that the animistic gods and the dead are the "true owners of the things and possessions of this world" and are therefore "one of the first with which human beings had to enter into contract" (G 20/90). All exchanges take place in the enabling context of "the spirits of the dead, the gods, things, animals, and nature" (G 18–19/87). If this context precedes any gift relation, then there cannot be a first generation whose appropriation of vacant lands gave them exclusive ownership and sole rights to intergenerational transfers, as Locke and Nozick have argued (Locke 1988; Nozick 1974). A first generation is a contradiction in terms, for while it might seem that it could generate *ex nihilo*, its not having been generated would be impossible and cast doubt on its capacity to generate.[9] Another way to put this, more in line with Mauss's text, is to say that a putative "first generation" would still have been preceded by nature and the ancestral spirits—that is, by spirits of the dead and of nature. Forming the inevitable backdrop and context of gift relations, these spirits are also addressed in every giving. The spirits are incited by the gift relation to be generous to humans: to give to another not only sets up a relation with that other person or group, but reestablishes contact between us, and the dead and nature. This is why the donors, as representatives of their tribes, often wear masks of their namesakes, the animistic nature gods and the spirits of the dead (G 20/90–91).

In several places, Mauss stresses that the elements and forces called gods, nature, and the dead can hardly be understood on the basis of assumptions that individuals are separate from each other and from their culture, their land, their ancestors, and so on. He stresses that these elements, indispensable to the gift relation, mix individuals and groups as well as spiritual and physical things in an ongoing traffic (G 17–18/85–86). This mélange, including the natural element, expresses the inappropriability of the gift on the part of both donor and recipient. And yet this inappropriable, unpossessable element in the gift is co-constitutive of the donor's subjectivity (her birth and origin). The donor's authority and very power to give depend on the context of emergence in the clan, the lineage, and the native soil.[10]

It is this unpossessable yet constitutive element that is crucial in explaining the second claim (b) that the recipient has to give back because the spirit of the thing wishes to return to its origin (G 15/81). The "origin" in question is not (principally) the individual donor but the entire temporally extended context of the gift's emergence: the "spirit." The spirit is thus first of all responsible for the identity of the donor—who she is—and *through* the donor, the spirit "passes into" the gift, and on to the recipient of the gift. The recipient is thereby tied to the donor and to the spirit of the donor: her land, clan, tradition, and ancestry.

For this reason, the recipient cannot just keep the gift for himself but must pass its "spirit" on. The giving does not make the gift belong, now, to the recipient alone, because, as we have learned, the donor was not the sole owner to begin with, and so did not have the exclusive power and right to give it. Consequently, the donor cannot transfer such rightful power to the recipient to keep it. This is the case even if the clan, the dead, and the nature gods in some way authorized the donor to give the gift, for what the donor could not fully appropriate could also not be fully made his own by the recipient. The recipient *cannot* (in all of its senses, from factual to normative) keep (all of) the gift because its *hau* makes it foreign to him, and not entirely assimilable. A normative claim follows from this ontological one: because the gift is not entirely assimilable, the recipient *should not try to fully assimilate it and make it his own alone.* Coming from the others, but not such that the thing given is fully separable from the donor, it keeps some of the others, and so remains foreign (G 16/82). There is something *inassimilable* or indigestible in the gift that does not belong to the recipient, and so he cannot and should not assimilate it and make it his own. This alterity, called in Mauss the spiritual force of the thing given—a natural force or the force of the ancestors that is also "law" and thus a normative force (G 13/78)—cannot be mastered or destroyed. It precedes the recipient as it precedes the donor, and as neither of them can fully own it, it not only precedes them but exceeds them toward a future: the recipient must pass it on.

As we can see, then, the obligation to reciprocate stems from the fact that in accepting the gift, the recipient assimilates that which will remain alien even as it co-constitutes his subjectivity as well as (though in a different way) that of the donor. The recipient assimilates something that was, or becomes, a part of him. And yet, as a result of the incompletability of the assimilation, something of the gift must pass on to (yet) others. In accepting the gift, the recipient acknowledges that this lack of full separation between donor-subject and gift also holds for him. The recipient, too, has always already received gifts from others, from his ancestors and from nature. The things that make him who he is and root him in a "native" soil, a habitat, a tribe, and a lineage have been *gifted* to him from others.

To be sure, the constitutive relation between gift and person appears much weaker for the recipient than for the donor, at least if there is no established gift practice between them or their groups. And indeed, the less he acknowledges the constitutive alterity (what I called the unpossessable) in the gift, and the less he has any previous or expected future dealings with the donor and her world of origin, the more the recipient may be inclined to dismiss the return obligation. Arrondel and Masson also note that "an extreme case occurs between 'strangers' playing only once," an extreme case we should, however, not take as a model (Arrondel and Masson 2006, 1022). Similarly, in his discussion of intergenerational reciprocity, Brian Barry has argued in the wake of Nozick: "If someone offers me a toffee apple, out of the blue, and I accept it, does my enjoyment of the toffee apple create even the tiniest obligation to distribute toffee apples to others? I do not see that it does" (Barry 1991, 232; see Nozick 1974, 95). In the absence of an explicit agreement to offer a return, it would then be unclear whether unsolicited (and thus involuntary) donations generate an obligation, either to the donor or to others. We will come back to this—but as we can already tell, the stipulation that the gift comes "out of the blue" is the crux of the matter, for its point is to deny any constitutive relation of the gift to the donor, and to isolate individuals from inherited contexts and from each other. Importantly, Barry acknowledges, where Nozick does not, that if the gift is part of an "established practice," the recipient will be obligated after all (Barry 1989, 232ff.). (We will see later that Derrida makes a similar argument.[11]) We can see here how crucial it is to pay attention to the context in which gifts take place, and to carefully consider the relation between contextual practices and individuals. For if we take many intergenerational practices as both "established" (habitual, culturally ingrained, traditional, part of a heritage) and indispensable to the formation of individuals as donor agents (such as infant care, linguistic and cultural education, and so on), we would be able to conclude, *pace* Barry's or Nozick's ultimate conclusion, that gifts of inheritance, broadly construed, obligate heirs to pass on gifts and benefits. As we will see, Derrida offers such an argument, though not at the level of cultural anthropology and developmental psychology—helpful as these are in this context—but at a more general, "quasi-transcendental" level at which we are to recognize that differential contexts stipulate the condition of possibility for the emergence of identity, including the personal identity without which there can be no sense of agency. (Derrida's qualified support for Mauss's account of the return obligation may thus also be seen to counter the objection that archaic, premodern mentalities cannot be applied to modern, highly differentiated societies.)

However, Derrida's gift will also help us to see the other side of this argument: namely, that identity also requires recontextualization, a breaking free from preceding, inherited contexts, contexts that may not be seen to predetermine agency. This is a point not entirely lost on Mauss. Precisely because they are gifts and not preestablished contracts, precisely because they involve an altruistic moment, gift chains always carry the risk of break-off. What is more, if every gift indebts the recipient, it must be seen to also provoke hostile responses in a recipient who wishes to avoid being thus indebted and, in a way, subordinated. Mauss underlines this negativity and "antagonism" (G 8/71), especially in his famous treatment of the potlatch and the *kula* ring. Arrondel and Masson see the elaboration of this "ambivalence of the gift" as the second significant contribution of his work, the first having been the introduction of indirectness or seriality into reciprocity. They apply this negativity to family relations, though it is not difficult to see that they hold for intergenerational relations more broadly:

> The first [key lesson to be learnt by economists from (especially French) anthropological studies], which has been underlined by Mauss (1950) in his famous *Essay on the Gift*, concerns the inherent ambivalence of any gift, which induces a double relation between donor and recipient: a *positive* relation of sharing and solidarity on the one hand; but also, a *negative* relation of superiority, domination, coercion or violence, the recipient becoming *in debt* to the giver and, to a certain extent, subordinate to her. This statement has strong implications in the case of parent-to-child gifts. Their primary objective should be to favor and speed up wealth transmission [this claim of course has to be understood against the background of the economists' self-imposed limit to material transfers, which they take to include time spent with others but not care, tradition, language, and so on], while strengthening family links. Instead, they have been repeatedly accused, through history, of destroying family links and generating conflicts, with children showing ingratitude, or parents wanting to manipulate and control children. (Arrondel and Masson 2006, 1023)

As we will see, the gift cannot be thought without what Derrida calls a "duty beyond duty" (GT 156/198; see GT 69–70/94; ON 7–8, 133), and so the intergenerational relation established by the gift should not be misconstrued as smooth, continuous, and without conflict.

But that does not mean the gift does not obligate; the discontinuity, and the need to recontextualize the gift, may in fact be one factor that motivates the indirectness of the return, the search for a new recipient, a third party in need or appropriately situated, for example in an intergenerational chain. Thus, unless the recipient—in the intergenerational chain, the heir—denies any constitutive context and insists on the self-generation of free individuals, he cannot avoid seeing the gift as inextricably stemming from a historical-worldly context that precedes him and that he cannot appropriate in toto. The gift is accepted, but on an elemental level remains foreign and inappropriable. As unpossessable, this "spiritual" element *cannot not* be passed on, and so the gift *must be* "returned." The "must" here is both ontological and normative: ontological in making up the being of individuals, and normative because in living and appropriating, individuals are understood to affirm and consent to that which makes up their being. And this "must"—what Derrida calls an *il faut*—pertains to both the appropriation of the gift (e.g., from ancestors, and so as to enable donor-subjects in the first place) and to the passing on of the gift due to its ultimate inappropriability. To indicate this ontological normativity in describing the archaic gift practices, Mauss and his fellow anthropologists frequently use the language of "possession," obsession, and haunting by spirits (e.g., G 50/142).

I.3. The Arche-Teleology of Nature

Crucial to the explanation, then, is what I have called the "third element": the world of production, context of inheritance, and established practices. This "third" precedes and exceeds donor, recipient, and their transaction. To then say, as Mauss does, that the "the recipient has to give back because the spirit of the thing wishes to return to its origin" (G 15/81) is not only to view the thing as animate, but to impose a circle on the excess: the thing desires to return to its "birthplace." This is understandable if life in general, before the nature-culture or nature-history divide, is seen as cyclical: all things and people would come to be from, and return to, the same sacred or mythical source, typically figured as the life-spirit.[12] The spirit of life or of nature would be seen as the ultimate foundation of social relations. The obligation to return the gift would then also be an obligation to return to nature as the single source of society and normativity.

Even if he does not himself advocate for this foundational naturalism in *The Gift*, Mauss does counsel a circular return, this time historical rather than natural. In our capitalist times in which, "[f]ortunately, everything is still not wholly categorised in terms of buying and selling" (G 83/213), the normative force inherent in returning the gift at a later time translates into the duty to return to the traditions of gift-giving. The study of the archaic practices that honor circular nature in this way is mandated by the return gift: "We can and must return to archaic society," Mauss writes in *The Gift*'s "Moral Conclusions," for "[t]his morality is eternal" (G 88–89/220). We "should return to laws of this kind" (G 88/219), laws that demand generosity and show that our modern lives "are still permeated with this same atmosphere of the gift." In the social insurance legislation of his day, which he sees as a form of "state socialism," Mauss recognizes that "we are returning to a group morality" (G 87/218). This morality—one that is not fully separable from political economy or foundational sociology—is that of the gift as "one of the human foundations on which our societies are built" (G 5/65–66). In understanding archaic society and morality as a "foundation," Mauss believes he has found a stable source, an origin of the gift, a beginning of history to which its goal must and should return. In the final analysis, gifts would circulate within a large natural-historical cycle, a circle that threatens to subordinate the altruistic, open-ended moment to exchange, commerce, and direct reciprocities.

However, we should note that early on, when considering the reason for returning the gift, Mauss is not content with this cyclical foundationalism and arche-teleology. He wonders why his principal source (a Maori elder famously cited by Elsdon Best) stresses that the recipient passes the gift on to a third party instead of returning it to the donor. Why this "intervention of a third person" (G 14–15/79), and the resulting priority of indirect over direct reciprocity? Mauss's explanation seems to be that the *hau* of the gift emerges, or becomes visible, in particular if the return gift is made to a third person: if A gives to B, and B to C, but C now still has the *hau* of A though she had no direct contact with A, then the spirit must indeed be in the thing given. This survival of the *hau*, even beyond a context in which A participates, could be explained by saying that it is still the same spirit (life force, nature, etc.) that remains identical to itself. But could it not also be that the survival of the spirit is not so much, or exclusively, that of an identity, but of an unpossessable alterity of which we could not simply say that it stays the same across different contexts?

Let us consider that the very relation established or renewed by the gift must alter donor and recipient if neither of them is totally separable from things given. In accepting an inassimilable alterity, even while passing it on, the recipient must be altered by it if the gift is also co-constitutive of subjectivity. This alteration comes to the fore for instance in the recipient's indebtedness to the donor, her clan and her native soil, and the bond (but also antagonism) that goes along with the gift (G 8/71). This alteration is related to the alterity that circulates, precedes and exceeds both, and gives it force. So even if B returned the gift to A instead of passing it on to C, A would no longer be exactly the same. A is thus not the stable origin of the gift, and "returning" the gift to A comes with the same aspect of inassimilablity as any other act of gift-giving. Strictly speaking, then, there would be no return of the spirit to its origin. The "circulation" of the spirit would be much more open-ended, an open-endedness that precisely (as we've seen) calls for renewed gifts, but also sets the recipient free to the extent that he is not just bound to the donor but will already have become a donor himself, connecting with yet others in a merely quasi-circular chain. The origin of the intergenerational chain would be untraceable, just as future generations would be both anticipated and beyond expectation and imagination. Similarly, nature or earth as the other element of the preceding world would be both a predictable, tangible and appropriable, even edible element, and yet remain too "spiritual," too large and too erratic to appropriate.

Although it is not foreign to his text, Mauss does not emphasize the constitutive nature and productivity of the gift relation, nor does he underline this move from alterity to alteration. This emphasis will surface in Derrida.

II. Derrida's Gift

II.1. The Dead and the Unborn

The ambiguity in the source of the gift, in particular the oscillation between nature and ancestry as both stable sources and unpossessable alterities, comes to the fore in Derrida's reading of Mauss. This reading is complex, and I cannot do it full justice here. The complexity is increased by the fact that *Given Time* is announced as only the first of two volumes, with the second never having been published.[13] Further, the text we do have presents a complex interweaving of Mauss's empirical-ethnographical studies of the gift in non-Western and premodern societies, and Heidegger's ontological account of the gift of being as wrested from the Western tradition and pitted against its modern occlusion in the technological epoch.

Derrida directly discusses Mauss in *Donner le temps*, but his discussion of the gift extends beyond this text. In *Specters of Marx*, Derrida associates the gift not only with time—an association we will explicate in a moment—but with intergenerational time and with intergenerational justice.[14] He argues, in a reading of Heidegger and Levinas on the gift, that we must recognize "the force and the necessity of thinking justice on the basis of the gift, that is, beyond right, calculation, and commerce . . . therefore the necessity (*without force*, precisely, [*justement*], without necessity, perhaps, and without law) of thinking the gift to the other as gift of that which one does not have and which thus, paradoxically, can only *come back* or belong to the other" (SM 32/55; emphasis in original). I will come back to this paradox of a gift beyond, but not without relation to, commerce and exchange, and this paradox of a giving of what one does not have—but before I do that, I want to stress that in this text on the gift as a source of justice, Derrida makes clear that intergenerational cannot be separated from intragenerational justice:

No *being-with* the other, no *socius*, without this *with* that makes *being-with* more enigmatic than ever for us. And this being-with-specters would also be, not only but also, a *politics* of memory, of inheritance and of generations. . . . [N]o ethics, no politics . . . seems possible and thinkable and *just* that does not recognize in its principle the respect for those others who are no longer or for those others who are not yet *there*, presently living, whether they are already dead or not yet born. . . . *[J]ustice* must carry beyond *present* life, life as *my* life or *our* life. *In general.* For it will be the same thing for the "my life" or "our life" tomorrow, that is, for the life of others, as it was yesterday for other others: *beyond therefore the living present in general.* (SM xviii/15; emphasis in original)[15]

I have analyzed the line of thinking that leads up to this passage in some detail elsewhere (Fritsch 2005, 2011b). Here I will only ask that we keep in mind the central claim: that sociality and justice are unthinkable without relation to the dead and to the unborn. This is a claim that Derrida, in different contexts, has in fact often made. For instance, Derrida contests Sartre's claim that a writer writes for her age by arguing *e contrario* that "one writes for the dead or for the in-nate. . . . [T]hose who are not yet living, "not yet born" are also the spectral addressees, irrecusable as well, of everything we address, of all our letters" (NII 394n7).[16] In volume 1 of *The Beast and the Sovereign*, Derrida argues that the source of ethics is connected to the finitude of life that therefore carries ethics not only toward the mortality of nonhuman animals but also toward nonpresent generations (BS1 108–111/154–159). In *Rogues* and in *For What Tomorrow* (a telling title) he argues that democratic citizenship and human rights ought to be rethought so as to include an engagement with animals, the dead, and the unborn (R 53–54/81–82; FWT 97–98/161–162).

In *Aporias*, Derrida further comments that it is a mistake to limit the belief in the spirits of the dead and their presence among the living to "the Primitives," as Paul Valéry does, and argues, as he does in the face of Marx (in SM), that the relation to the dead and a politics of mourning engage all political communities, perhaps even the essence of the political (A 61–62/112). The text on Mauss, then, might be thought to give us a bit more detail about this "politics or ethics of memory and of generations" (SM xviii/15) that turns the present to the past as well as to the future, this "topolitology of the sepulcher" (A 62/112) that explains the present as constitutively related to the specters of the dead and the unborn. As I have suggested, in the context of Mauss's gift and the archaic societies he studied, this spectral ethics and politics morally ties generations to one another only if it can explain the obligation to give back.

To forgo a lengthy reconstitution of Derrida's text on Mauss, then, I will begin by focusing on the way that it seeks to explain the obligatory nature of the return gift, paying particular attention to the role of what

I called the unpossessable. As we will see, what I just called the unpossessable alterity and its normative force—the thing demands to be passed on from the recipient—as well as its role in constituting subjects will be linked to *différance*. In fact, when Mauss stresses that "time" is logically implied in returning gifts (they cannot be returned right away; G 46/66), Derrida equates time with *différance* (GT 39/57, see 12/24, 40/58, 42/62). Later in the text, he writes that "[t]his "logic" and this "aporetics" of the gift here deploy those of *différance*" (GT 127n1/163n1). Let us then take a brief look at this "logic" in view of the gift and of *différance*.[17]

II.2. Différance and Time

Différance names the quasi-transcendental condition of the identity of things as well as subjects. The term seeks to articulate both the movement of differentiation that characterizes any mark or identity in a system of referral, and the inescapable deferral of the self-reference or self-affirmation of identity. Difference and deferral—or, as Derrida also says, temporalization and spacing [*temporalisation et espacement*] (MP 8/8; see also R 32/58ff.)—entail the need for contexts as well as the inexhaustibility of, and independence from, contexts. If an identity can come to be established only as a result of spacing, that is, by differing from other elements, then these other identities form a necessary and necessarily preceding context. As the previous chapter argued, partly against Levinas, histories, traditions, languages, ancestors, and parents are indispensable in the case of human subjects in giving birth to agents who may become donors themselves. Contexts co-determine identities so that they carry within themselves contextual factors. People drag their inheritance along as a surfacing whale does its wake.

However, preceding contexts do not determine identity conclusively. Identity is not enclosed in a given horizon, because the context consists only of ongoing processes of differentiation. Contexts themselves change with every repeated self-affirmation of an identity in that context. Affirmation involves iterated appropriations from merely comparatively stable circumstances and the novel uses and futural projections of contextual elements. An identity exists only by changing; it never "is" stable but is only always in the process of being stabilized. Vintage Derridean terms such as "trace," "specter," the prefix "quasi-" and the many locutions of the form "X without X" (e.g., PF 47n15/56n1, 81/99) are meant to capture this condition between identity and difference, presence and absence, past and future. Identities are differing-deferring to an unforeseeable future that we know will never arrive as such.[18]

It may already have become evident how relevant this brief review of *différance* is to Mauss's discussion of the gift. In this spectral ontology—which Derrida here pits against "French structuralism of the 60s," in which Lévi-Strauss's removal of "magical and affective notions" in favor of "underlying structures" is said to have exerted "influence" on Lacan, Foucault, Barthes, and Althusser (GT 76/101)—in this spectrality, the vexed and contested notion of "spirit" (*hau, mana, wakan,* etc.) should be seen as less problematic, though perhaps no less difficult to comprehend. The elements that I identified in Mauss as crucial to the return obligation are redeployed by differential iterability, by the "logic" of *différance*: first, the necessity of preceding contexts and their role in gift-giving; second, against this enabling background, the inseparability of donor and thing given; finally, the donor and the recipient's appropriation of what in the end remains unpossessable, and therefore cannot but be passed on toward an open-ended future to come.

On Derrida's account, a gift proceeds from three interrelated, conjointly necessary sources: a subjectivity capable of *intending* to give (GT 11/22–23, 27/42–43, 101/131–132, 123/157); the gift of being (Heidegger's *es gibt Sein*, "there is being," but literally "it gives being"), which Derrida reformulates as *différance* (GT 19–20/32–34); and what I just called the context in histories, traditions, ancestors, and groups, clans, or tribes—if you wish, the "empirical" sources of the donor's capacity to give. These three elements are not fully separable because, as explained above, the identity, the very subjectivity, of the donor-subject requires a differential context for its emergence. Similarly, *différance* cannot be thought independently of identities-in-process and their contexts because it merely names the "gap," the temporalizing spacing, between them: no relation without *relata*. *Différance* in the gift is only ever traced in "empirical" history, as its very temporalization, its binding of or hold on subjects.

How can this account help us to understand the normative force of the gift, the obligatory nature of the return? Derrida leaves no doubt that, because "différance *is inscribed in the thing itself* that is given or exchanged," donor and donee are compelled to recognize a "mysterious force" that "demands gift *and* restitution" (GT 40/58–59; emphasis in original). And this demand, he argues, governs all theoretical—anthropological, sociological, economic, and philosophical—discourses on gift-giving, however much they strive to refrain from prescribing or taking sides, for or against gift practices, for instance. For the discourses on the gift, too, owe themselves to previous accounts, to the inheritance of a language, a tradition, and so on. (Mauss's essay in particular depends on the ethnographical studies he himself did not undertake, but those too depend on the Maori, the Trobrianders, the Haida and the Tlingit, the Yuit and the Inuit, the Romans and the Germanic tribes, and so on.) There is no truly objective and neutral meta-level from which to describe the gift; any essay on the gift is "a priori a piece . . . of a performative, prescriptive and normative operation" (GT 62/85). Derrida sums up the content of this normativity in its very aporetics:

One must opt *for* the gift, for generosity, for noble expenditure, for a practice and a morality of the gift ("one must give"). [*Il faut opter pour le don, pour la générosité, pour la dépense noble, pour une pratique et une morale du don ("il faut donner").*] . . . But—because with the gift there is always a "but"—the contrary is also necessary: One must [*il faut*] limit the excess of the gift and of generosity, to limit them by economy, profitability, work, exchange. (GT 62/85–86, translation modified; see also GT 30/47)

Put schematically, *différance* gives rise to normative force owing to the fact that, as we've seen, a subject cannot but appropriate things from others. But such appropriation is never complete and will not return full circle to the subject; it is what Derrida calls an "ex-appropriation" (GT 81/108, 151/191) that always leaves a remainder. An appropriation is also an investment in one's context, a giving (back) to it, an implication in something larger that precedes and exceeds the self. As Derrida puts it elsewhere: "Only a finite being inherits, and his [*sic*] finitude obliges him. It obliges him to receive what is larger and older and more powerful and more durable than he. [*Elle l'oblige à recevoir ce qui est plus grand et plus vieux et plus puissant et plus durable que lui.*]" (FWT 5/18). Given that identity is not plainly given, that subjectivity is not simply there to begin with, to be at all means to seek to come back to oneself from the context of appropriation to which *différance* turns and opens the self again and again. A subject's appropriation from context, its self-affirmation, implies a limit to the gift and demands that one calculate what comes back to oneself; it thus implies exchange, work, (restricted) economy, and profitability, as well as responsibly giving an account of oneself and one's gifts (GT 63/86; see GT 30/47, 101/131–132).

But given the deferral implied in *différance*, the calculation is opened to an incalculable or disseminative future even though, *qua* incalculable, it co-constitutes the calculating subject. The gift breaks open the intended circle of return. There is "an essential passage between the gift and this dissemination" as that which "does not return to the father, or that which does not *return* in general" (GT 47/68). Even if the donor always calculates some return, the disseminative *différance* of the gift implies its unpossessability and nonreturn. If all giving is enabled by the differing-deferring that entails context-boundedness as well as disseminative context-transcendence, but dissemination also thwarts subjective efforts at anticipating, let alone controlling, how the gift is received, understood, and what is done with it (GT 122/156), then dissemination makes of every gift a gift without return to the donor. A gift binds and obligates the recipient, but also releases and unbinds her, lets her loose to do with it what the donor cannot expect or control, by deferring and opening the social practice to an unknowable future. If A's gift, inseparably stemming from contexts exceeding both A and B, is co-constitutive of B, then B cannot ever fully repay the debt; the gift remains inappropriable, excessive, and asymmetrical for B. (I will get back to this sense of asymmetry.)

The theme of "the unpossessable" I stressed in Mauss thus returns here as "the incalculable" and the "something larger, older, more powerful and more durable" (FWT 5–6/18): a gift's context of emergence and production, understood itself as an unobjectifiable gift of inheritance that works its way into every particular gift. The self cannot fully appropriate this gift of inheritance, even if it must do so to some extent; on account of its greater power and durability, but also its differential, disjointed, and discontinuous temporality, it will always exceed appropriators toward an incalculable future. As the deferral to an open-ended future that co-constitutes the present, the unpossessable divides the heir's identity against itself, and thereby sets in motion its economizing and calculative exchange-gifting in the first place. The heir does not precede her inheritance, but comes about only in its appropriation, an appropriation that, to the extent it is constitutive, cannot be completed: final appropriation would amount to the death of the heir. Hence, the temporality of the self, her noncoincidence with herself, first commits her to taking up an inheritance she cannot finalize but only (discontinuously) continue. Inheriting is thus also an effort that, given its motivation by noncoincidence, must also consist in making the gift one's own, in coming back to oneself, in calculating a return for oneself. But such a calculation cannot but be traversed by the incalculable, by the unpossessable that exceeds the heir, and asks her to pass on the gift to others: she must give to an open-ended future, one that is not her own and will not return to her but one to which she nonetheless owes an account, a responsibility, a calculation.

Thus reconstituted, the unpossessable is a dominant theme in Derrida's reading of Mauss: *Donner le temps* is framed by reference to it in the form of the enigma of a "giving of what one does not have." Both Lacan and (especially) Heidegger, but also Madame de Maintenon (discussed in the epigraph) speak of such a paradoxical gift, cited at the opening and the end of the book (GT 2–3n2/12–14n1, 159n28/201n1), as well as in the middle (48/69, 69n23/94n1).[19] Because a donor is also, and first, a recipient, she gives a gift that neither she nor the recipient or the recipient of her gift can have or take in its entirety. Despite the appropriation from the past, the thing remains beset by a future beyond the grasp of the present. The duty to return the gift is then a "duty beyond duty," an indebtedness (GT 62/85) without debt (GT 13/26, 69/94, 156/198) and—I will come back to this below—without reciprocity (GT 12/24).

Drawing on Heidegger's account of being, then, Derrida's quasi-transcendental argument, his "spectral" ontology (or "hauntology"; SM 10/31) supports Mauss's explanation of normative force in the indigenous beliefs he presents in his study without paying the price of accepting at face value the "magical notions" of which Lévi-Strauss complained, but also without falling for a naïve empiricism or positivism, that is, a presentism without specters. The resulting concept of the gift, however, may account for ongoing socialization, but it cannot provide a firm "bedrock" for social relations. With this reference to foundations, we return to the issues of nature and history, and the arche-teleology we mentioned above.

I will here first discuss Derrida's treatment of nature in this text, looking ahead to the final chapter on earth (Chapter 5), and then turn to a more detailed rapprochement between Derrida's gift and economists' and philosophers' accounts of intergenerational indirect reciprocities, spelling out what I mean by asymmetrical reciprocity.

II.3. The "Gift of Nature" in Derrida

While we have seen a few common themes in Mauss's and Derrida's treatments of the gift—notably that of the unpossessable—Derrida reserves a strong criticism for Mauss's alleged foundationalism and the role of a circular return to archaic origins and to nature. While *différance* may be seen to bolster Mauss's argument regarding the "spirit," differing-deferring specters will not return to any origin. Rather, the "origin" becomes a temporalizing spacing-out among elements whose differentiations can only be traced in their effects, without the traces ever hitting rock bottom. To be sure, given that *différance* can only operate in and through histories and contexts, we can seek to trace gifts to their donors. But within every identified source (this or that ancestor, say, or this or that territory), there is an untraceable, unidentifiable force at work that multiplies the genealogies and opens them to contestation. An inheritance can have a hold on donors only to the extent that they cannot exhaust the inheritance, leaving a future to be read by others.

That is why we are not surprised to find Derrida, exasperated and perhaps a bit wearied, teasing out Mauss's references to archaic origins, circular returns, and nature:

The anthropologist proposes to *give back* and to *come back* in a circular manner to the good example, to return to the good inheritance that archaic societies have given or rather bequeathed us. The inheritance that is thus passed down is nothing other, finally, than nature. It is nature that gives, and one must show oneself worthy of this gift. One must take and learn the gift of nature. [*Le don de la nature, il faut le prendre et l'apprendre.*] From giving nature, one must learn to give, in a manner that is both generous and ordered; and by giving as nature says one must give, one will give it back its due, one will show oneself to be worthy, one will mark the right equivalence. . . . Archaic society, the archaic, or the originary in general can be replaced by *anything whatsoever* (by X or by Chi), by nature, the mother, father, creator, supreme being, prime mover, *logos*, masculine or feminine possessor of the *phallus*: One will always find again the same schema. (GT 66/90; this schema is also called "Rousseauist" a bit earlier on the same page, and attributed to both Mauss and Lévi-Strauss)

The text goes on to interrogate the links among normativity (*il faut*), the equivalence of reciprocity (with nature and among humans), and natural necessity. The links amount to the idea, so fundamental in Western political theory and economy, that it is natural to "give back what one owes," as the first definition of justice in Plato's *Republic* puts it.[20] Derrida's provisional conclusion suggests that it is precisely the *il faut*, despite the ineradicable temptation to lead it back to nature, or otherwise make it a regress-stopper, that marks an excess over natural and circular equivalence. This excess permits the gift an escape from the circularity of debt and restitution, but also exposes it to counterfeiting and fiction; whence the further discussion of Baudelaire's well-known short story "La fausse monnaie," regarding the counterfeit coin given to a beggar.

Rather than focus on that discussion, I would like to ask whether we are not missing something when we associate the references to nature exclusively with circularity and foundationalism. I will argue that the indeed problematic nature of the Rousseauist (or Hobbesian, or Lockean) naturalism, and the many attempts to derive the social contract from the state of nature, should not lead us to overlook the role of the "natural" in gifts. As we have seen, in Mauss's reading of the indigenous, nature also names, beyond the desire for the origin, the unpossessable elemental that turns and re-turns, noncyclically, in all gifts. Is there any room for this "natural" unpossessable in Derrida? Let us pursue this question by asking why Derrida appears to privilege the deferral of the time that it takes to give a gift over the spacing that seems equally required. I detect this privilege not only in the title of the book (*Donner le temps* [*Given Time*]) but also in the passages in which Derrida tries to show that *différance* is already at work in Mauss's text, and not just imposed, in a heavy-handed manner, from without.

To be sure, *différance* is not a master concept and does not govern discourses from a removed, context-transcendent meta-level. Hence, its effects can only be traced in the issue and texts at hand. In this context, the issue is the thinking of the gift in Mauss, where it is said that giving takes time. If the gift was returned right away, no giving would have taken place. As Derrida comments, "[T]he gift only gives to the extent it gives time. . . . The gift gives, demands, and takes time" (GT 41/60). The quotation marks that Mauss in some places puts around the word "time" are read by Derrida as an indication of the anthropologist's awareness that "beneath the word time, it is no doubt a matter, in the homogeneous element of chronology, of a more complex and qualitatively more heterogeneous structure of delay, of interval, of maturation, or of différance" (GT 39/57). Derrida then underscores the relation between *différance*, time, and gift, glossing the former as "time," "term," "delay," "interval" of temporization, the becoming-temporization of temporalization" (GT 40/58–59).

This gloss inevitably recalls the account in the 1968 essay "Différance" to which Derrida refers later in *Given Time* (GT 127/163). In the earlier essay, we read that *différance* is to be thought as a "temporization [that] is also temporalization and spacing, the becoming-time of space and the becoming-space of time, the 'originary constitution' of time and space" (MP 8/8). Time cannot be thought independently of a spacing that refers temporalization to necessarily material, spatial contexts; there is no time as such. In the contemporaneous "Ousia and Grammē" (also in *Margins of Philosophy*), Derrida examines the spatial metaphors the history of philosophy uses to describe time (point, line, plane, and in particular, circle) and deconstructs the priority Heidegger's *Being and Time* grants to Dasein's temporalization over its spatiality. Heidegger, however, retracted this priority in his later "On Time and Being" (GA 14),[21] the very text on which Derrida's *Given Time* draws to show that a gift can only be thought as different from exchange if related to Heidegger's gift of being, for the nonsubjective forgetting and self-withdrawal of the ontological gift allows gifts to be given without full recognition and return by donor and recipient (GT 20–23/34–38). Heidegger suggests that the gift of being be figured as a *Zeitspielraum*: literally, a time-play-space, that is, a temporal leeway or temporal-spatial playing field in which being gives beings to presence (GA 65, 242/191). It is being as "timespace" (GA 14, 14/19, 16/21, 22/27) that enables any coming to presence, including the giving of presents and the making present of gifts.[22]

It seems to me that, in the published portion of Derrida's reading of Mauss, this spacing recedes in favor of the gift of time. As mentioned, the strategic-contextual reasons for this may be found in Mauss's text itself, but that text also, as we saw earlier, underlines the role of natural elements—the forest, the land, the earth, the sea, the animals—in the "spirit" that the donor's context transfers to the recipient's and that neither of them can fully make their own. In the reading of Mauss, these references to natural elements come under the stricture of a cyclical foundationalism and the "Rousseauist schema" (GT 66/90): the attempt to trace society and normativity back to nature whose foundational status and cyclical turning ensures the gift returns to its origin. However, if Mauss's time of giving is read in terms of an unpossessable *différance*, which articulates the spacing of time and the temporizing of space, then we would expect Mauss's *space of giving* to resurface in Derrida's interpretation. This space, as we've seen, especially in its ultimately unpossessable, spectral dimension, is discussed as the native soil, the forest and its birds, the sea and the earth.

One may object that Derrida's spacing is not yet (physical) space, and certainly not anything we might call nature, land, sea, or earth. Spacing, however, does require elements that it spaces out and thereby temporizes, whether these be linguistic graphemes or phonemes, mathematical symbols, biological DNA, living organisms, human identities, or physical things.[23] According to Derrida's argument, *différance* permits in its very spacing the formation of the oppositions that feed logocentrist discourses, including the vexed oppositions between nature and culture, and the physical and the mental (MP 17/18). But in its temporizing of space, *différance* also defers these oppositions, that is, it undermines their settling into binary dichotomies. The gift of *différance* is neither natural nor unnatural, precisely because *différance* is neither pure space nor pure time. Every gift gives time in being given time (by being or by *différance*), a time whose "moments" are spaced out by a "spacing" without which there could not be any gift (GT 122/156). As Derrida underlines in the reading of Baudelaire's story, if there was no unmasterable "distance" or "step" between donor and recipient, there could be no gift relation across that distance (GT 122/156). Despite the fact that Mauss notes such distance by stressing that the sociality established by giving is always more or less antagonistic (G 8/71, 45/131), in Derrida's reading of Mauss, the spacing of time and the timing of space are not related back to indigenous accounts of the gift as proceeding from the space of giving and the "spirit" of the forest and its birds.

But perhaps the space of the gift *is* referred to nature after all, just not in the reading of Mauss but in the subsequent reading of Baudelaire's short story. There, Derrida's emphasis on the possible fictitiousness of the gift—a gift *qua* gift (so as distinct from calculative exchange) must be unrecognizable as gift, and so possibly counterfeit—leads him to a discussion of fortune, chance, and nature. If a gift requires an intentional subject who intends to give, but the very intention also returns some gift to her (for she congratulates herself for the gift, consciously or unconsciously), thereby annulling the gift as gift, then one way in which *différance* can help make the gift possible is by introducing chance and fortune, even if these are "re-intentionalized" (GT 133/169). The fate of the counterfeit coin in the hands of the beggar is unforeseeable, and the encounter between the friends and the beggar is by chance. It is also an accident that the friends happen to have coins to spare, that they were *born* into sufficient wealth, and so on. This relation between what is given at birth and the aleatory is what Derrida comes to call fortune as nature (GT 126/162). He recalls the relation between gift and nature prevalent both in premodern societies (nature as donor to which everything returns) and in the "Cartesian epoch" (nature as the given, the order of natural necessities as opposed to history and culture) (GT 127/163). Alluding to Heidegger's interpretation of the pre-Socratic *physis*, he associates the latter with nature as "the donation of what gives birth, the originary productivity that engenders, causes to grow or increase, brings to light and flowering [*fait pousser ou croître, porte au jour et à l'épanouissement*]." In this giving nature, "fortune (fate, chance, luck, *fors*, fortuity) and necessity are not opposed" (GT 128/163).

In giving us this nature to think, and beyond Baudelaire's own diatribes against modern progress and what he called "Americanization" (GT 130/166), the short story leaves us with "both a physical and an ethical question," a question whose full quasi-ontological and environmental-ethical import we should not overlook today: "How is one to behave with regard to this originary productivity, chance and necessity of donating nature [*la nature donatrice*]?" (GT 128/163).

We should revisit this understanding of nature on the reading of Mauss. Mixed in with the layers of his text that present themselves as foundationalist with respect to nature and arche-teleological with respect to history, reading *The Gift* in terms of *différance* would rediscover in every gift a differential nature—in Chapter 5, we will call it "earth" as history and habit of "lifedeath"—characterized by a productivity that gives while also withholding from appropriation and mastery. Donors and recipients find themselves born into its vagaries, their appropriations of it hovering between intentional planning and fearful contingency. While it necessarily precedes gifts and the social relations they establish, this nature also exceeds them precisely by its unpredictability and withdrawal. Understood in neither a premodern nor a post-Cartesian way, nature is a possible name for the context in which alone subjectivities, human and nonhuman, can come to affirm themselves. While selves cannot be entirely removed from nature, their iterated ex-appropriations and futural recontextualizations cannot but seek independence from it—hence, we may say, the ineradicable fear of being devoured alive by the animals, the earth, or the sea (a fear to which we will return in the final chapter). Hence, also, the attempt to stay sovereign in the face of nature, for instance by seeking mastery over the elements or by seeking to avert or defer the return of one's corpse to the earth or the sea. Much is at stake in how we respond to a fear-inspiring nature into which we are given over by the unpossessable and finite timespace of *différance*. The task would be, it seems to me, to respond to fear and finitude by discovering its inseparability from a promise in nature to pass on to the future the gift of a human world, or human earth, despite its own finitude. In Derrida's words, the task is to respond to "the finite promise *of the* world, as world: it is up to 'us' to make the world survive . . . to let survive that which 'we' inadequately call the human earth" (AV 47/39).

The world, then, that is passed on to the future is suffused with a promise to give it in a form that lets it survive as human earth. This promise, this gift of the world as humanly habitable earth, returns us to justice between generations.

III. Asymmetrical Intergenerational Reciprocity

III.1. Four Types of Reciprocity

With this discussion of the gift in mind, we can see how one might explain its specific relevance for an account of justice between generations.

If one generation, however we define it and account for its unity, can become what it is only by accepting gifts from previous generations, and if this acceptance obliges a return, then paying it forward, as the apt English expression has it, appears as the most obvious way to attempt to meet one's intergenerational obligations. And in fact, this "descending" (Gosseries 2009) or "backward-looking downward-transferring" reciprocity (Arrondel and Masson 2006) is the most intuitive type of intergenerational reciprocity (Arrondel and Masson 2006, 1010–1012). There are, however, three other forms of intergenerational reciprocity that, independent of Heidegger's, Levinas's, and Derrida's account of temporalization, add other layers to the seeming onward linearity of descending transfers. I discuss all four forms here to indicate the thickness and complexity, as it were, of the intergenerational composition of the living present. I understand this thickness as a way of fleshing out Derrida's claim that there is "no *socius*," no sociality, without a "being-with-specters that would also be, not only but also, a *politics* of memory, of inheritance, and of generations" and that "no ethics, no politics . . . seems possible and thinkable and *just* that does not recognize in its principle the respect for those others who are no longer or for those others who are not yet *there*, presently living, whether they are already dead or not yet born" (SM Xviii/15; emphasis in original). But I will also suggest that the differential gift of inheritance should be thought of as, if you wish, the groundless ground of the four types: a condition of possibility that reinscribes and exceeds the typology and its temporal distinctions.

If we stay with Arrondel and Masson's typology (Arrondel and Masson 2006, 977, 1026; see also the table at 1028), we obtain four reciprocity types by combining the results of two distinctions: first, the distinction regarding the orientation in time from which one's model, content, or motivation for giving is drawn (backward- or forward-looking), and second, the direction of transfer (upward to the previous generation, downward to the subsequent one). A backward-looking orientation means a generation (let's call it G_3) gives in view of what previous generations (G_2, G_1) gave. They give, that is, in view of having received and thus being obligated by what happened in the past (often called the "rebound effect" or the "Descartes effect"; see, e.g., Kolm 2006). Restricting ourselves for the moment only to intergenerational gifts, G_3 may then give to G_2 and/or

G1 (e.g., retirement support), in which case we have the backward-upward type. It may also give to G4 or G5 (etc.), (e.g., caring for and educating the generation of children in its midst because G3 had been helped by their parents); then we have the backward-downward, or descending type.

Gifting is said to be forward-looking when G3 gives in view of what G4 or G5 are expected to do, that is, in view of inducing an obligation to give, which some economists call "the propagation effect" (see, e.g., Kolm 1984). G3's forward-looking gifts may also be to the past (upward to G2 and/or G1, etc.) or to the future (downward to G4 and/or G6, etc.). The former type (forward-looking upward gifting) obtains when G3, for instance, supports G2 in old age in order to "mold" G4 to help G3 in old age. In the forward-looking downward type, G3, for example, raises G4 in order to get G4 to raise G5 in a certain way. This type is sometimes called "dynastic altruism" (Becker and Barro 1986), for it permits a generation to reach out to an indefinite, even in principle infinite number of future generations. While the title may sound derogatory, I've already underlined the intergenerational importance of this type (which should still be understood as a type of reciprocity; see Arrondel and Masson 2006, 982, 1034ff.) in the previous chapter in discussing the notion of "infinity" in Levinas ("fecundity engendering fecundity"; TI 269/302).

I will now proceed to address some worries about the language of reciprocity, especially from a Levinasian and Derridean point of view, and confront this typology with the account of "timespace" given above. This will permit us to refine the typology and clarify what I mean by "asymmetrical" intergenerational reciprocities. First, however, I will seek to clarify its relation to so-called chain models of justice between generations.

III.2. The Serial Chain Model

The present account of intergenerational reciprocities may be perceived to give some precedence to gifts and responsibilities among overlapping generations (children, the elderly, parents, teachers, students, care workers, and so on), but it is not restricted to them. I can see three ways in which we can explain the reach beyond overlap. First, we have the relations of interlocking chains that have been explored, in helpful ways, by intergenerational philosophers (Passmore 1974; de-Shalit 1995; Howarth 1992; Gauthier 1986, McCormick 2009). If we take those living at one time to consist of three generations, then the first of these (say, G_4, of the set G_4-G_5-G_6) interlocks with the previous link in the chain (with G_3, of the set G_1-G_2-G_3), and the last interlocks with the future (G_6 with G_7). In this way, all generations are connected with each other, namely, in this form of the chain. The chain model is often criticized for its perceived inability to handle responsibilities that skip intermediate generations. Suppose a type of environmental pollution started by G_3 is known to become a problem, perhaps due to threshold effects, only for G_8, not yet for G_4. On the chain model, however, G_3's gift obligations do not reach this far (Page 2006, 118). Jamieson claims in this context that, according to the *Stern Review*, "perhaps 90% of climate change damages will occur after 2200" (Jamieson 2014, 165).

The way intergenerational reciprocities are discussed here, we can respond by pointing to two further ways in which they reach beyond overlapping generations. We already mentioned the "dynastic" or "infinite" nature of these relations, which in fact points in both temporal directions. The gift from my parents and ancestors was enabled, though of course not caused or determined, by their parents and ancestors, and so on; at some point the line becomes untraceable. Similarly, in taking over responsibility for my own children (or those of my sister or of my friends or of strangers), I asymmetrically assume responsibility for their future responsibilities and gifts, including their responsibilities for the responsibilities of their children and children's children, and so on (see Chapter 2). Thus, G_3 is asked to enable G_4-to-G_7's responsibilities to G_8, for example, with respect to climate and biosphere in general.

Secondly, and partly because of this ultimate untraceability or infinity, we can always, and with some legitimacy, begin to abstract from the personal relations. If I owe my philosophy teacher a specific debt for what she taught me, she could have done it only because of her teachers and the tradition that stands behind her like a giant, so that I may feel I owe a debt to teachers, or even previous generations in general and the philosophical past in general, a debt that is to be paid forward to students and future generations in general.

Indirect reciprocity thus connects with the idea of an intergenerational chain: each generation addresses the next as one that is to carry on the project of justice in an iterative manner. Given the dependency of life on inherited contexts, each generation should see itself as similarly addressed by the preceding generation. If the present sees itself as also a link in this chain—in the next chapter, we will speak of each generation taking its "turn"—then its owing to the future is in part explained and specified by its having received from preceding links in the chain. In my view, no account of intergenerational justice, no matter how abstractly it proceeds, can avoid reliance on the chain: the overlapping and non-overlapping next generation is more favorably positioned, epistemically and in practice, and so cannot be bypassed in the production and continuing transfer of gifts and benefits. It is in fact critical that G3 focus on G4 in enabling it to meet its obligations to G5, even if the primary and ultimate objective is to assist G8. For the reasons indicated, the chain that results from the intergenerational reciprocities has denser moral and political relations, and extends beyond the two adjacent chains owing to the "infinity" that is not limited to interlocking pairs (as in Gauthier or McCormick). And even if, for certain at-times-legitimate purposes, we abstract from overlap and stress the universality of duties to future generations, we must also undo the abstraction in focusing, for theoretical and practical reasons, on the G3-G4 relation.

III.3. Reservations about Reciprocity

As indicated in Chapter 2, Levinas and Derrida often reject the language of reciprocity. They do so because of several objections that, I believe, do not apply to my conception of asymmetrical reciprocity. In fact, because of its temporally disjointed relation among at least three parties, and its combination of self-regarding and other-regarding aspects, I believe it presents a dynamic integration of gift and exchange that helps us to operationalize and flesh out intergenerational justice. Let me make this more precise.

(i) Altruistic gift and self-interested exchange: We've become acquainted with Derrida's argument that the gift must be understood "without reciprocity" (GT 12/24), and indeed, much of his effort in reading Mauss is devoted to distinguishing two concepts that are not clearly set apart in Mauss, namely, "gift" and "exchange." To the extent it does not return to the donor, the former is called a "pure gift [*le don pur*]" (GT 64/88, 137/174, 147/187), and Derrida is often read as arguing for the superiority, especially

the moral superiority, of the pure gift over economic exchange and reciprocity. (For references, see Fritsch 2011a, which seeks to mediate in the corresponding debate about interpreting Derrida.) However, as we've seen, the purity of the gift is only an aspect, not a separate instance, of gift-giving; that is why Derrida often writes "the pure gift (if there is any)" (e.g., GT 134/170), and explains why Mauss had to learn that the "pure gift" could also turn into the bad, even the worst (GT 64/88). For Derrida also argues that, because "différance *is inscribed in the thing itself* that is given or exchanged," giving "demands gift *and* restitution [*demande le don et la restitution*]" (GT 40/58–59; emphasis in original). The gift is given *or* exchanged, and its normativity calls for both the excessive, "purely" generous aspect of giving and for restitution, return, giving back, calculation, rendering a responsible account of one's giving, and so on.

We explained above how this can be. Subjects can become subjects only in responding to the differential spacing of time by attempting to come back to themselves, by calculating a return; this seeking to come back to itself, says Derrida, should be understood as "the very definition of the *subject as such*" (GT 101/132; emphasis in original; see also GT 10/23). But *différance* also makes of the gift a "dissemination without return" (GT 40/58). An intending subject will always congratulate herself for giving, even if unconsciously, Derrida argues, so as a consequence, there will be some return on her gift (GT 142/180).[24] A gift cannot but also be a psychological, economic, social, or political investment in one's own personality or context. In addition, there will be no purely generous gift, because gifts take place in the context of "established practices" (see above) that obligate the recipient, thus thwarting both pure altruism and pure generosity (GT 137/174). But the donor cannot calculate a full return even if she intended an exchange of equivalents, as the future of what is given is beyond her, enmeshed in a context or a "world" that she cannot foresee or master, discontinuously continuing a "more powerful and more durable" gift of inheritance that is subject to an ongoing process of differentiation and deferral. That is why, despite the subjective calculation and the indebtedness, the gift can also be said to be "without reciprocity" (GT 12/24). The gift must be thought in relation to economy, but remains beyond it (GT 7/18).

At this level of generality, then, the account of the gift disallows a binary distinction between altruism and self-interest—a distinction that Mauss as well as Arrondel and Masson also find wanting. Plenty of room remains to make pertinent and useful distinctions at other levels of analysis and in circumscribed contexts—one thinks of the great distance between, say, market exchanges and infant care—but as necessarily proceeding from differential contexts, neither will be free from return and dissemination beyond return. (Indeed, *Given Time* reinscribes Aristotle's distinction between market chrematistics and family economics, between the alleged infinity of desire and the supposed finiteness of need and care, in the differential, "infinite-finite" gift: without a relation between the two, the family—whose fecundity, as argued in the previous chapter, Levinas opposes to the totalizations of politics and history in too binary a fashion—would be closed in on itself and thus incapable of any sort of gift, hospitality, and care [GT 158/200ff.].[25] We will come back to this below.) Asymmetrical reciprocity is meant to capture this "dynamic synthesis" of altruism and reciprocity, a synthesis that Arrondel and Masson argue is necessary to explain empirically observable intergenerational gifting. (Similarly, Wade-Benzoni [2002, 2009] argues for mixed motivations when it comes to future people. "Reciprocal altruism" is also a much-discussed phenomenon in evolutionary accounts of the origin of morality; see, e.g., Heath 2008; Rutte and Pfeiffer 2009; Singer 1998). In relation to future people, then, asymmetrical reciprocity demands generous, open-ended conduct, but does not sever this generosity from either future-regarding hope of continuity and meaning or past-regarding gratitude and indebtedness. Rendering reciprocity indirect in fact opens it to future-regarding "altruistic" supplements, such as concern for future people for their own sake (see Fritsch, forthcoming). For in contrast to direct reciprocity, where the recipient is specified by the interaction (A-B, B-A), indirect reciprocity calls for an open-ended identification of the third party, C, both as to its identity and as to what is to be given. Only if one were to insist that the content of what is to be given to C is fixed by what A gave to B would we not need supplementation by other moral, possibly altruistic considerations, such as who needs gifts the most and which kinds. And such strict equivalence is put into doubt by the "dissemination without return" that, as indicated, is not just an accident befalling gifts, but is demanded by them.[26]

(ii) Asymmetry and symmetry: Another reservation with respect to reciprocity stems from its seeming presumption of symmetrically situated parties. In (esp. feminist) literature on the social contract tradition and on reciprocity (as referenced in the previous two chapters), this starting point that assumes what Martha Nussbaum calls "rough equality" has been widely criticized for assuming that justice is a matter of bargaining between parties of equal power (Nussbaum 2001, 2006). This would be especially problematic in the case of intergenerationl relations, which (as we saw in Chapter 1) are typically characterized by asymmetries in power and responsibility, to the point that some have argued that asymmetry should be our model for responsibility, rather than equality (e.g., Jonas 1984; Brumlik 2004).

In those rare instances in which Derrida uses reciprocity in a positive sense, he clarifies that we should not equate reciprocity and symmetry. He writes, for example, that one cannot but "prefer," even if simply on a practical level, the language and culture, even the nation and citizenship, into which one is born, which one has been gifted and is asked (by the gift of inheritance) to carry on. By speaking French, or by writing as I do here in English, I carry these languages and their legacies into the future in a way I do not for other languages, the many languages and cultures threatened by the homogenizations of globalization, for instance. However, Derrida continues, one must allow one's inheritance to be "crossed" by universal demands, and also respect and be hospitable to the other. He writes: "And reciprocally [so universal norms must be crossed by the exigencies of singularity[27]], but reciprocity is not symmetry and first of all because we have no neutral measure here, no common measure given by a third party" (PI 363/374).

Asymmetrical reciprocity seeks to respect moral and social asymmetries already in its very name. Given the "disjointure" in time that gives rise to the call for responsibility in the first place, given the differential "timespace" in which it situates the intra- and intergenerational relations established by gifts, it does not assume that the parties are situated in the same time and space. It does not promote an ideal theory approach in which parties are placed in a counterfactual, ahistorical situation to determine what they might owe each other. Such situations tend to make it very difficult to then integrate histories of oppression, such as racial, colonial, sexist, and class oppression, into a theory that begins by screening out historical realities, as Charles Mills has argued in relation to Rawls (see Mills 2014).

In addition, asymmetrical reciprocity seeks to respect the absence of a "common measure" by understanding that the subject can never be equal to the demand placed upon it in its historical situation. In Levinas's words, the demand comes from "on high," not because it is simply too demanding—a common misunderstanding of Levinas and Derrida—let alone because we are surreptitiously endorsing divine-command theory, but because the injunction is in itself aporetic and torn between self and other, past and future, debt and generosity; its precise content and source cannot be foreseen (Derrida 2007b, 451, 461). It calls for historically specific inventions that attempt anew to do justice to what one has been given and to what the future demands. Such inventions cannot be measured in advance and thus refuse a good conscience for the one who takes the measure.

(iii) Shared and disjointed time: Another objection one might raise with respect to reciprocity would claim that it assumes shared time. In glossing Mauss, remember, Derrida writes: "The difference between a gift and every other operation of pure and simple exchange is that the gift gives time. *There where there is gift, there is time*" (GT 41/60, Derrida's emphasis). The implication is that in "pure" or "simple" exchange—which, of course, Derrida argues exists in its purity no more than the pure gift—there would be no time. The conceptual ideal of exchange is that it takes no time: you give me X and I give you Y at the same time, without time in between in which one is indebted to the other, without one being superior and the other, dependent, owing, and so on. In this sense, the model of exchange or barter among self-interested parties (a model we already encountered in Mauss's critique of "Western individual notions") assumes sovereign, self-identical, independent actors who are either indifferent to time or share a common time.

Reciprocity might thus come under an attack similar to the one Nietzsche directed at revenge. Pure reciprocity could be understood as a more general category of which revenge would be a species; revenge is the return not of a benefit, but of a wrong. Nietzsche famously argued of revenge, and Heidegger agreed, that it is marked by "an ill will [*Widerwille*] against time."[28] Revenge and reciprocity would, on this extended account, be animated by the desire to annul time so as to set up a sovereign will in the present that is not subject to finite time, and thus not vulnerable to others and not dependent on contexts. For Nietzsche, Heidegger, Levinas, and Derrida, however, time implies the finite subjection to change, and thus vulnerability and dependence. For instance, in his account of capital punishment—the death penalty is often seen as restituting a wrong—Derrida argues, perceptively I believe, that the model of sovereignty behind the death penalty, especially the idea of instant execution, consists in the attempt to "kill time." In execution, sovereignty dreams of contracting its own power into an instant, turning around its own axis like a perfectly round wheel, so as to immunize itself against being affected by others. While taking time implies receptivity to the outside, instantaneity and anaesthesia, Derrida argues, are indissociable (DP1 225–226/308; see R 109/153–155).

If, however, every event is made possible by Heidegger's being as "timespace," or Derrida's *différance* as "the becoming-time of space and the becoming-space of time," then it cannot be the case that time could be annulled or suspended. There is no pure simultaneity, in the sense that presence is spaced out in its coming to be from the past and its passing toward the future (what we will discuss as time taking turns in Chapter 4). Even exchange takes time, and so involves a present "stretched-out" between a past and a future that "give" the present its turn. In this sense, in "asymmetry" we should hear the anachrony and disjointure of time that, as discussed, gives rise to historical subjects and their responsibilities in the first place. It will be important, too, not to import the assumption of shared time, of contemporaneity, into the definition of "generation." Generations are abstractions from the ongoing reconstitution of subjectivities and the birthing and dying that make up the *socius* we then wish to divide into intra- and intergenerational relations.[29] Nonetheless, such abstractions, as I suggested in Chapter 1, are legitimate for certain purposes.

(iv) Indirect over direct reciprocity: Another point follows from this account of differential-iterative time as constitutive of the identity of historical subjects: namely, the priority of indirect over direct reciprocity, or

exchange. One may have thought that indirect reciprocity is merely an extension of the direct version, legitimate for specific intentions perhaps, but leaving intact, as the core idea of reciprocity, a two-party relation situated in shared time and space. Further, if we assume that individuals stay the "same" as they go through the usual stages of life (childhood, maturing, adulthood, aging, old age), then some versions of some of the four types of intergenerational reciprocities are not indirect but direct forms of reciprocity (see, e.g., Gosseries 2009; but note that, in contrast to Gosseries, Arrondel and Masson 2006 and Kolm 2006 do not make this assumption). For instance, on the forward-looking downward type, I may care for my children only to induce them to care for me in old age. However, if we treat the parties as changing over time, or we treat reciprocities as holding between stations in life (childhood, old age, adulthood) or social roles (educator-child, teacher-student, and so on), then these reciprocities remain indirect and hold between three parties.[30]

As we can see by reaching back to the account of differential iterability above (see II.2 in this chapter), Mauss's gift and Derrida's work contest the assumption of personal identity over time, as does much other work in this area. On this view, a subject comes to be only by responding to its originary disjointure and displacement. Identity is not a substance or *hypokeimenon*, but is to be won in an ongoing process. Subjectivity exists only in the mode of coming back to itself from its differential contexts, without ever coming back full circle or having returned to a fixed station. We cannot simply assume that individuals are the same, especially not over longer time spans and with differing life stations and social roles. Thus, *différance* makes it impossible to distinguish, with any sort of precision, direct from indirect reciprocity; at most we would have a gradual scale. For each other is undergoing change over time, in part as a result of the very gift, so that a perfect case of direct reciprocity, like the "simple" simultaneous exchange discussed above, could not obtain. On this view, then, the initial contributor and the final beneficiary cannot be identical to one another, as is perhaps acceptable in the case of pension schemes (with regard to which many a retiree hopes that her earlier self had been more like her in terms of spending habits).

(v) Backward- and forward-looking temporalities in asymmetry: The objection with respect to time might continue, however, by pointing out

that indirect reciprocity assumes not a disjointed timespace, but a linear time: past A gives to present B who passes on the gift to future C. Even the thicker account of four types of intergenerational and possibly overlapping reciprocities results from distinctions inscribed on linear time: backward- and forward-looking, upward or downward transfers. To respond to this charge, I begin by supplementing the four types with Levinas's account of "diachronic" time.

In discussing Levinas's fecundity in Chapter 2, I stressed that his "being-for-beyond-my-death" involves the general and constitutive expectation that there will be a world beyond one's death, and that therefore one's efforts and actions will not come to an end with death. If death is not nothingness, but on the face of the other calls on me to let the other live, then my responsibility, but also my hope and horizon of expectation, is extended to a world beyond my life. Although this hope and expectation of meaningfulness could be characterized as an advance credit that the present always draws from the future, it is to my knowledge not discussed by economists, who typically limit their discussion to material transfers. Nonetheless, we should understand this projection of future horizons as a general background disclosure of "world" within which all specific types of reciprocity can make sense in the first place. As a general condition of reciprocity, then, this responsibilizing expectation nonetheless also appears as a form of reciprocity: I draw meaningfulness from regarding, with at least some care, (overlapping and/or non-overlapping) future people beyond my death. If we now ask how this form of reciprocity fits into the typology outlined above, we discover that it does not fit neatly, as it upsets its founding distinctions.

Most important, it seems to me that neither Levinas's "being-for-beyond-my-death," read in the way I did in Chapter 2, nor Derrida's differential gift of inheritance or gift of world can be assigned to either the forward- or the backward-looking type. This is because, as indicated, it names the "groundless ground" of the four types of reciprocities. And at a certain level of analysis, this temporality of world disclosure confounds distinctions between past, present, and future to the extent these rely on linear time. As we've seen, the context or world with which and "in" which gifts co-constitute and obligate donors and recipients is inherited as to be reenacted from the future. Inheritance—and we *are* our inheritance,

Derrida argues (SM 68/94)—is not to be understood as a tied-up, finite bundle given by the past (see ET). If that is what it was, and we were still to maintain its constitutive nature, then it would predetermine action, and so leave no room for it as the beginning of the new. Inheritance, then, is to be understood not on the model of a privileged presence—it is what it is—but as *to be*, actualizable from the future *to come*. In this sense, the "larger and older" and "more durable" gift of world within which alone gifts gain normative force renders this force both past- and future-oriented. At times, Derrida puts this in the form of a "double before":

Only a finite being inherits, and his finitude obliges him. It obliges him to receive what is larger and older and more powerful and more durable than he. . . . The concept of responsibility has no sense at all outside of an experience of inheritance. . . . One is responsible before what comes before one but also before what is to come, and therefore before oneself. A double before, one that is also a debt, as when we say *devant ce qu'il doit*: before what he ought to do and owing what he owes, once and for all, the heir is doubly indebted. (FWT 5–6/18; see also the play on *devant* in Derrida 2002a, 122, and in AV)

What we could, on the model of the middle voice (i.e., neither active nor passive voice) of *différance* or *restance* (MP 9/9), call *devance* names this precedence of the gift of inheritance that is also a futural excess and overflow, a to-come. We saw above that the excess of the gift entails that, despite its constitutively necessary appropriation by heirs, it remains inassimilable. This inappropriability is, we've seen, central to its normative force: the heir must appropriate, but also must leave to the future. Thus the *devance* of inheritance upsets the distinction between looking backward and looking forward. The past from which a generation necessarily receives is not only the past of empirically identifiable generations (parents, caregivers, teachers, role models, forebears, ancestors, and so on), but (in both Levinas's and Derrida's terms) an "immemorial past" excessive to all economizing and bookkeeping. Because it cannot be appropriated and repaid—for the gift is inappropriable and ahead of the heir—the excess looks at us and implores us generational beings from the future. Levinas's "being-for-beyond-my-life" as well as Derrida's account of a justice, a hospitality, and a gift excessive to law and norms call on us from what the latter calls the future-to-come (*l'à-venir de l'avenir*, or just *l'à-venir* (SM xix/16; see SM 177n5 for the translator's note on the translation as "future-to-come").

The usual way of distinguishing past and future people in determining debt and repayment obligations in accounts of indirect reciprocity, as practiced by economists and philosophers, is thus insufficient. Every obligation and transfer to future generations involves (without exhausting) repaying a debt to the past, but a debt from which agents cannot but also break free in opening themselves to a future. Speaking of "asymmetry" in intergenerational reciprocity is meant to address the resulting impossibility of clearly assigning intergenerational obligation to either the past or the future. Asymmetrical reciprocity is thus not as vulnerable as indirect reciprocity to the objection that it cannot account for direct obligations to future people. For while it may be acknowledged that indirect reciprocity can avoid some ontological problems, namely, by not taking not-yet-existing future people to be independent claimants (see Chapter 1), the price it pays for this, the objection continues, is heavy: its obligation to future people is merely indirect, much weaker than a direct one.

By contrast, in insisting that in every relation to future generations there is an element of past debt, asymmetrical reciprocity necessitates further specifications of owing forward, as we've seen, including what I've called other-regarding future-oriented duties. But these specifications are to take our Janus-faced generational entanglements seriously.[31] In accepting my motivation for giving to the future from the future, for example, an element of indebtedness to the past is also at work; I could not ascribe my gift to the future just to myself, or just to the "present" generation. Conversely, in orienting my motivation to the past even when giving "upward," the needs of the future tug at me. Similar entanglements obtain when combining forward-looking motivation with upward donation, and a retrospective regard with downward transfers.

This does not mean that we cannot distinguish which regard and which direction of giving is primary in particular instances; the conclusion here is rather that the normative force cannot be pinned down in time and space. The gift asks for a return from a time without time, without assignable place on a linear time line divided into past-present-future. Its "origin" is not at our disposal or knowledge. The motivations and norms governing gift practices, perhaps especially those primarily regarding generations, are at times barely conscious, to be brought to explicit reflection only with difficulty and directed effort. Indirect reciprocities are often not *purely* voluntary or consciously intentional, for even the most material and overtly given gifts cannot be isolated, as we have argued, from an in toto unpossessable, given-giving heritage whose differential constitution links it to an "immemorial" past and an unforeseeable future "to-come." Inheritance, therefore, tends to have imitative effects and set precedents, and to entail implicit or explicit norms of gifting (see Arrondel and Masson 2006, 977). As we saw in Chapter 1, it is important to keep in mind this world-constituting and preference-forming aspect of intergenerational justice. The task is to raise awareness of the possibly imitative nature of the actions of one's generations, and the sometimes oppressive implications of inherited lifeworlds, without thereby losing sight of the limits of such awareness, and without displacing all normativity from the facts of inheritance, leaving us to seek the sources of morality in ahistorical procedures, as some have argued is typical of Western modernity.[32] Asymmetrical reciprocity points to a historical-ontological reality as much as to its normativity. That is also why there is always the risk of paying forward what will come to be perceived as nonbenefits or harms. Paying attention to historical reciprocity at least has the advantage of calling for vigilance on the part of heirs, in particular in view of asymmetrically positioned future generations. Asymmetrical reciprocity recognizes their "spectral" presence with "us contemporaries" as demanding of us, as noted, normative, other-regarding supplements that often have to be bent against the continuation of inherited wrongs.

(vi) Gift and economy: The last objection I address returns us to the worry that the differential gift blurs significant boundaries between gift and exchange, and between private life and the world of commerce. There is here a danger of dissolving morality in economy, of spreading exchange and calculation beyond its proper bounds. Indeed, we've seen that asymmetrical reciprocity disallows binary divisions between other-regarding generosity and self-regarding exchange, and thus between gift and economy. In conclusion, I would like to respond by returning to what I have called "the gift of nature." For in indeed blurring the distinctions to which we are so accustomed, I believe, an opportunity may be recognized to rethink the gift relations not only among generations but also among social spheres, and indeed between the intergenerational "chains" and nature.

We've already indicated that *Given Time* suggests that the gift points to the fact that neither family nor "chrematistic" economy (whether capitalistic or not) can be isolated from each other. While the family depends on the circulation of goods, the economy cannot just assume the givenness of individuals on the market. The upshot of this, as some have argued, is that unpaid care work should be recognized as an unacceptable externality even if we do not wish to marketize care (Kittay 1999; Held 2006). Interrogating intergenerational reciprocities can thus also lead to undoing an economistic starting point that begins with isolated individuals who owe their talents and their labor power to no one (see Macpherson 1962). More broadly, then, the Maussian-Derridean gift not so much blurs important sociological and normative distinctions as asks about the conditions of economic production and distribution for return, commerce and exchange, exposing it as, in Bataille's term, "restricted" (GT 105n24/136n1, 147/186, 159/201; see also "From Restricted to General Economy," in WD). To say that an economy, in practice or in theory, is restricted is to point out its focus on returns to the investor, on calculative exchange, commercial circulation, and the utility-maximizing agents presupposed by it. To "generalize" economy is then to confront it with the gift as its enabling condition, that is, with *différance*, dissemination, and "the problematic of the trace" (GT 100/131). It is to call out the externalizations of restricted economy (see Wood 2007).

It is also in this sense that Derrida's claim that the gift sets the economic circle in motion should be understood (GT 30–31/47). It casts in new light the opening question of Derrida's text, "What is economy?" (GT 6/17). Confronting economic circulation with the gift beyond return amounts to asking, "Is there economy?" As we've seen, economics and economic activity, on this view, depend on a prior gift of world that co-constitutes individuals, but as inextricably related to each other and to things given, such as land (see the excellent analysis in Mei 2017 on the "ontological" presupposition of land as *given* by today's economists). By insisting on a gift prior to, and thus also within, exchange, Derrida asks, as German economist Wolf Dieter Enkelmann has argued, about the conditions of possibility of economics as science. Enkelmann writes:

[Derrida's] question regarding the *gift of the given* is, in its subject matter, a question about the *economics* or *ecology of resources*. For like economic theory, economic practices assume many givens. They always refer to something that for them is simply *present*, such as nature with its raw materials or the world with its unlimited possibilities, and also human beings in the form of individual, [rational] beings. (Enkelmann 2010, 27, my translation; emphasis in original)

Understood in this way, to generalize economy is to confront it with its starting conditions in nature, inheritance, and family. It is to politicize its externalities. Enkelmann goes on to claim, helpfully, that Derrida's ecological question about economy makes of the latter science a political science about world:

It is then [when asking "Is there economics?"] inevitable to integrate the external factors. In the end, what is at stake is a kind of sustainable world economy. The question regarding the gift of the given brings into economics the question of how there is the world, instead of simply pre-economically presupposing the world as given by nature or by God. World economy then becomes economy *of the world* instead of just being economy *in the world*, for whose existence and maintenance one is, on this assumption, not responsible. (Enkelmann 2010, 28, my translation; emphasis in original)

The point would then be to understand economy not only on the model of blood circulation, but on the model of metabolism. As the ecological economist Herman Daly puts it, "Economists have focused too much on the economy's circulatory system and have neglected to study its digestive tract. . . . Throughput growth means pushing more of the same food through an ever larger digestive tract; development means eating better food and digesting it more thoroughly" (Daly 2008; see also Raworth 2017). But as Derrida insisted, especially when rethinking organic individuality and its relation to what we will call earth, metabolism cannot be thought without waste products, from breathing out to vomit, defecation, and the corpse. To generalize economy is then, as we will explore in Chapter 5, to confront it not only with its starting conditions, but also with its remains and its waste as inadvertent gifts. Not the least question with respect to the gift of nature and generation may thus be: "What is it to make a gift of a corpse [*qu'est-ce que faire d'un cadavre cadeau*]?" (GL 143/163).

4

Double Turn-Taking among Generations and with Earth

The previous chapter argued for asymmetrical reciprocity as a model of intergenerational justice that does justice to the social-ontological and the normative significance of the co-implication of the past and the future in the present, as elaborated in Chapters 1 and 2. Asymmetrical reciprocity captures the sense that indebtedness to previous generations and to nature plays a role in giving to future people, no matter how asymmetrical and altruistic the gift to the future is taken to be.

Chapter 4 presents a second way of modeling the social-ontological and normative significance of the historicity of human subjectivity and social relations. This second model conceives of generations as taking turns with quasi-holistic "objects" of intergenerational sharing, such as nature or what we will here call the earth. There are several reasons why I introduce this second model. First, it is useful to show that there are ways other than reciprocity and the gift to think the spectral presence of the dead and the unborn in the present. Like the gift, as we will see, taking turns is an "ontological" notion in that it permits us to think the very being of social-historical time: each moment receives its turn from a previous one while already turning over to the next.

Second, turn-taking will be argued to better respect the nature of the earth and other quasi-holistic "objects" (such as institutions, languages, and traditions). Reciprocity, even if indirect and altruistic in the ways we discussed, suggests that one owes "at least as much" as one received, where the benefit or gift is often a nonrenewable (e.g., finite resources) or a consumable (e.g., food) that one can no longer pass on. Thus, one owes an equivalent among substitutables, and at some point needs a common metric to calculate such equivalencies. Substitutability, however, is notoriously difficult to reconcile with concerns about the sustainability of the natural environment (see Holland 1997, 1999), for it is doubtful that, for instance, productivity gains or improved infrastructure can count as an equivalent for forests or a stable climate. As we will see, taking turns can help here, for it changes the normative question from "What kind of equivalent do we owe forward?" to "What is it to take a fair turn with X?"

Third, taking turns lends itself better to presenting questions of intergenerational justice as inherently political questions. As I will argue, this is because a second source of taking turns as a model of justice (the first is social-historical time) lies in the sharing of (equally indivisible or nonsubstitutable) political offices, as theorized especially in Aristotle's *Politics*, and in particular with respect to democracy. When nominally free equals seek to share an "object" that can neither be cut up like a cake nor be "used" or occupied by the sharers at the same time, then sharing should take the temporal form of taking turns (κατά μέρος, *kata meros*; Aristotle, *Politics*, e.g., 2.2, 1261a; 3.16, 1287a). As I will argue, this basic idea of sharing by turns—which has received very little attention in the literature[1]—can be expanded to apply not only to (democratic) offices and institutions but also to other holistic, long-term "objects" of intergenerational sharing, especially the earth as habitat of life.

In his work on democracy, in particular, Derrida has linked the issue of the being of social-historical time and Aristotle's discussion of sharing by turn-taking. For this reason, this chapter takes its cue from Derrida's rethinking of political life as lifedeath by arguing that taking turns helps in conceptualizing the intra- and intergenerationally shared nature of democratic institutions. While democracy has often been accused of favoring the present at the expense of the future, and of inheriting an anthropocentric model of sovereignty, my argument that democracy should be rethought as a matter of taking turns (an elaboration of my earlier argument; see Fritsch 2011b) is meant to counter democratic presentism and human exceptionalism at the same time. My principal concern is to show that, not only do rulers take turns with the ruled in the ancient idea of democracy, as discussed by Derrida in *Rogues*, but the present generation takes turns with the preceding and following generations in governing the democratic institutions that express sovereign power. Taking turns offers an appropriate way of conceptualizing the intra- and intergenerationally shared nature of democratic institutions. Further, the generational taking turns with democratic power must be thought in conjunction with an environmental turning: not only do human generations seek to share sovereignty over subjects and the earth, but such human sovereignty is dependent upon, and crisscrossed by, a lateral turning with the earth. Stressing this second turning in the first, I argue, allows us to conceive deconstructive "double" affirmation as an affirmation of *survivance*, or life as lifedeath. As such, affirmation affirms the improper of the human and the vulnerable passivity or precariousness that exposes each of us to other humans as well as to the nonhuman.

I. Democracy's Presentism

Particularly in the context of the environmental crisis and justice for future people, the concept and practice of democracy, like modernity generally, has frequently been accused of presentism, the favoring of the present at the expense of the future. Derrida's "democracy-to-come" contests both the metaphysics and the politics of this presentism, and hence may contribute to a rethinking of environmental and intergenerational justice. In this chapter, I investigate democracy's presentism by suggesting that dominant layers in the democratic legacy conceptualize death as the end point of life, both so that death does not really affect life while living (it's merely the end of it), and so as to conceive of death as a point in linear time. This bolsters a faith in—even a passionate attachment to— the belief that we can pinpoint the instant of death. In his death penalty seminars (DP1, DP2), for instance, Derrida seeks to show that this belief is powerfully at work in the modern-democratic expression of sovereign power over putting to death by way of the guillotine and the electric chair (death without cruelty because instantaneous), and also underwrites the much more complicated distinctions made among suicide, murder, and capital punishment (DP1, DP2).

It is in this sense that we should understand Derrida's otherwise somewhat surprising claim that the death penalty is the "keystone" of the political (FWT 147–148/239–240): capital punishment is the hallmark of the faith in the possibility of the human mastery of death. That is also why the conception of sovereignty that is expressed in capital punishment, as sovereign mastery of death, is so intimately linked to human exceptionalism and the traditional idea—dominant from Plato to Kant, Hegel, Heidegger, and Levinas—that animals, though living and thus by definition mortal, have no access to death, properly speaking. If what is proper to human beings is an appropriative and heroic relation to death, as shown, for example, in war or in the idea that every murderer deserves his death, then properly human sovereignty affirms itself also as mastery over the nonhuman. And when it comes to intergenerational relations, faith in the instantaneity of death—death as an instant in time that separates life from death—supports belief in firm distinctions among the living, the dead, and the unborn. We may thus ask what the deconstruction of presentism tells us about the relation between democratic sovereignty and relations among the generations—without, however, supposing that generations are merely human, and keeping in view the problematic relations among sovereignty, mastery over (animal) death, and a view of time that permits clear distinctions among the present, the past, and the future.

This rethinking of democratic sovereignty comes at a time when intergenerational and environmental duties are high on the agenda of global publics. What is particularly noteworthy, I think, is the urgency of our situation and its unique place in history. As a result of climate change and environmental degradation more broadly, we the presently living—a "we" that is never given—may be the first generation to have the very real and massive power of affecting future generations drastically by business as usual; in addition, we know about these effects, more or less conclusively. This knowledge now stretches back (by ice-core drilling and deep sedimentary rock analysis) and forward (by climate modeling) hundreds of thousands of years, in some cases even millions of years.[2] As discussed in the Introduction, the notion of the "Anthropocene" suggests that humanity should now be understood to constitute a geological power in its own right. Stretching human history into the deep past of the earth and unimaginably far futures asks us to reconceptualize human power and sovereignty in relation to the geological and atmospheric forces on which we depend, but also to position "our" present time in the context of long-term intergenerational relations. We must see ourselves as only one generation among many others before and after us, while *also* seeing ourselves as unique in being singled out by a special responsibility. We have to do this despite the difficulty, discussed in Chapter 1, of actually singling out any one generation, since birth and death occur at every instant. I will suggest double turn-taking as the best model for this situation.

What should give us pause is that the intergenerational and environmental problems, together with their attendant duties, are to be handled by a political form of government that stands accused of a presentist bias. Well-known democratic theorist Dennis Thompson, for instance, argues that "[d]emocracies are systematically biased in favor of the present" (Thompson 2005, 267). Timothy Clark diagnoses "a deep and systematic injustice in the workings of contemporary government, political thinking, and many modes of thought and analysis in the universities and daily life," an injustice he claims comes to a head in "the lack of political representation of future generations" (Clark 2008, 45).[3] Stephen Gardiner suggests that democracies suffer not only from the much-discussed "tyranny of the majority" but also from a lesser known "tyranny of the contemporary" (Gardiner 2011a, 36; see 143ff.). Democracy's rather poor record on sustainable practices and combating climate change has prompted some to speak of a "failure of democracy" that would demand that we urgently replace sovereign democratic freedoms, in particular those regarding individual and collective self-determination, with "survival" as "the most fundamental value" (Shearman and Smith 2007, 133; see Giddens 2009, 73; Tremmel 2006).

Various reasons have been given for this priority granted to the present. Michael McKenzie suggests "four potential sources of short-termism in democratic systems: 1) short-sighted voters; 2) politicians with short-term incentives; 3) special interest groups with short-term objectives; and 4) the fact that future generations cannot be included in decision-making processes today" (MacKenzie 2016, 24). Presentism has also been related to the short-term thinking said to be brought on by democracy's relation to free market competition (in particular in post-Fordist capitalism; see Harvey 1990), and by the fact that state power is beholden to special economic interests.[4] These interests are often pushed by economic actors that exert a lot of power on states (e.g., by way of the dependence on corporate taxes and investment and the creation of employment) and on politicians (in particular if public financing of elections is insufficient). Under competitive conditions, these economic agents often operate with very short and accelerating time frames.

Further, increasingly competitive conditions may lead to an instrumentalization of action (as the first and second generation of the so-called Frankfurt School argued; see Horkheimer and Adorno 2002; Horkheimer 1974; Habermas 1987), and thus a favoring of one's own position in the present. The instrumentalization of action orientations applies in particular to economic agents, individual and collective, but also to democratic nation-states to the extent they compete with each other for attracting capital investments (Przeworski and Wallerstein 1988; Przeworski 2010). To all this, we no doubt have to add the growing social acceleration that has gripped all societies in the process of industrialization, in particular since World War II, and led to calls for "slow politics" and "slow science" (Scheuerman 2004; Rosa 2010). Long-term thinking, we may surmise, has a hard time installing itself in motivational apparatuses if these are already overstimulated and overstressed. Democracy is particularly vulnerable to acceleration; Rosa and others have argued that technology and economy affect society much faster than democratic (especially deliberative) processes, which merely play catch-up. Information-gathering and deliberation simply take time, as does the verification of legislative proposals against normative standards, existing law, and long-standing policies. In response to this desynchronization, political scientists have noted an increasing displacement of decisions away from elected democratic bodies toward faster but less democratic agencies, from the legislative to the executive branch, to courts, and above all to the private sector, to corporations, and to the economic sphere (Rosa 2012, 357–373). Presentism consists, then, in a favoring of the present rather than the future, but this present is itself fleeting, swiftly giving way to the ever-new future and its latest gadgets.

Presentism has also been related to the frequent changings of the guard required by the electoral cycles of representative democracy (see Gardiner 2006; Garvey 2008; Dryzek 1996; Wood 2008). Simon Caney speaks in this context of "harmful short-termism" (Caney 2017, 135), and political scientists King and Crewe argue pointedly: "[P]oliticians lack accountability for the future impacts of their policies, and this leads them not to think policy through, often with disastrous results" (King and Crewe 2014, 356–359, 395). Some also argue there is a presentist time preference on the part of the (some add: an increasingly instrumentally oriented or consumerist) populace, perhaps justifying the implementation of a positive social discount rate on the part of its representatives (Thompson 2005, 2010). In this context, we could mention a number of psychological, all-too-human factors bearing down on democratic citizens: the difficulty of noticing and properly acting on so-called creeping problems, the unidentifiability or invisibility of the future victim, weakness of will, a tendency to procrastination, and so on (see Chapter 1).

In Chapter 1, I also discussed the intergenerational intensification of the type of collective action problems known as the "tragedy of the commons" (Gardiner 2011a 37, 143ff.). I suggested that if we accept the assumption of largely self-interested, instrumentally oriented agents, part of the conclusion is that we need powerful democratic institutions with sanctioning power to counter the presentist effects. These institutions would have to be more independent of economic power and have global reach (to address a global tragedy of the commons), but they should also survive the generational discontinuities and takeovers. Democracies must be able to sustain their sovereignty over time, but they must also understand sovereign power as globally and intergenerationally shared.

I want to suggest that Derrida's rethinking of democratic sovereignty by way of the figure of turning can be of enormous help in addressing presentism. Deconstruction has always sought to question and subvert the "metaphysics of presence," and so offers its own account of the emergence of presentism.[5] This account can be approached most usefully by way of the deconstructive concept of democracy, which not by accident refers to the future in its very name (*la democratie à venir*). As we will see, democracy-to-come questions the power of the present over the past and future along with the power over the nonhuman, the beast and the earth. Just as much as the deconstruction of anthropocentric humanism not only, or even primarily, finds that some animals share what was thought of as exclusively human properties (from thought and language to mourning and burial), but also, from the other side of the divide that is to be multiplied, questions the property of the human, such as access to language, meaning, thought, and death as such (see Derrida's *The Animal That Therefore I Am*), so the deconstruction of presentism not only gives some presence to the past and the future, but "depresentifies" (or "spectralizes") the presence of contemporaries to each other. In other words, if we rethink life as not a matter of life *and* death or even life *versus* death but as a matter of *lifedeath* (or even *lifedeathbirth*; see Fritsch 2017b), then the dividing line between the presently living and the nonliving will become less secure and singular. Further, questioning the divide between life and death, I will try to show, not only reconceives the relations among the living and nonliving human generations, but also the relations among the human sovereign and nonhuman living beings.

Let me now explore double turn-taking as undermining democracy's presentism.

II. The Space-Time of Double Turning

The deconstruction of presentism yields both an ontological (better: quasi-ontological or "hauntological") and a political, normative reason for reconceiving "our" time, the time of our power, as a time of taking turns among generations. The normative reason is the attempt to reconcile the equality and freedom of citizens: to share political offices equally even when all at the same time cannot occupy them, citizens take turns with power. I have suggested elsewhere why this intragenerational turn-taking should be understood to include generations (Fritsch 2011b), and I will further elaborate below. The "hauntological" reason—"hauntology" being Derrida's rewriting of an ontology of presence toward one of the interplay of presence and absence, thus one of haunting ghosts, spectrality, the structure of the trace, and *différance* (see *Specters of Marx* and Chapter 2 on *différance*)—reconceives the time of democratic sovereignty as the "space-time of the 'by turns' [*l'espace-temps d'un tour-à-tour*]" (R 24/47). The notion of taking turns (the wheel, *la tour*; the turn, *le tour*) among governed and governing is discussed in *Rogues*, then, not only because Plato and Aristotle introduced it to reconcile equality and freedom, but also as a way of thinking time (R 25/47–48; see BS2 130/193).

Why this relation between (generational) time and taking turns? We can address this question by taking as our springboard Aristotle's famous exoteric aporia of time in chapter 4 of the *Physics* (*Physics* 4.10–14, 217bff.), discussed extensively (without as of yet discussing the turn) in Derrida's early essay "Ousia and Grammē" (in MP). After discussing prevalent views of time, Aristotle arrives at this conundrum of time as follows. While we can think of time as divisible into parts (the now, *nun*), there are also reasons to deny that the now is a "part" (*meros*). If time "is" (has being), then it must be in the form of the "now" as its part. However, the "now" is either "no longer" or "not yet," for if the nows were all present nows, then we would have only presence, and so no passing of time nor any change or movement, which are equally central to what we mean by time. Thus, time must consist of (indivisible) parts, and each now is different from the others. But time is also passing and succession, so each now must also be divisible or decomposable such that it can give way to another now. As the aporia has it, the now is part and not part of time; time is divisible and yet not divisible. As Johannes Fritsche put it, referring to the famous definition of time as "a number of motion in respect to the before and after" (*Physics* 219b2): "For Aristotle, number is a discrete quantum (*Cat.* 6, 4b20–31). Motion, on the other hand, and along with it time, are continuous quantities (see e.g. *Physics* 220a4–11). How, then, can we think discreteness and continuity as united in time?" (Fritsche 1994, 101; see also Coope 2005, 18–20).

As we can see here, we need an account of time that does justice both to what we might call the presentness of the present, and to temporal succession. It cannot be that one moment is *first* present in itself (an indivisible now in Aristotle's aporia), and only *then* comes to pass away, giving way to another; every instant ceases to be as soon as it comes to be. And yet, if time were nothing but flow, or pure negativity, then nothing could maintain itself in being, as there was no presence, and no difference between one time and another. Now, one way of addressing this aporia is by thinking time as a taking of turns: each time has its unique and irreplaceable turn, but the "now" as this singular turn consists only in turning toward or around itself in coming to be from other times, and turning toward another by passing away into yet other times. Singular presentness is here not thought, as with indivisibility, in essential or substantive opposition to flow and movement, but as resulting from its very torsion. Taking turns, then, is a way of grasping the relation between irreplaceability and replacement, or singularity and multiplicity: what is irreplaceable each time is its turn, but such a turn consists only in a granting of presence by past and future.[6]

As an indication for thinking time in this way,[7] Derrida (R 6–7/25–26) traces the etymology of the French *fois*, meaning "once," "one time" or "times" (as in *trois fois*, "three times"), to the Latin *vicis*, the uses of which range from "by turns" (*per vices*) and "in turn" (*vicissim*) to "succession," "alternation," "change," "reciprocally," and "in place of" (*in vicem*), giving rise to the uses in English of "vice versa," "vicarious," "vicissitude," and "vicious circle." Derrida refers to his essay "Shibboleth" for further discussion of "the vicissitudes of latinity," and he writes, referring to the aporia of time as the "im-possible": "[e]ach time [*C'est chaque fois*] in order to confirm a dangerous law of supplementarity or iterability that forces the impossible by forcing the replacement of the irreplaceable [*en forçant au remplacement de l'irremplaçable*]" (R 7/26). In fact, the English *week* and the German *Woche* are also derived from *vicis*: time taking turns with time, week by week, one singled-out presence coming to replace a previous one while already being in the process of being replaced by another. Time and identity over time call on us to do justice to the singularity of each time, but this singularity can "be" only as iterated next time, repeated and to be repeated on the revolutions of the calendar, and generation by generation.

The ontological (or, as we said, hauntological) reason for reconceiving the time of sovereign power as a time of taking turns among generations thus lies in the attempt to think time as a succession in which one's time consists in being born and dying away. If time does not coincide with itself from the beginning—the present shares its time with the nonpresent past and future—and so consists in taking turns, then this must also be seen to apply to identity, that of a living organism, an institution, or a collective self such as a democratic nation or a generation, for instance. Life forms, singular or collective, exist in the mode of taking turns, with themselves (a past self giving place to a present self giving place to a future self), but also with others. Temporally speaking, every self consists in turning around itself. If a self was simply identical to itself over time, then it's hard to see how it could ever have come to be, undergo any sort of change, and pass away. This means we have to think both identity over time and its change together. Taking turns with oneself is one way to reconcile these two demands: a self turns toward the future as other in order to turn back on itself as it has been.

However, as argued in Chapter 3, we have to avoid construing or modeling time independently of space, and as noted, Derrida refers democratic sovereignty to the "space-time of the 'by turns' [*l'espace-temps d'un tour-à-tour*]" (R 24/47). In this context, on the basis of our discussion of time, we can motivate the crucial reference to space by recalling that temporal succession can be thought only if there is a way of relating different times to one another; otherwise, we would once more be left with mere flow. A dominant way to do this is of course to introduce some kind of consciousness that synthesizes different modes of time by way of memory, attention, and expectation: hence, one may argue, Aristotle's references to the "soul" that counts the numbers of time or perceives the motion of time for there to be time at all (*Physics* 223a16–29). The difficulty, as Heidegger has argued, is that this move leaves unclear the temporal-ontological constitution of this consciousness itself—hence, *Being and Time*'s existential analytic of human existence in terms of temporality and being-toward-death, the notion that we saw Levinas rewrite as being-for-beyond-my-death, and that we connected with being-from-others. Toward the end of Chapter 2, I effected this connection with the help of *différance*, which, we recall, Derrida presents as the becoming-time of space and becoming-space of time (MP 8/8), and which he discusses in the context of democracy by reference to Jean-Luc Nancy's account of what has been lacking in "the philosophy of democracy" up until now, namely, an account of the "sharing [of singularities, of singular individuals] as spacing (or, as I would say, as space-time, the becoming-space of time or becoming-time of space" (R 48/73).

With respect to this problem of the synthesis of time's modalities, space refers to that which remains, that which permits time's modalities to be inscribed and possibly retrieved as iterable traces (see Hägglund 2008, 2016). It is for this reason that, for Derrida, time cannot be thought without inscription in space. The experience of time crucially depends on the material supports and techniques of inscription available at a given time, making possible the social acceleration we discussed above (for Derrida's own account of the speed of the social, see Derrida 1984). What is most relevant in our context, however, is the conclusion that generational turning takes place both in environments we characterize as cultural, political, and institutional, and in those we call terrestrial and evolutionary. As *Of Grammatology* puts it in discussing the work of French paleontologist and anthropologist Leroi-Gourhan, life in *différance* is a life in modes of inscription, from the

> "genetic inscription and the "short programmatic chains" regulating the life of the amoeba and the annelid up to the passage beyond alphabetic writing to the orders of the logos and of a certain *homo sapiens*. . . . [O]ne could speak of a "liberation of memory," of an exteriorization always already begun but always larger than the trace which, beginning from the elementary programs of so-called "instinctive" behavior up to the constitution of electronic card-indexes and reading machines, enlarges *différance* and the possibility of putting in reserve: it at once and in the same movement constitutes and effaces so-called conscious subjectivity, its logos, and its theological attributes. (OG 84/125)

As an account of space-time, *différance* makes possible the conscious subject of memorization and anticipation (needed on many accounts for recording time, as we've seen), but only by inscribing it in environments that precede and exceed conscious life. Lifedeath is situated in the intergenerational evolution of sociopolitical institutions as well as on earth as the history and habitat of life in general.

The notion of life can thus be said to be "the enigma of the political around which we endlessly turn" (R 4/22). Democratic politics is to be understood and practiced in the space-time of turning around intergenerational and terrestrial life. To make this more precise, and to unfold its inherent normativity, I will distinguish for analytic purposes two forms of turning that in life are co-implicated. For if an entity does not just coincide with itself but exists in the mode of taking turns, then its differential or hauntological constitution implies a certain basic performativity or normativity, in fact a double normativity. At the most general level, this normativity of what we called, in Chapter 1, double affirmation (see also Fritsch 2017b), applies to every mode of identity, subjectivity, or sovereignty, whether individual citizen, the political sovereign (the *demos* or the people of a democracy, for example), or a generation, whether individuated at the domestic or global political level.

Turn-Taking 1 (T1): Given the noncoincidence of the present time, no identity is simply given. Any self must, from the beginning, seek to return to itself, promising itself to its future self. If a subject's temporality is turning, coming to be and passing away, then it must seek to resist the dissipative or disseminative side of this movement and establish its identity over time by bending the turning back toward itself. To make its self, to constitute its power, sovereignty has to resist sharing its time with others. To a greater or lesser extent, sovereignty involves both "the suicidal illusion . . . of giving birth to oneself" (NW 101), as perhaps in Kant's conception of freedom as "self-beginning,"[8] and the resistance to giving way to an other, to let a future self have its turn. At both the level of individual citizen and the level of political institutions, we find this attempted re-turn and rotation:

For democracy to be effective, for it to give rise to a system of law that can carry the day, which is to say, for it to give rise to an effective power, the *cracy* [rule, power] of the *demos* [the people] . . . is required. . . . A pure sovereignty is indivisible or it is not at all, as all the theoreticians of sovereignty have rightly recognized. . . . This indivisibility excludes it in principle from being shared, from time and from language. (R 100–101/143–144)

The ipsocratic need for bending the turn back toward the sovereign self, so *Rogues* suggests, stands behind the model of sovereignty that Western metaphysics has favored, namely, a god who circles around himself in perfectly undisturbed rotation. And part of the problem of democratic presentism, we may say, lies in having inherited this model of a "conscious subjectivity, its logos and its theological attributes" (OG 84/125), of a sovereignty that is so intimately tied to human exceptionalism. For the dominant Western concept of democratic sovereignty, the one that today is so unevenly and problematically being globalized, is a notion inherited from the idea of God as the absolute power and true sovereign to whom belongs the unconditional right over the life and death of all living things, above any norm and beyond any positive law. This idea is fed by Plato's notion of the Good beyond being (R 137–140/191–194), Aristotle's unmoved mover as "the life that exceeds the life of human beings" (R 15/35), and the way these came to be interpreted in light of the Judeo-Christian, biblical creator-god. Although less linear than I can suggest here, we may thus trace a genealogy from ancient Athens and Jerusalem to the medieval God as sovereign ruler over creation, and then from the divine right of the king as God's representative on earth to the democratic revolution that, despite beheading the king, replaces God with "the people" as an indivisible sovereign. As evidence, Derrida cites Tocqueville's *Democracy in America* (1825): "The people reign over the American political world as God rules over the universe" (Tocqueville, cited in R 14/34).

Turn-Taking 2 (T2): However, this circulation of the sovereign around itself is subject to a "double circulation" (R 24/47): the turn back to itself or around its axis is upset by the constitutive turn to the other, to time, inheritance, and the future. There is no guarantee that the future self will be the same self, and in fact, given the differential constitution of identity in a life-sustaining context, to seek to return to oneself is also (at the "same" time) to turn toward the other. The attempted re-turn passes into the differential context without which there could be no self. Despite the sovereign bending, the turning never comes around full circle; it remains a "half-turn [*demi-tour*]" (R 111/156) or a "quasi-circular return or rotation toward the self" (R 10/30). To affirm oneself as oneself is to affirm the context without which one could not be what one is, and that means to welcome unconditionally the future to-come as an alterity within oneself. The welcome is extended to others, ranging from one's future self to other living humans, even to noncontemporary humans (the dead and the unborn) and to nonhuman others, including the inorganic. Democracy involves a turn toward the singular and unpredictable "each one," and this "other truth" of democracy (R 14/35) provokes the question, "How far is democracy to be extended, the *people* of demo*cracy*, and the 'each "one"' of democracy? To the dead, to animals, to trees and rocks?" (R 54/82).

It is important to understand that these two turnings (T1 and T2) do not present us with a decision as to which one to favor. For good or for bad, sovereignty is only established as double circulation. Democratic constitutions and institutions demand both circulations at once, even if their conjunction is contradictory or "auto-immune": the turn toward the other and the performative assertion of indivisible power with its attendant belief, always to some extent illusory, in freely beginning with itself (R 100/142–143).[9] Despite this performativity, however, we can distinguish different self-conceptions of democratic power, some of them more hospitable to unconditional alterity than others. In Derrida's words, deconstruction attempts to "separate," despite their "inseparability," the "exigency of sovereignty in general" from "the unconditional exigency of the unconditioned" (R 141/195–196). If I here insist on double circulation and turn-taking as constitutive of sovereignty, and if I elaborate (beyond Derrida's own work) the normativity involved in it, it is to render democratic power less perfectly round, and more welcoming of its inevitable unconditional exposure to other times and life-sustaining environments.

In this spirit, let us apply double turning to democracy as placed in intergenerational and environmental contexts. By doing so, we obtain the following.

T1: Political sovereigns, democratic or not, have to establish their continuation over time despite the fact that individual office-holders die and give way to those born after them. The noncoincidence of the sovereign with itself lies, to pick up the terms used in earlier chapters, in its natality and in its mortality. Natality implies that the sovereign has been given its turn by another and now has to make that turn its own, appropriating inherited political power for itself, without ever fully being able to incorporate the inheritance and its dead. Mortality may be resisted in the case of generations and collective identities by seeking to pass on sovereign power to a successor that, despite representing an alternation and alteration, promises to maintain the sovereign power and re-close the circle, hence the attempt to restrict the successor to citizens who are tied to the same constitution and institutions. It is a well-known paradox that freedom-granting constitutions also restrict the freedom of future people (for discussion and further references, see Fritsch 2013a). A collective self, such as a family or a nation, may further seek to reestablish itself despite the mortality of individual members by tracing bloodlines, making bequests only to the oldest son, or at the national level, by (in the absolutist case) passing sovereignty from king to his son or (in the democratic case) restricting national membership to those who belong to it by blood or by birth; hence, the link between democracy and fraternity and the hegemony given to the figure of the natural-born brother that Derrida seeks to loosen up in *The Politics of Friendship*.

T2: As indicated, natality and mortality—the fact that individual sovereigns die and new ones are born—necessitate the turn toward the other who is not yet prefigured as one's own child, the brother, the co-national equally bound by the constitution, the skilled worker, the employable immigrant, and so on. The second turning implies hospitality to the indeterminate future other; it entails the gift of giving way to another, letting another generation have its turn as one had one's own. Along these lines, as noted in the previous chapter, Derrida argues in the exordium to *Specters of Marx* that "learning to live" means learning to come to terms with death, the death in life that disallows life to coincide with itself, delivering it over to the other and the other others. Coming to terms with death means accepting to co-inhabit the world with vulnerable others whose very mortality calls for "nonviolence" (RDP 83), and for an "anterior affirmation of being-together" (PF 249) as the "law of originary sociability" (PF 231). Learning to live means learning to live justly; no realpolitik can avoid having to come to terms with the others it cannot but welcome. Justice, however, is never restricted to one generation but is an intergenerational issue: "[N]o ethics, no politics . . . seems possible and thinkable and *just* that does not recognize in its principle the respect for those others who are no longer or for those others who are not yet *there*, presently living, whether they are already dead or not yet born" (SM xix/17; emphasis in original).

To grasp one's life as one's own, then, can only be done justly by understanding that one seeks to affirm it as one's turn with life. This means, on my telling, that I grasp "my" life as ongoingly received from others for whom I am a member of the then-nonpresent future generation, and as continuously (voluntarily and involuntarily) passing it on to others for whom I am a member of the nonpresent past generation. Derrida continues: "The possibility of the question, which is perhaps no longer a question and which we are calling here *justice*, must carry beyond *present* life, life as *my* life or *our* life. *In general*. For it will be the same thing for the "my life" or "our life" tomorrow, that is, for the life of others, as it was yesterday for other others: *beyond therefore the living present in general*" (SM xix/17; emphasis in original).

Tomorrow, then (though it is already coming), the present generation will be the dead for the next generation. And yesterday (though it is not yet entirely dead and gone), the present generation was the future for the generation now dead. If the disjointure of time renders possible identities in their social relationality, and thus makes justice an issue, it also relates generations to one another. Social life is intergenerational life, and so justice in general must from the beginning be seen as intergenerational. The turn-taking nature of time shows us that generational overlap, the relation of the young and the old in what is no longer a mere contemporaneousness, is not a mere accident from which theories of intergenerational justice may abstract. Time is the time of sur-vival, or survivance, each time sur-viving life's dying but never coinciding with itself, a life or lifedeath that therefore consists in taking turns. Life involves exchanging positions and stations in life, as the young become the old and the unborn become the dead. The democratic assent to letting the others have their turn in governing is thus enabled by the turning nature of time. But the consent has also—quietly, perhaps, but necessarily—been extended to a generational, rather than just individual, turn-taking.

III. Generations Taking Turns

In this application of double turning to the intergenerational context, as I noted at the outset, we should avoid an uncritical anthropocentrism. We should not proceed as if humans took turns only with humans, remaining more or less external to the biosphere with which they take turns. As we've seen, the turn toward the other in T2 is highly ambiguous. On the one hand, it always takes place under the self's attempt to predetermine it (even if minimally) and to restrict it to what is perceived as the self and its extensions. This is no bad thing, for it belongs to subjectivity to seek such separation from its context, in this area, of the human from its environment. On the other hand, the turn toward the other is a turn to that which ultimately cannot be foreseen or controlled; as indicated, the "anyone" incoming may range from the co-national "brother" to the stranger, the dead, the unborn, animals, trees, or rocks. The other toward which the self (re)turns in T2 (and from which it emerged in natality) is a life-sustaining context that includes other humans, but is not restricted

Double Turn-Taking among Generations and with Earth 171

to them; it is also the biosphere of which the self always remained a part in some way.

To better capture this ambiguity (though without wishing to remove it, for it belongs to what we are trying to think here), we may want to speak of another (a second) duality in turning:

Intergenerational Turning (T1G-T2G) (where T stands for "turning" and G for "generation"): Individuated generations take turns in inhabiting the biosphere. The turn to the self (T1G) is here a turn to one's own generation in the present. However, as a result of the disjointed, turning nature of time, this attempted re-turn finds itself always already displaced or rerouted toward a turn to nonpresent, or spectrally present, generations, overlapping and non-overlapping (T2G).

Environmental or Terrestrial Turning (T1E-T2E) (where E stands for "earth"): Individuals and generations turn in and out of nature, or the earth, from which they are born, with which they must engage in metabolic exchanges, and to which they return upon death. Seeking to turn toward themselves from a space they need but also need to separate themselves from (T1E), individuals encounter a counterturning (T2E), the earth turning them about, what we will elaborate in Chapter 5 as the claim of the earth upon the living: the earth demands that a turn be left for earth others, in breathing out, in defecation, in the corpse.

Graphically, the interplay between T1 and T2 could be represented by a single generational turning, rather than by two turnings, generational and terrestrial. If we had only a single turning, we could seek to represent the fact that the generations are not simply external to the "object" of turn-taking by expressing the "use" as carving, as it were, into the object as well as into the turn-takers. However, I think it more productive, and graphically more helpful, to speak of two turnings—generational and environmental—that turn in and against each other in a "double turn." Two turnings address a certain degree of separateness between intergenerational and environmental concerns, despite their constitutive co-implication While the degree of separation between these turnings is, typically, exaggerated, I believe it to be an important point and will take the time to justify it a bit further.

I see three reasons to separate and then re-relate the two turnings: generations taking turns with each other with respect to a certain holistic or quasi-holistic object (here, above all political institutions and the earth), and the terrestrial turning of individuals and generations with the earth. The first is the ontological reason that lies in the fact that, for any living identity (individual or collective, human or nonhuman), to be means to seek to re-turn to itself (in the sense of T1, discussed above). It belongs to its being to resist its dissipation into the context in which it lives, even if (as per T2) such dissipation tugs at its return and puts up resistance of its own. The separation between human generations and their environment thus need not be seen as the mere result of anthropocentric bias. The second reason is more or less moral: many problems facing us today are, as Stephen Gardiner has argued, best captured by conceiving human beings as broken up into generations, with earlier ones passing on costs to later ones (Gardiner 2011a, 143ff.). This is because, against the background of the power asymmetry we discussed in Chapter 1 and the existence of temporally extended "goods" shared over the long term, the division into earlier and later generations is best placed to reveal moral concerns that Gardiner aptly titles "intergenerational buck-passing" (154).

The third reason is strategic and political: most publics and policy makers today (as well as most social scientists) see long-term problems, including environmental ones, in intergenerational terms, often related to community belonging (Wade-Benzoni 2009). A philosophical approach need not be bound to these preferences, of course, and may indeed have good reason to trouble them, but it should also, in my view, not just bypass such realities, especially in light of the moral and quasi-ontological reasons we just discussed. Philosophical argument and moral traction need not be opposed. The point here is to show that concern for future generations, at the individual, communal, national-institutional, or global human level, can be usefully expressed in terms of taking turns with communally shared institutions and with the earth. In fact, intergenerational communities, especially those that are broadly democratically institutionalized, exist in a mode of turn-taking that also takes turns with the natural environment, and whose normativity may be explored on this basis.

Thus we obtain the intergenerational and the environmental double turning. This second duality in turning means we must now distinguish four aspects of historical turn-taking, aspects which are always intermeshed in reality but which may be analytically distinguished:

T1G: the attempted self-return in and through birth from previous generations and inherited circumstances;

T2G: the turn toward the other, specifically the next generation(s);

T1E: the attempted self-return in and through birth from the earth and the consumption of biospherical resources, from air to food and shelter;

T2E: the turn toward the earth upon death, but also throughout life's continuous exchange with nature.

While the next chapter will discuss the terrestrial turning in greater detail, I now elaborate the intergenerational turning. I will do so by discussing the ontological and normative benefits that I think this way of modeling intergenerational relations promises, a discussion that will also help us to further flesh out turn-taking. Keeping the focus on democracy in mind, here I further explore the question of how to share governance with past and, specifically, future generations. Why address such sharing as a turn-taking? One reason we have given stems from the fact that the doubly turning constitution of sovereign power has always already made an intergenerational affair of the democratic assent to taking turns with others in governing. Saying yes to turn-taking means accepting that I receive power from previous others and will leave it to others. Even if, as we've said, democratic electoral cycles are sometime blamed, among other things, for the short-term thinking we urgently need to overcome, the principled consent to permitting another cycle, to exchanging power, comes to have intergenerational significance once we realize that the democratic assent may be seen as proceeding from the time of birth and death, which characterizes social relations in general.

But there is another reason why the intergenerational sharing of democratic governance may be conceived as taking turns. We said above that turn-taking is motivated both by a hauntological reason (time as made up of presents that take turns), and by a normative political reason. We indicated the latter by referring to Aristotle's *Politics*: in order to share political institutions among nominal equals who cannot, all at the same time, be the ones to occupy the institutional offices, citizens take turns with power. This basic idea, however, can be extended from institutions to other objects of sharing, provided the object meets certain criteria. Sharing in general is often thought along the lines of a division into parts that is not appropriate in all contexts, and particularly unhelpful when the sharing concerns institutions and the environment. The major reason for this inappropriateness is the holistic nature of the object: dividing it into parts would destroy it as the functioning object it is. While we usually cut up a cake to share it, we do not normally dismantle a bicycle or a house to share its parts. Rather, if selling is not an option, we take turns riding or inhabiting it. Apart from this indicator, there are a few others that suggest turn-taking as a more appropriate form of sharing, such as the inability of any one user to appropriate or consume the thing to be shared in toto; here, too, eating may be a misleading model.[10] Further indicators are the merely temporary use or usefulness of the shared thing, and the fact that it was received from others earlier in time and is to be left to others thereafter. If the thing to be shared precedes and exceeds the present use of the user, then it may be better shared by turns.

Thus, drawing in part on the excellent work by Allen Habib (2013), we can in general share an object (X) by parts or by turns.[11] The latter seems more appropriate if, singly or jointly, the following conditions are met: (i) X is owned in common but cannot very well be shared by parts (e.g., disassembling a bike to distribute its parts renders it unusable, though we can indirectly share it by parts if we have a common metric, like money: we can then rent it out or sell it and share the proceeds by parts); (ii) X's use or usefulness is temporary (e.g., we don't need a bicycle twenty-four hours a day, hence the popularity of bike-sharing services); (iii) X was received from others earlier in time and is to be left to others thereafter; and (iv) X cannot be appropriated or consumed in toto, or it contains an unpossessable element. In some cases, one of these conditions may suffice to render sharing by turns more appropriate. For instance, I may have to share a house by turns even if (i) but not (ii) is met; this changes when the house is a vacation home or a mountain cottage that users only need at certain times, so that sharing by turns becomes the obvious solution. If in the case of a house, only (i) is met, we may want to rent or sell the house if we can (such a possibility being another important indicator), were it not for the fact that (iii) our grandparents built the house and bequeathed it in the hope it would stay in the extended family.

Now, I think some things meet these indicators in particularly salient ways, such as a tradition, a language, an institution, and the natural environment. The major reason why Aristotle in particular suggests that, under some constitutions such as the democratic, citizens share political power and institutions by taking turns is, as indicated, that the offices can neither be occupied (or "used") by all free and equal citizens at the same time, nor be shared by division directly (each gets a part of the office and its power) or indirectly (citizens sell the office and share the proceeds).[12] Political offices and institutions are also typically meant to unify a body politic despite generational turnover; they precede and survive their present subjects.

Similarly, the natural environment displays the indicators for sharing by turns. The biosphere that sustains life precedes and exceeds its present occupants, in that it was received and cannot but be left (though likely in better or worse shape than when it was received) for future others. It displays the temporality of a larger sphere into which one is born and into which one passes. Its "use" is temporary owing to the time of birth and death. As the background condition of life that is always already presupposed, the biosphere cannot ever be consumed in toto. Like the language that one must presuppose in every speaking and that therefore always leaves an inappropriable remainder that Derrida calls *restance* (R 90; PI 322), the earth will remain beyond the grasp of human power and political sovereignty. Natality and mortality imply the at least generationally common usufruct ownership of the earth, a "use" or "owning" that constantly slips away from present toward future. Finally, like the bike or the house, the biosphere is a complex holistic system that, on pain of destroying it, cannot entirely be shared by parts, even as individuals must appropriate parts from it.

In addition to the doubly turning nature of timespace, then, we have good reason to think of the intergenerational sharing of both democratic institutions and the natural environment in terms of taking turns among generations. No one generation can or should fully and exclusively possess democratic power or the earth, let alone power *over* the earth. A generation owns only its turn with power. The advantage of this conception is thus that it expresses a certain humility of power: the finite, natal-mortal character of sovereignty. From the vantage point of this finitude as the origin of normative sociality, we can begin to see that certain holistic, encompassing elements that we share are no mere instruments of human endeavors. Let me discuss some of the advantages of turn-taking as a model of sharing, specifically the intergenerational kind.

First, we may say that turn-taking is readily accessible to common intuitions that may be elaborated as normative principles. If many grasp the justice of taking turns, they can fill the idea with further normative content with respect to what it demands. This, we may say, is due to the fundamental role turn-taking plays in socialization and language learning. Turn-taking may be seen as a basic and crosscultural social behavior and a major developmental milestone for children (Sheridan et al. 2014) that has also been observed in animals, for instance, some birds in flight formation and certain fish species (Harcourt et al. 2010; Voelkl et al. 2015). In economics, it is associated with efficiency gains in certain situations (see Leo 2017). It has been argued to be central to conversation and thus to sharing language as another common holistic object, in which one takes turns in speaking and listening (Hayashi 2012).

In the case of generations taking turns, however, there are also some differences to consider. In most cases of intragenerational turn-taking, users expect or get a second turn. Part of their moral motivation may very well reflect this. Further, given overlap among generations, the switchover in the case of generational turn-taking is not as clear-cut. In the example of the mountain hut, we would have a case not of all users leaving at the same time to make room for new occupants, but of some people departing while others are staying to welcome new arrivals. While this raises again the question of the individuation of generations, which I will discuss further below, I do not think these differences from intragenerational turn-taking undermine common intuitions and normative traction.

Second, turn-taking emerges out of an ontological condition of human life, namely, the generational time of birth and death. Just as "nows" take turns with each other, generations take turns by birth and death. If one indicator for sharing by turns is the temporary nature of the "use," birth and death of course impose this on generations. I suggested in Chapter 1 that theories of justice ought to meet both normative and ontological demands, and so I think turn-taking meets this dual challenge in a particularly salient way. To this sense of hauntological attunement, we can add that time as turn-taking captures the sense that individuals and generations are preceded by a life-supporting context (earth, traditions, institutions, etc.) that they must appropriate and make their own, but that constantly slips away, temporally and spatially, toward the future, undoing the appropriation and the ownership. (In the previous chapters, we discussed this as "ex-appropriation.") The sense of slipping away in the very grasping is captured by the well-known saying (whose origin I have been unable to trace): "Treat the earth well: it was not given to you by your parents, it was loaned to you by your children." Of course the earth was also in some sense handed down by the parents, but I believe that the stress of the saying on the earth's being on loan from the future is justified: a generation's "use" of the earth is already slipping away toward the next one. Turn-taking does justice to this sense by suggesting that a generation owns a turn, but not the thing with which it takes turns. While still allowing some agency, control, and use, turn-taking captures this temporal "humility"—the closeness to the earth, as we will see in the next chapter—of human agency and political sovereignty.

Third, as Allen Habib has argued convincingly, unlike the sharing of parts, turn-sharing does not require mereological accounting, and so no quantitative metric to compare the value of parts to one another (Habib 2013). (However, we should add that such accounting cannot be eliminated entirely, e.g., for intragenerational sharing and for nonrenewables.) This makes it especially suited to sharing things that cannot (easily) be shared by division, and to respecting the holistic nature of certain objects. This respect often finds expression in the idea of an intrinsic value of, most commonly, nature, life as such, or the earth as the biosphere of life. But turn-taking also does not require us to decide whether democratic institutions, or nature, have value in themselves, so that we can then ground duties to—or at least with respect to—those institutions or nature itself. As is well known, when it comes to nature this is a point on which ecologists, on one side, and economists and policy makers, on the other, often disagree. Turn-taking disallows welfare trade-offs because it entails duties not just to future turn-takers but to the "thing" with which a turn is to be taken. What is owed is not an equivalent for something used up from a common fund, but a turn with the "object." For example, I may owe you a turn with the bike even if your poor back means riding it will not be good for you; the bus ticket I give you instead does not count as a turn with the bike. Similarly, we could say, increases in the rate of productivity, or in overall GDP, do not count as appropriate equivalents for impoverished democratic institutions, for instance, those dominated by private interests, or for a polluted environment or much hotter climate. This is so not simply because democracy or a clean environment is more valuable than economic growth, at least at a certain threshold of well-being, but because what contemporaries owe the future is a fair turn with the governance of these institutions in the public and long-term interest, and the inhabiting of the environment.

Politically (and this is my fourth advantage), turn-taking encourages a generation to think of itself as a unity with collective responsibility, although not with sole ownership over the "object" of sharing: as we said, a generation merely owns its turn. The "turn" permits thinking together both the intergenerational dispersion of ownership and the politically vital unification of a generation as turn-taker. As indicated in the Introduction, such unification could be thought to proceed from a crisis in the "object" of sharing, such as climate change: all those currently sharing in democratic power as adult citizens are called upon to preserve that which is intergenerationally shared. A generation owns its turn, not the "object" constantly slipping away toward the future. This last point returns us to the challenge with which I opened this chapter, namely, the task of thinking our generation as singled out by a special responsibility, and yet as only one among many other generations preceding and following us. Taking turns encourages both long-range thinking into the past and especially the future, as demanded by climate change: we are just one generation among many others. But turn-taking does not thereby undermine the urgency and special situation of our generation, one that is indeed morally (though, alas, not politically) unified by its unique responsibility. We the presently living, whether American or Chinese, African or European, Indian or Bangladeshi, must act in concert out of concern for our collective turn and future turn-takers.

If turn-taking encourages a generation to think of itself as a unity with collective responsibility, this raises the question of how to individuate a generation in the face of individual births and deaths (see the Introduction and Chapter 1). It seems we have two options to relate turn-taking and generational individuation. First, we treat all those living at any given time (or all adult contemporaries) as a single turn-taker. This requires that we either treat generations as coming onto and exiting the historical stage *en bloc* (a strategy against which I argued in Chapter 1 on the grounds that it abstracts from overlap), or that we see individuals as hopping on and off an existing turn. On this latter interpretation, we have not really individuated a generation, for there would be only one continuous turn. Turn-taking, it would seem, could then only apply to individuals.

Therefore, in line with the definition of generation favored in Chapter 1 (the idealized familial definition), we should accept that at any given time, there is more than one overlapping, turn-taking generation. While G1 may be on its second turn (with the same object), G2 is starting its first turn with the same object of intergenerational sharing (see the table in Chapter 1). This view has the additional advantage of being able to distinguish the turns of G1 and G2. Stressing two (or in fact three) overlapping turn-takers not only allows us a beginning and end to individuated generational turns, but also permits us to stress that G1's second turn (the one that overlaps with G2's first) may have additional responsibilities, not only to turn-takers after its death (G4+) but to co-turn-takers during its lifetime, for example, to draw on its experience in order to educate and advise G2 (and eventually G3) with respect to what turn-taking with this object requires at this time. This differentiation does not prevent us from saying, for certain purposes, that G1, G2, and G3 are collectively responsible for their fair turn at time period 3.

IV. Fair Turns

Let me return to the issue of what it is to take a fair turn. In terms of normative content, I said, turn-taking changes the question of the content of intergenerational justice. Habib argues that "the distribution problem between generations of people has been conceived (tacitly) as one of indirect part sharing," as in the case of selling a house to share the proceeds (Habib 2013, 758–759). Nature as a whole is construed as a collection of parts, each of which may be assigned values that we can compare in a common metric. But turn-taking does not translate nature as a whole, for instance, into capital so as to compare the values of parts, as many sustainability theories do. On this model it's no longer just a question of what kinds of things and how many of them, or how much in terms of equivalents, we owe future people, but of what it is to take a fair turn with holistic objects with future people. While I will not discuss this question in great detail here, obvious answers are the following: First, a turn-taker may be said to owe X forward in the condition in which she received it. While this would fit with the typical content of reciprocity (to give at least as much as was received), the difference between reciprocity and turn-taking here would be that the former typically allows substitutions, or what we have here called indirect part sharing (e.g., improved infrastructure for nonrenewables), whereas turn-taking looks to the overall state of the object in which it was received.

This first answer to the question about fair turn-taking does not mean, of course, that a present turn-taker may not come under an obligation to improve the condition of X. For instance, if a previous user damaged a bicycle by overuse but made some profit of the overuse (e.g., by delivering newspapers with the bike), which she also passed on, then, ceteris paribus, we might say the next turn-taker should use the inherited profits to fix the damage for the sake of the third turn-taker. With respect to climate change, I would argue that this is the situation in which the current generation in the developed world finds itself: having inherited the benefits of industrialization, it must now pay for the associated climate damages (see Baer 2010).

Such an argument from liability for compensation can, of course, be bolstered by the second answer to the question as to what it is to take a fair turn: X, one might say, must function well for the next turn-taker, however that is specified. In the last chapter I argued that asymmetrical reciprocity is Janus-faced, looking both to the past and the future, even if that makes our normative answers more overdetermined. Here, too, the specific needs and responsibilities of the next generation (including responsibilities to their next generations) must be kept in mind. The turn captures particularly well the temporary use or appropriation of an inheritance that will be passed on. Finally, we can say that the X must be, as Habib puts it, "flourishing" or "healthy" as the kind of thing it is (2013, 761–762). In the case of a bike, we owe not just a functioning bike, but a bike that meets the objective standards of bike-ness. In the case of nature or the earth, ecologists and other experts would then have to define what ecological health is.

In addressing the question of what it is to take a fair turn, we have thus raised the question, at least implicitly, of the relation between asymmetrical reciprocity and taking turns, the two models of IGJ I have defended. As this raises the question of different levels of what I have called ontological (or hauntological) normativity, I begin by reviewing the overall argument in this respect. In Chapter 2, I re-elaborated Levinas's being-for-beyond-my-death as entailing being-from-others, and then formulated this in Derrida's terms as double affirmation. Affirmation of the preceding context—in Levinas's text, the earth and the habitable dwelling—must affirm the self along with the other, and the other along with the self. But it is also double in a temporal sense: to affirm oneself requires that one affirm one's past as promised to the future, the future being constituted in part out of the past (see Fritsch 2017b). In view of specifically intergenerational concerns, we then saw asymmetrical reciprocity and taking turns as arising with double affirmation (or, to coin a mouthful, with being-from-others-for-beyond-my-death). I then asked further about the normative content of intergenerational reciprocity and taking turns.

For analytical purposes, then, and without implying relations of foundation and grounding, we may want to distinguish three levels of normativity here (a distinction not to be found in Derrida). At the first, most "quasi-ontological" level, we have double affirmation as the very mode of existence of life forms, including organic individuals and human beings, but also at work in collective identities such as species or democratic institutions. At the second level, we find elaborations of double affirmation, such as my asymmetrical reciprocity and taking turns, in view of certain issues, such as intergenerational justice (though the divisibility of IGJ from intragenerational issues remains an issue we should not remove from critical attention by the elaboration at this second level).[13] At the third, most explicitly normative level, we flesh out the concepts or models at the second level in greater detail. At this level, we ask, for instance, in what does fair reciprocity consist (equivalence? giving at least as much and as good as one received?), or what it is to take a fair turn (e.g., leaving the object of turn-taking in the state in which one received it? ensuring it works for the purposes of future turn-takers? or letting the object flourish as the thing it is). Answering these questions at this level gives us quite distinct norms, norms that of course have to be weighed against other norms, intra- or intergenerational.

In terms of this framework, reciprocity and turn-taking are situated on the same level. And yet turn-taking may be said to enjoy a certain priority, albeit one that stems not from a different relationship to ontological normativity as such, but merely from the "object" of the relation between normative parties. For taking turns is an elaboration in view of quasi-holistic objects, such as the earth, within which reciprocity relations take place. As we said at the outset of this chapter, reciprocity, even if indirect and altruistic in the ways elaborated in Chapter 3, is generally taken to imply the idea that one owes at least as much as one received. Given that what was received is usually a nonrenewable (e.g., finite resources) or a consumable (e.g., food), the recipient owes an equivalent value, and so needs a common metric to calculate such equivalencies. Turn-taking avoids a common metric as not being helpful when it comes to complex, interrelated wholes. Reciprocity thus has to respect the functioning or flourishing conditions specified by fair turns.[14]

To further articulate this priority, allow me to briefly return to Allen Habib's account of turn-taking. For him, whether we share by turns or by parts is always a question of normative choice. For instance, we can share the cake by turns (looking at it? rubbing our faces in it?), and the bike by parts (by disassembling it). Habib concludes from this that the distributive theorist or practitioner has a normative choice in those cases just as much as in the nature case. However, it seems that in this latter case at least, (a) our temporal constitution (we die and we are born) as well as (b) the holistic and necessarily preceding nature of the object (nature co-constitutes us as living beings, potential moral agents, and thus as turn-takers) force us to share nature by turns. This is true even if we try to share it by parts, or imagine doing so: (a) willy-nilly, we the currently living will die and leave nature to future turn-takers, just as we inherited it from others; and (b) the ecosystemic services on which we depend precede all human generations and exceed them, too. If we do not remain external to the "object" but depend on it and its preceding and exceeding us, then turn-taking (at least with the earth, but also other aspects of a gifted inheritance, such as language, traditions, and community-forming institutions), is ontologically prior to part-sharing, and so not just a normative choice. To think of it as merely a choice is to misunderstand the beings that we are, and to downplay our relations of dependency on the earth and on previous generations. That is why, we may say, it is important to relate turn-taking, as we did here, to the very being of identity in time and space. On the basis of these hauntological considerations pertaining to the space-time of a "by turns," we developed not only the intergenerational turn-taking, but the terrestrial turning on which generations depend. Before rephrasing terrestrial turning as the claim of the earth upon the living in the next chapter, I shall return to it here in closing.

V. The Environment Turning about Generations

Despite the advantages promised by generational turning as a model of intergenerational relations, there remains a sense here that justice among generations is a concern only for and among human beings. While humans are de-presentified and deprivileged by the rift in time that makes it never quite present to itself but always in the process of coming to be from the past and passing away into the future, sharing and taking turns on this model, as more generally on so-called stewardship models (humans as stewards or trustees of the earth), still takes place among humans only, humans who are more or less indifferent to the "object" with which they take turns. To disrupt that humanism, taking turns must be complicated so as to take into account that the environment also takes turns with us. Let me begin to further justify this complication and thus the introduction of the lateral, environmental turning.

First, I would like to address the objection that the environmental turn remains anthropocentric in a problematic way, down to its very name. In environmental philosophy, in deep ecology, for instance, the term "environment" has frequently been subject to criticism for its anthropocentric bias.[15] One may object that the very word "environment" implies a center, and that this center would inevitably remain the human in its generational turnings. The environmental turning would then be a mere turning around the human. Indeed, the very word "environment" comes, by way of Old French, from Latin *en* ("in") and *vertere* ("to turn," *virer* in Old French, also linked to the *vicis* of which we said above that we should hear it in *une fois*, "one time"). The notion of an "environment" thus implies the verb "to surround, encircle, encompass." To speak of an "environmental turning" is pleonastic in this sense; environing is already a turning.

But as I will try to indicate, in the context of the intergenerational turning, the environmental turning is not a turning "around" the human, but a turning in which the environment turns *with* the human, or turns about the human. The human comes to be from, and passes away into, the earth. In this second turning, the "environment" is the other (as in T2, above) from which and toward which the human turns, in breathing and eating as well as in birthing and dying. In this sense, the environmental turning in fact subverts or veers off the linearity and continuity of the circular line of the generational turning: the Old French *virer* ("to turn") also gives "to veer," as in the nautical sense "to turn about, to change course," and the Latin *vertere* is the root of the English "to subvert, to invert." The environmental turning sustains, but also crosses and interrupts, the attempts of human sovereigns to remain sovereign despite the passing away of individuals. In conclusion, and thus in all brevity, I will try to justify this understanding, according to which the generational turning remains enabled by the environmental turning while also being turned about by it.

We can make this point by returning to the reason for introducing "by turns" to think the space-time of political life. Given the turning nature of time, the self is constituted in seeking to return to itself. But such a re-turn is always a repetition in difference, or a turning in context, and so brings with it change and the risk of death. The attempted re-turn is necessarily a de-tour that passes through a web of differences. But the relata of these differences do not only include humans of different generations (the dead, the living, and the unborn), but also the difference between the living and the nonliving, between humans and animals, plants, viruses, and the inorganic.[16] In other words, in seeking to come back to itself, the self must turn toward its context, the world—ranging from traditions, languages, and socioeconomic circumstances to its environment, prior to any nature-culture split. From this world, the self must appropriate, even consume it literally, in order to feed its self-circling. However, given that the detour through the web of differences never comes back to the same starting point, in this appropriation and consumption, there is always a remainder, an indigestible, inappropriable rest that signifies that the self is part of a larger context to which it is tied in a metabolic exchange.

Political sovereignty, including democratic power, constitutes itself by claiming ownership over its territory, but ownership requires appropriation, and appropriation is what Derrida calls an ex-appropriation (NII 171; GT 151/191), as a remainder is left behind that marks the unmasterable belonging of the human to the earth. The unmasterable and antagonistic belonging is marked in the taking turns of breathing in–breathing out, drinking-urinating, eating-defecating, dwelling and going out into the world, being born and dying. Daily turnings anchor the generational turning in the environmental. That which "we" the presently living cannot make our own was received from others—and the much-famed "first occupant" with due rights of appropriation should be figured as animal rather than human (see AA 18/37)—and is, willy-nilly, promised to the future other.

To conclude, environmental turning crisscrosses generational turn-taking, which is already a turning toward self and other. The sovereign generational turn-taker wobbles in response to environmental turning. With each new birth and death, but also with each new breath, the lateral turning makes the generational turning vibrate. Generational turning thus has to steady and reconstitute itself—until it, too, comes to an end.

5

Interment

Chapter 1 argued that intergenerational relations must take into account the question of world formation: when thinking about the future, generations cannot presuppose a given world, but must reflect on the sources and shape of worlds left for the future. Apart from specific normative issues—from the number and identity of future people to socioeconomic infrastructure, institutions, and the environment—the issue includes ontological questions about what a world is, how a world is sustained over time, and what its relation to the natural environment may be. Subsequent chapters then presented two models for reconceiving justice between generations. In each case, I stressed the importance of the fact that intergenerational relations take place in a context—a world or worlds—that both precedes each generation and surpasses it toward the future. Chapter 3 argued for reciprocity obligations backward and forward, but stressed that the benefits received from past generations are inseparable from gifts of nature. Chapter 4 detailed taking turns with the earth as a model of justice, but emphasized toward the end that generational turn-taking depends on a lateral turning of the earth with human turn-takers.

This final chapter elaborates the relation thus indicated between earth and worlds. The overall argument is that, if living beings in general have their being constituted by turning to contextual others in seeking to return to themselves, then these contextual others are not just nonpresent human generations, but nature or earth. Earth is one name for the "hetero" in the auto-hetero-affection that defines life.

I. Globe and World

Today, humanity uses the equivalent of 1.6 earths to provide its resources and absorb its waste. It now takes the earth just over one year and six months to regenerate what we humans use in a year. This figure, calculated by the Global Footprint Network, varies greatly from country to country. For instance, if everyone lived like a resident of the US, we would need over four earths; if instead we all lived like residents of India, that figure would be 0.49.[1] So-called Earth Overshoot Day—the day humanity as a whole uses up the terrestrial resources available that year, if we are to need no more than one earth to sustain ourselves—is reached earlier each year. Perhaps we should understand the recent intensification of, and attention around, the search for exoplanets—planets believed to be sufficiently similar to earth to sustain life as we know it—against this background: if we humans don't love earth (anymore), or earth doesn't love us back, perhaps we can leave it.

It seems to me, though I will not argue it here, that such reveries should be linked to the belief—central to the account of the human-nature interface in the Enlightenment, especially in Kant (see Oliver 2018, 2014)—that humanity can (and will) be unified to the extent it lives only on the surface of the earth. Superficiality on a spherical earth means that humans will come into contact, and so will have to interact with one another in view of a living space they have to share from a common vantage point.[2] This unifying vantage point makes of the earth a superficial globe that today affords an increasingly fast-paced, techno-scientific, and economic *globalization* that tends to take the earth and its resources as given—as opposed to, in the words of Jean-Luc Nancy, a *mondialisation* (a "world-wide-ization") in which the natal-mortal formation of human and terrestrial worlds is foregrounded (Nancy 2007; Gratton and Morin 2012) and, as we do here, linked to its intergenerational and environmental sources (on Derrida's use of the contrast globalization vs. *mondialisation*, see Li 2007). The globalized vantage point distances humanity one step from the earth, turning it, in the well-known words of Kant's *Critique of Practical Reason*, toward "the starry skies above me and the moral law within me" (Kant 1992, 1).[3] Kant's friends chose this passage for the tombstone to mark the place where his corpse is buried in the earth.

Given the overuse of the earth, it is incumbent upon our times to rethink the relation between the human world and the earth. To do so, the remarks that follow take their lead from Derrida's cursory but significant references to the earth-world relation in the last seminar he gave (*The Beast and the Sovereign*, volume 2), a seminar in which he reflects on human sovereignty, mortality, and burial in the earth (*enterrement*). My argument in this last chapter will proceed in the following three steps: If (as Derrida argues in many places, including BS2) it is as if I am already dead while living (BS2 50/87; see GL 19/26, 84/97; VP 82–83/108–109), and if, second, my corpse—whether inhumed or cremated, or in some other way—will be claimed by terrestrial elements, then I am living my life as *already* interred: in-earthed-in-earthing, *enterré-enterrant, beerdigt-beerdigend*. I am living with others *in* (and not merely on) the earth. Humans are both interred (agonistically belonging to a larger time and space here called earth) and interring (marked from the beginning by outliving and being outlived, and that means by responsibilities for returning others as well as one's remains to earth).

In the face of the tremendous un-earthing of fossil fuels and its intergenerational consequences, from environmental degradation and loss of biodiversity to climate change, we will want to consider this condition of interment in its association with what Derrida calls the promise of the earthy bond between singular lives.[4] Perhaps the human condition is not so much un-earthing in the sense of disclosive, or un-earthed and erect in the sense of revealed or opened to revelation; perhaps it is closer to the earth than we tend to think. I will take these three claims in this order and discuss their inferential links: first, (a) life as what we have called, with Derrida, lifedeath or lifedeathbirth; second, (b) the terrestrial claim over the mortal body, and third (c) life conceived as interred and interring. I use "interred" in the sense of indelibly and co-constitutively linked to a preceding, unpossessable, and fear-inspiring context that we may call earth. "Interring" is meant in the sense that each member of a generation is charged with handling remains and corpses, as it is already in the process of, in turn leaving its legacies and remains to another generation. I will here begin by introducing the three claims that will be elaborated further in subsequent sections.

(a) The first claim is that life is lifedeath: life depends on the "gift of death," as the English title to one of Derrida's books has it (GD). While robbing the living of the plenitude of and mastery over life, death, as we've seen Heidegger and others argue, also gives life in making its world possible. Life may prefer life—and self-reference or self-affirmation has always been one way to mark off the living from the dead and inorganic—but only in differing-deferring death; thus, death is not simply opposed to life, as if it were located on its outside. An immortal life, a life without death, would have nothing to give, to itself or to the other (see BS2 100n13/153n2). The disclosure of the phenomenological "living present" depends on a being-toward-death that Derrida argues is, in Heidegger as well as in Levinas, still too humanist, too removed from life, animality, and earth. The world is the world of life *and* death.

(b) The second claim is that the earth, from sea to land and air, will absorb the corpse whose life it sustained. Earth here names the organic and inorganic context of living beings, a context that is co-constitutive of life, both in the sense of history and evolution, and in the more spatial-material sense of habitat. Derrida reminds us that life has always been defined by its self-referencing or auto-affection, but he insists that it must instead be thought as an auto-*hetero*-affection (BS2 170/244; AA 133/95). As we saw in the previous chapter, the attempted re-turn to the self, the *autos*, is always already re-routed through others, the *hetero*.[5] Earth, I will argue, is one name—though of course not the only name—of the *hetero* that cannot be taken up by life without remainder.

(c) The first two claims entail the third claim: that the terrestrial absorption of life—the earth's claim to the body—does not merely happen at the so-called end of life, as if before death the *body* was in the firm possession of its living bearer. Not by accident, as we will see, do we find this phantasm of sovereign mastery over the mortal body in early modern texts such as *Robinson Crusoe* and Locke's *Second Treatise of Government*, the latter with its famous argument that labor extends ownership from the body to territory on the earth (Locke 1988, sec. 27). This dream of mastery is the principal target of both the death penalty seminars (DP1, DP2) and the seminars *The Beast and the Sovereign* (BS1, BS2). To expose sovereignty to unconditionality, as Derrida puts it programmatically in

Rogues (R 141/195–196), is to expose the living body to its corpse-like and terrestrial corporeality—and that means, as I will propose, to the earth.

Death as the end of life—to which we have access, as Michael Naas has shown in several of his recent works, only phantasmatically and never as such (see Naas 2008, especially the essay "Comme si comme ça")—works on the body as the earth nibbles away at life at each of its moments. To say that we are reborn at every moment is also to say that we die away with each breath, each drink, and each morsel of food that we exchange with the earth. Earth, then, may name the unpossessable and ungovernable context within which sovereignty seeks to assert itself.

Normatively and politically, I will conclude, sovereignty should be rethought as that which seeks to govern an earth that will not submit to becoming mere territory. The organization of politics into the state turns around the unpossessable earth while being turned about by it. The sovereignty of Eurocentric humanism consists in seeking to master death by pinpointing it as the end of life, by dreaming of "killing time," and with it affectability by others, as Derrida puts it near the end of the first year of *The Death Penalty* (DP1 226/308; see also R 109/154). Because subjection to time and change signals receptivity, suffering, and relation to others, to contract time into an instant is to attempt to master time, to *kill* it, and to render the self sovereign, invulnerable to alterity. Instantaneity and anaesthesia go together here, as Peggy Kamuf has stressed (Kamuf 2012). Analyzing "a certain Cartesianism of [Dr.] Guillotin," the inventor of the eponymous, allegedly painless killing machines—from the "instantaneism" of time as composed of "simple, discontinuous, discrete, and undecomposable instants" to mind-body dualism, mechanicism, and individualism (DP1 225/307)—Derrida underlines that the ideal of capital punishment in our onto-theological heritage is a death that is painless because instantaneous, an instant that is conceived as dividing life from death as sharply as the guillotine's blade. Moreover, because it is a death that aims only at the head ("capital" comes from *caput*, head), it is a death that is meant to sever the head from its vulnerable, embodied connections to earth others: a death that is meant to un-earth us.

By contrast, and of course without doing away with sovereignty altogether, democracy-to-come articulates a different understanding of sovereignty. Putting this thought to work in the context of the environmental crisis, I proposed a thinking of time as nonmasterable turning or even a taking-turns: each time takes turns with the past and the future, with the dead and the unborn, *as well as* with the earth that turns us toward alterity, toward the others of human territorial mastery.

II. The Différance of the Earth

I will now elaborate and justify the first two claims—(a) life as lifedeath and (b) the terrestrial claim over the corpse—on the basis of my discussion of deferral and differentiation in Chapter 3. There I sought to show that, despite the seeming priority granted to time in the discussion of the intergenerational gift, *différance* also names a spacing that ties every gift to a material context and to nature as "the donation of what gives birth, the originary productivity" (GT 128/163). As briefly discussed there, deconstruction's always to some extent historical and genealogical point of departure is to view an object as emerging out of its differential relations to others. These relations of difference are taken to be constitutive of the object; that is, the object is not seen as preexisting its context, but as owing itself to the environment of its emergence and being. Difference, as Saussure had it, is prior to identity. This priority may already counsel a certain caution with regard to the language of entity and context, self and environment, sovereignty and earth, a caution well-known in environmental philosophy (e.g., in Arne Naess's critique of the "man-in-environment" model; Naess 1973).

But the context is not itself exhaustively analyzable, as if we could enumerate all of its elements in a complete list. A complete list would stabilize identity despite its constitutive relationality, because the relations would be bounded and travel along the same lines. Even if A needed to reference B to come to be "itself," A and B would be fixed by their references. By contrast, the claim here is that the context is inexhaustible, not just because the list would be too long to itemize, but rather for the more essential reason that the context is itself undergoing change as it constitutes the elements of which it is made up.[6] Each element in the context is in a similar position of changing with its context, the context changing with them, so that no element can be, or rely on another element to be, a stable identity. (The entrance of A into relation with B makes of B a B' and of A an A'. A, then, like B, is only ever *between* A and A', or A' and A<dp>, and so on.) Further, and for the same reason, the dependence on a constitutive context is not fully determining for an element, since it can be recontextualized; an entity can—indeed, it cannot but—shift from context to context.

It is these two moments of differentiation and recontextualizability (or iterability) that Derrida sought to capture economically with the neologism *différance*. The term is used to encompass both difference and deferral, that is, situation in context but without final determinability; anticipation of future environments (for not anything goes), but also exposure to the open-ended future the elements in an ongoing system cannot know or master. And despite having first developed it primarily in the context of structuralist accounts of language and culture, it is the notion of *différance* that Derrida sees as "co-extensive" with mortal life (Derrida 2001a 108; FW 16). He has from the beginning insisted that it holds wherever there are elements in a more or less holistic system, including genetic DNA and cellular and organismic life forms in an environment.[7] That is why we can seek to think life in general along the lines of *différance*, as Francesco Vitale's "biodeconstruction" suggests Derrida always did (Vitale 2014, 2018), and as I do below in terms of lifedeath.

Life in *différance* is a life born mortal, stretched between birth and death without thereby marking off, as we have been arguing all along, a presence or a "mineness" of individual life cut off from the time before birth and the time after death. A life that does not coincide with itself, that lives only by being stretched out toward the other as to another time, is a life that lives off dying and rebirthing every moment:[8] a sur-viving [*sur-vivance*]" (see "Living On: Borderlines," in P), a "lifedeath [*la vie la mort*],"[9] or a lifedeathbirth (Fritsch 2017b). This lifedeath draws both on its natality and its mortality to set itself up as separate from its environment and its predecessors, but without ever being able to fully appropriate its birth, its death, and thus its life as fully its own. It responds to this tension between appropriation and expropriation by developing phantasms of self-birthing[10] and of its own proper or authentic dying (PC 359/381–382; BS2 157/229). It is a spectral life that differs from itself since birth, and defers its proper self to a future it cannot make its own, a future that outlives the propriety of "my life" or "our life."

With the help of *différance*, we can thus better understand the first claim of my overall argument in this chapter, the claim that life and death are not separated by a razor-sharp dividing line (such as the guillotine's blade), but instead are co-implicated. In BS2, Derrida makes this point by arguing that, as co-constitutive of the world of the living (as Heidegger famously argued), death is not "merely the end of life" (BS2 93/145), and that its pleasures are "stillborn [*mort-né*]" (53/90). As we saw in previous chapters, life is a natal mortality or mortal natality, and thus constitutively related to nonpresent generations, the dead and the unborn, who are thus not simply absent. We are born into the light of day, but born only as mortal, mortally related to the other who gives birth to, or survives, the newborn. Birth and death thus take place in a world, a preceding-exceeding context that, as we will see below, will not remain unaffected by the births and deaths taking place not just "in" the world but as its very happening.

Let me then conclude my claim that life is essentially mortal. The timespace of *différance* is the reason Derrida speaks of life as *survivance*—"sur-vival" or "living-on": life lives only by overcoming death at each turn. Identity must of necessity be repeated, for an identity is never given once and for all. Each affirmation is already promised to a repetition that brings in the other once more (hence we should speak of iteration), so that the promise of return to oneself can never be finally fulfilled; it is a promise made to a future forever to come. As the "first time" that is to be repeated likewise never took place as such, life is a "living-on" suspended between the "absolute past" and "future to come," neither of which took place or will take place as such, in the present. It is on this basis that Derrida may write that "it is as if I am already dead" (BS2 50/87; see *Glas* 19/26; SP 95).

III. The Terrestrial Claim to the Corpse

III.1. The Quasi-Ontological and Normative Claim

Life, then, is stillborn, dead-born, *totgeboren*. Its natal mortality links it from the inside to an outside, a constitutive exterior that includes (human and nonhuman) generations of the dead and the unborn. In this section, I would like to present my second claim: that the constitutive outside may also be called *earth*—the history and habitat of life—as the context in which *différance* plays out.

This second premise maintains that earth is one name for that which absorbs and claims the body of life. If *différance* is, as was argued in Chapters 3 and 4, timespace (the becoming space of time and the becoming time of space), then the unmasterable ties in which it casts living beings are not only temporal but also spatial, material, and fleshly. We are indeed born into different birth cohorts and generations, and one friend dies before the other. But we are also born in and of the earth. The earth emerges as that which relates and separates living beings and their worlds. Above all, it is that which receives and claims the corpse. To be mortal means to be inextricably inserted into a material space that precedes and exceeds a living-dying organism.

However, in using "earth" or "nature" to refer to this constitutive space, some precautions have to be taken: both earth and nature are often pre-comprehended as stable referents that resist cultural change and historical development, forever turning around themselves (see Chapter 3 on "nature" in Derrida's *Given Time*). If, for instance, we track the references to "earth" in the death penalty seminars, the word is used (exclusively, I believe) in contrast with heaven, for example in the claim that here on earth, capital punishment is final and irreversible, some permitting themselves to believe, however, that by putting someone to death they are merely handing him over to God.[11]

But in a few other places, we do find a different use of common environmental or ecological terms such as "nature" and, in BS2 in particular and as we will examine shortly, "earth" (BS2 264/364–365ff.). In these more charged contexts, however, the terms are—and this should not surprise us—not used to denote the opposite of a binary, such as culture-nature, history-nature, man-earth, human-animal, and so on. In keeping with our discussion of *différance*, the term, as I will seek to show, denotes the context that is not just around but also inside the thing of which it is the context. It is the outside that is the inside spacing of life, demanding its overcoming of and turn toward the outside. This is the major reason why the second claim (that the earth claims the corpse) already entails the third (that the earth claims the living body). In the passages we will examine, earth names the mortal condition of life, and as such, earth is thus closely associated with receiving the corpse, whether buried, cremated, or whatever.

As habitat and natural history, then, earth may name that which absorbs and claims the body. By absorption, I do not just mean that the body decomposes and returns to the earth, as the Bible stresses, for instance.[12] Rather, I understand this second claim in a *quasi-ontological* (and thus also quasi-empirical) sense following from what I said about *différance* above. We said that death is "inscribed" in life as its spacing or self-difference. This difference from itself forces life, in its very constitution, to be always already turned to its context of inscription without possibility of a return full circle. Even though a living self has to attempt it, there cannot be such a return to the self's starting point, because the self-difference is constitutive and cannot be overcome. It is constitutive because the self can relate to itself only by relating to the other, "other" understood in a broad sense (i.e., not restricted to another self). The *hetero* in auto-affection always already inserted the living self, what Derrida calls ipseity, *into* a co-constitutive history, a context, an environment.

Calling the earth's relation to the corpse and the body a *claim* (an address, an interpellation, a demand) should help us to avoid a likely misunderstanding. In BS2, Derrida cautions us not to take this "in" or "into" in the sense of a container. In the phrase "beast and sovereign both live *in* the same world," "in" the earth should not be understood as if the terrestrial outside *remained* outside, *external* to life. Rather, they live in the earth as "*that within which* all these living beings are carried" (BS2 264–265/365). Auto-affection entails a being *of* something that is also a being *in* something larger than oneself that generates the fear of being swallowed alive, a fear but also a desire that Derrida tracks in his reading of *Robinson Crusoe*: from his fear of drowning as his shipmates did, to the earthquake opening up the ground to swallow him, to the beasts or the cannibals visiting his island, coming, he thinks, to eat him. The differential reading of auto-affection shows that life requires a larger context that precedes and exceeds the living individual and always threatens to nibble away at it or devour it. Crusoe here, as we will stress again later, is read as emblematic of Western individualism and imperialism, the one that responds to its fear of death by seeking to master the island-earth and animals.

By the homonymic relation between *dans* (in) and *dents* (teeth), Derrida then links auto-affection to the mouth, to food, and to "self-taste" (see Elizabeth Rottenberg's excellent analysis of this motif of orality and devouring in Rottenberg 2011).[13] If auto-affection is only as an auto-*hetero*-affective relation (BS2 170/244), then tasting oneself is inseparable from being tasty to others, in particular to beasts. This being tasty to animals—or also, as in Crusoe's case, to cannibals—is *tasteless* to the individualist and humanist conception Derrida is diagnosing here: being tasty is anathema to the dignity of the human who sees himself removed from the earth and its other inhabitants. As James Hatley puts it, humanizing nature above all consists in the (necessarily failing) attempt to "make over the space in which we live as if humans had become inedible and everything else is revealed to be more or less available for ingestion." However, he argues, "the relative success of this endeavor should not fool us into assuming that the underlying predatory nature of the earthly space we inhabit no longer makes its claim upon us" (Hatley 2004, 15).[14] Similarly, in her "Tasteless: Toward a Food-Based Approach to Death" (now collected posthumously in *The Eye of the Crocodile*), Val Plumwood famously discusses her experience of being attacked by a saltwater crocodile, an experience that made her rethink the relationship between the earth and its food chain. What she calls "the Western problematic of death" conceives the self either in its reductive naturalist version as ending completely with death, or as a disembodied spirit, one that sees life as a battle against death rather than *also* accepting that death is a part of life. Against this, she proposes a third way, in which the sovereign human learns to appreciate the corpse as a gift to the earth in a "chain of reciprocity" (Plumwood 2012, 19).

What is it, Derrida asks in *Glas*, to make a gift of the corpse? (GL 143/163). When Derrida complains, in *The Animal That Therefore I Am*, that much of Western phallo-logo-carno-centrism conceives of animals as so separate from humanity that they are unable even to look at us sovereign humans, we should add that much of Western culture conceives of our mortality as unconnected to the earth. In Plumwood's words, we conceive of ourselves "[a]s eaters of [earth] others who can never ourselves be eaten in turn by them" (Plumwood 2012, 19). Against this one-sided Western conception of death, then, Plumwood pits what she calls the "indigenous imaginary":

By understanding life as in circulation, as a gift from a community of ancestors, we can see death as recycling, a flowing on into an ecological and ancestral community of origins. In place of the Western war of life against death whose battleground has been variously the spirit-identified afterlife and the reduced, medicalised material life, the Indigenous imaginary sees death as part of life, partly through narrative, and partly because death is a return to the (highly narrativised) land that nurtures life. (Plumwood 2012, 19–20)

Note that Plumwood's "community of ancestors" is both ancestral and ecological. While the distinction between humans, on the one hand and, on the other, animals, plants, fungi, bacteria, and so on, is not thereby undone, seeing death as part of life inserts all living beings in the larger context of life, here called earth. The earth's claim on the living being it supports is thus connected to the normative finitude that both prompts each to turn toward itself as well as to turn toward the others. For if a living identity does not come into the world ready-made, or nonrelationally, identical to itself, then it must strive for that identity, for its time and its space, for its world. Provoked by the environing context,[15] it seeks to build a wall around the self that first of all marks the difference between self and world. With this striving for identity that is a response to self-difference, a striving that Nietzsche called will-to-power, what Derrida calls an "unconditional ethical obligation" (BS1 110/157) comes into the world.[16] And this obligation out of alterity has relevance for both intergenerational and environmental ethics.

For we should note that life as lifedeath critically undermines not only the distinction between the human and nonhuman living being—the basis of humanism—but also the separation of past, present, and future generations into distinct entities. In the first volume of *The Beast and the Sovereign*, Derrida criticizes Lacan's typical claim that only man is capable of law and crime (and thus of the death penalty). If that were so, ethics would consist essentially in human fellowship and "fraternity." In response, Derrida argues that extending this fellowship to the animal would not be sufficient.

[I]t is not enough to say that this unconditional ethical obligation, if there is one, binds me to the life of any living being in general. It also binds me twice over to something nonliving, namely to the present nonlife or the nonpresent life of those who are not living, present living beings, living beings in the present, contemporaries—i.e. dead living beings and living beings not yet born, nonpresent-living-beings or living beings that are not present. One must therefore inscribe death in the concept of life. (BS1 110/157)

We can gloss this passage by saying that ethics emerges with the unrecognizable, the *méconnaissable* (BS1 108/155), which is essentially tied to the death in life that makes life vulnerable to other forces beyond it. But if life is lifedeath, and is ethical only as lifedeath, then *all* mortals, and not just human beings, share a place in the moral universe. Note, however, that this conclusion is precisely not made by making this trait (the mortality of lifedeath), as is customary in environmental ethics, a nonrelational property as entry ticket into the moral universe. Death in life is precisely not a property, not something a being possesses as an ability or capacity. Rather, it names the nonpower, the unpossessable and unshareable source of ethical bonds by which we have always already been affected and related to earth others.[17]

What should be of further note here is that this depriveleging of the human goes along with a depriveleging of the present, the time of the living or sovereign present, as if our time was owned by our generation. If the present is not fully present to itself—if lifedeath relates the living to the nonliving—then justice cannot just be for the present generation but must from the very beginning take account of the dead and the unborn, the future generations that stand to suffer the most from the treatment of the earth as a human possession. On this view, as indicated, humanism, presentism, and territorialism are intimately linked, even if the links are also historical and contingent.

On the alternative view proposed here, the generations of the dead and the unborn are not thought of as exclusively and exceptionally human, though we must also not permit ourselves to think of life in an undifferentiated form, without species and species preferences (see AA). The point is to recognize that tying the source of obligation to death in life, to the corpse-like nature of the body, and thus to an inappropriable nonpresence, upsets human exceptionalism and generational presentism. The *différance* of the earth contests, in a single blow, both presentism and humanism. To have recognized the former (presentism) but not deconstructed the latter (humanism) is the upshot of Derrida's mini-essay on Levinas's "humanism of the other man" in *L'Animal* (AA 102–118).

As we saw in Chapter 2, Derrida agrees with Heidegger that the call of conscience—the call to responsibly disclose and appropriate possibilities for being, acting, and understanding—stems from the noncoincidence of finite time, from a being that is always ahead of itself in being toward death, a death not shared by others. To flee from death by attributing death only to *das Man*, the "they" (along the lines of "one dies but not me, not now"), is to flee from one's responsibility to oneself as stretched out in time, that is, as dying and being reborn at every moment (GA 2, §53, 297/336).

Derrida, however, also takes note of Levinas's famous response to Heidegger, which is that death is first of all the other's death: it is not accessible *as such* for my own appropriation, and so the call to responsibility is first of all to let the other live. Derrida's thought radicalizes Levinas's insight by making death even more other. First, volume 2 of *The Beast and the Sovereign* stresses with Freud and against Heidegger that we cannot think our death without presupposing us as thinking it, such that we don't have access to death as such but only phantasmatically (BS2 157/227). Further, the alterity of death means that death is no longer tied only to the human face, thus overcoming a human exceptionalism that Heidegger and Levinas share. Ethics then begins with a call to responsibility that comes from alterity, without a primordial answer to the question, Why be moral?, so without a "because" whose scope reason determines and masters, the reason that has always been the reason of "man," human and virile.

The alterity that prompts this response lies then in the other's vulnerability. Levinas characterizes this vulnerability as a nonresponse: the death in life that shows the other's "im-power" to respond, there where there are bodies that will be, that will have been, corpses. As Derrida argues, "Even if we were inclined to follow Heidegger when he speaks of "being capable" of our own death [*'pouvoir' notre propre mort*], it is certain that we are "not capable" of our own corpse, we will never see it and feel it" (BS2 161/233). If ethics, then, begins in mortal alterity, the moral call cannot be restricted to the human face. The call should not be seen to be extendable to animals, but should in fact "privilege," as Derrida puts it provocatively in *The Animal That Therefore I Am*, the command to responsibility of the animal. This is not because animals are more valuable than human beings, but is the upshot of hearing the call of the human being herself differently. The call will then no longer come directly and exclusively from the human, the humanity of man, but from an even more ulterior and anterior place: a call that "calls within us outside of us, from the most far away, before us after us, preceding and pursuing us in an unavoidable way" (AA 113/156).

While the "before" in this passage cannot be reduced to an empirical natural history, it is as little separable from it as the gift of *différance* was seen (in Chapter 3) to be inseparable from a gift of ancestors. Nonhuman life on earth indeed precedes human generations taking turns with earth: this is one of the meanings of *L'Animal que donc je suis*, the animal that therefore I follow (AA 10–11/27–28). Having been born as occupants of the earth before humans—and thus being before me, behind me, after me, surrounding me—the animals (themselves preceded by other forms of life such as plants and bacteria) looked at us before we looked at them (AA 17–18/36–37).

As history and habitat of life, then, earth is inseparable from earth others. The claim to what we take to be "our" lives, the claim of the earth upon the living-dying body, is articulated by the hungry eye of the crocodile, and in fact not only when the body has become a corpse. That is why we can flip perspectives at times, and see cats as domesticating *humans* for their well-being, or wheat, rice, and potatoes as having grown *us* since the agricultural revolution to better populate the earth with their species, as Yuval Harari did (Harari 2014, 77ff.) The differential *hetero* in the auto-affection that defines life turns the inside of the self-relation to the outside and the outside to the inside, such that earth, nature, or environment name that which cannot be fully absorbed by the self. Rather, the environment is that which exceeds the self as the very result of its mortality, its self-difference as self-other splitting. The tie to what I here call earth (and I will soon try to justify this use of "earth" with respect to Derrida) cannot be overcome.

This is not in the first instance for the empirical reason that the earth is biologically needed, or too large and too cosmic to absorb—though of course all of this is true, and important. But these truths flesh out the quasi-ontological point (the "quasi" here indicating that the ontological and the empirical cannot be neatly distinguished) that absorbing the earth would mean that there would no longer be any outside to turn to, no other to permit the return to self, and thus no longer any self.

An objection may be raised that this "grounding" of an empirical truth in a quasi-ontological one (however weak the "grounding" is to be understood by adding further precautions) adds nothing but obfuscation. Earth is, the objection might continue, empirically and objectively a necessary backdrop to human life. My first response to this objection is that I fear this empirical objectivity makes it harder for us to think earth as the inside of life, as its constitutive finitude. Precisely by maintaining an objective standpoint above the empirical earth, it may suggest that with the help of objective science we may leave earth, or see it as merely one possible home for us, for now.

Further, one important thing the quasi-ontological considerations permit us to see is another aspect to the normativity that is usually sucked right out of empirical truths, stated as they are from a removed observer's viewpoint that is then hard to account for. On the deconstructive view of earth, there can be higher levels of analysis, but there is no ultimate meta-level. Even the observer is engaged in the appropriation from context; in fact, observation is another mode of such appropriation. And this further permits us to say that the observer, too, is caught up in the *ex-appropriation* that *demands* that a remainder be left for others (on "ex-appropriation," see Chapter 3 on the gift and its general economy). To put this in the terms used above, if the self cannot but appropriate from the earth while having to leave a remainder, an excess, then the earth must be left for others to appropriate. We cannot but—and also *must*—make a gift of the earth to future people and future animals, future plants and future fungi, bacteria, and so on.

This gift as (voluntary or involuntary) excess over economizing and appropriation may be stated from the viewpoint of the earth: it *claims* the (living or dead) corpse as its own. I've argued that self-affirmation does not actually begin with the self, but is in fact a *response* to insertion in context, even if the context would also not be a context without the self-affirmation that seeks to separate self and context. In this sense, the normativity of the relation between life and environment cannot be clearly located on one side only. As a result of its mortality, life claims earth, but earth also claims life. It demands that we breathe out for breathing in, defecate for consuming food, and be edible by other beings.

III.2. Earth and World

There are two instances in *The Beast and the Sovereign* in which this claim of the earth upon the living is particularly marked. I discuss the first one here; the second instance is discussed in the next section.

Toward the end of BS2, Derrida returns to the question with which he opened the seminar, that of world as shared—or not—between humans and animals, among human individuals of different cultures, or simply individuals, human or not (BS2 8–9/31). One of the things he says in response to this question of world in the last session—and I am not claiming it's the only or a full response—is that, *pace* Heidegger, humans and animals both live as mortals, and that means that they co-in-habit the same world. In this world, humans and nonhumans are, Derrida writes,

> co-diers [*commourans*], as Montaigne might have said, not that they die at the same moment, but they die together. . . . [T]these ones not far from those ones and in the same space (water, earth, air, fire) as those ones. . . . [T]he beast and the sovereign both turn out to be living beings that find themselves in the situation either of dying of old age, or else of finding death at any moment, and so they live and die together. . . . [T]hey co-habit the world that is the same. . . . This co- of the co-habitant presupposes a habitat, whether one calls it the earth (including sky and sea) or else the world of life-death. (BS2 263–264/363–365)[18]

When it comes to thinking life as inseparable from habitat, "the world of lifedeath" and "earth" (earth including sky and sea) name the same place: the space into which the living are born, live, and die. Already in the first session, we read that living beings "have in common the finitude of their life, and therefore, among other features of finitude, their mortality in the place they inhabit, whether one calls that place world or earth (earth including sky and sea)" (BS2 10/33). Here again, earth names the "mortality of place" that living beings share. Given that alterity is, in BS2, defined by reference to surviving the dead and receiving their corpse, earth as "mortality of place" is here one of the recipients of the corpse (BS2 126–127/188–189). If my mortality means that others decide over me and possess me in what Derrida calls "an irreducible *non–habeas corpus*" (BS2 144/210), then death is the (nonpresent) source of both vulnerable-ethical and sovereign-political connections among living beings, connections that also link life and death, the organic and the inorganic, me and the earth.

When Derrida says that earth is shared as the habitat of co-mortals, he does not, I think, intend "shared" in the manner of an objective empiricism or naturalist realism, for that would flatly contradict the phenomenological-deconstructive meaning of world as worlding (*die Welt weltet*, Heidegger writes [GA 7, 181; GA 77, 149], and Derrida agrees up to a point [BS2 12/36]). The "world worlds": it opens a horizon of intelligibility from within which anything like "earth," or nature or reality in the objective sense, becomes accessible first of all.[19]

In fact, we should recall that in the Tenth Session, only a page after the passage on earth I just cited, Derrida claims that the very human, very common idea of a shared world that is the same for all and that continues as the same with or without me, should be thought of as a way of denying death in "the name of a life insurance policy for living beings losing their world." The "presumed community of the world" is a "refined utilitarian nominalism that is nothing more than an animal ruse of life, a life common to the beast and the sovereign" (BS2 267/367–369). Derrida does not just understand this useful presumption of a world untouched by death as a phantasmatic denial of death, I believe, but also as a quasi-transcendentally necessary projection of a common horizon of sense, without which the disseminative multiplicity of worlds could hardly be thought (BS2 265/366).[20]

Derrida sets over against this ineluctable phantasm, or this legitimate horizonal projection, of a shared world (call it world 2) two further senses of world: the world as island (world 1) and the world of lifedeath (world 3). Remember that he also calls this world "earth," understood as one feature of finitude, namely, the mortality in the place of inhabiting. The solitary world 1 is the result of coming to understand that "the community of the world is always constructed, simulated by a set of stabilizing apparatuses, more or less stable, then, and never natural . . . always deconstructible" (BS2 8–9/31). The deconstruction of this construction removes the orderliness of world: in Latin and Greek, *mundus* and *cosmos* not only mean "world" but also "order," that is, proper, good arrangement, harmony, and cleanliness (as in *émondage*, which means, for instance, tree pruning, trimming, and training). The result of this deconstruction of a common world is an insight into the fact that each living mortal engenders, at each turn, a different sense of world. Here, world is "the absolutely unshareable . . . the abyssal unshareable . . . separated like one island from another" (BS2 266/367).

But what is the position and role of world 3, the world of lifedeath or earth, with respect to worlds 1 and 2? Derrida does not pose the question in this form, but I think we can reconstruct it fairly along the following lines. Recall that lifedeath names the inscription of death in life, the self-difference that first of all provokes life *qua* life to seek to separate itself from its environing world, thereby "constructing" both itself in self-affirmation and the world in other-affirmation. World 1, the world as island, is the consequence of each living being projecting its world, from its unique positioning in context, and in response to its attempt to return to itself from out of the finite-mortal environment. It is along these lines that a common world (in the sense of world 2) may be assumed to ensure "the longest *survival*" (BS2 267/368), even if it remains phantasmatic and merely assumed. World 1, the world as island, can emerge only in the difference from other worlds, just as islands are unthinkable without the sea that connects, but also separates and engulfs, them.

The earth, then, as the world of lifedeath, and including the sea names the self-difference within the island that differentially connects with other islands. The island is an island only by belonging to the sea, which in turn belongs to the earth. But earth here does not indicate the stable shore as compared to the tumultuous sea in which human life so easily drowns, and whose visceral envelopment of the skin so touchingly and emblematically symbolizes the autoimmune attraction and repulsion that makes up our embodied being-in-the-world. If Robinson Crusoe felt saved from the sea by being stranded on an island, the feeling doesn't last long. He soon discovers that the island is subject to earthquakes: it opens up, divides and differentiates itself, leaving a gaping wound, an open mouth ready to swallow him just as the sea devoured his shipmates: "When the earthquake happens, Robinson [is] terrorized by the earth itself, terrified by the earth and by the possible interring of his living life [*Au moment du tremblement de terre, Robinson [est] terrorisé par la terre même, terrifié par la terre et par l'enterrement possible de sa vie vivante*]" (BS2 79/125). So when Derrida says the earth is shared as the world of lifedeath, as the place of co-dying, death is that which both separates and relates, across an abyss, individual living beings to each other. If earth

Interment 205

as habitat is shared, it is shared not as a common possession from which we are removed. As we saw above, we are not united, as in Kant, by our shared sovereign ownership of the earth's surface on (rather than "in") which we live (see Derrida 2000, 16n12[21]). Rather, the earth is shared as that which no one can possess: the unpossessable, the im-power of death at the heart of life, the *hetero* in auto-hetero-affection. Earth names the nonpower of sovereignty, its unconditional exposure to alterity, its mortal body or its corpse. The corpse—we cannot even write "my corpse"—signifies above all that agency, the power to live, move, go out into the world (of the earth) and come back to oneself, comes to an absolute limit with the interred condition of the corpse. The corpse signifies death as nonresponse, the incapacity and passivity that ties the living body to that which it cannot absorb, interiorize, and incorporate, but which will have engulfed it, if we can say so, from the inside out. Earth is one name, even if only one, for the preceding and exceeding context of lifedeath that I cannot appropriate for myself but must *leave* for the other, the surviving sovereigns as well as the earth as recipient of the corpse.

When, in the Fifth Session of BS2, Derrida lists the others that Crusoe is afraid will bury him or swallow him alive, and to which his life is in fact "delivered over, in his body, defenseless, to the other," Derrida first names, before beasts and cannibals, the quaking earth "as a kind of external and foreign element" (BS2 138/203). In fact, we should recall that each time Derrida writes, as he does here, of Crusoe's fear of "being buried [*enterré ou englouti*] alive," there is a reference to the earth [*terre*]. "Earth" names the way in which the living body is claimed by its other, by the other par excellence claiming the living body.[22]

III.3. Posthuming

The second place where what I've called the claim of the earth upon the living is marked in the seminars, and that I single out here, is to be found in Derrida's discussion of the curious term "posthumous." Here, too, he mentions earthquakes as something that certain animals can sense or sniff out better than humans can. Sensing by smell, as in breathing in to sniff out, is *humer* in French, a term Derrida relates to "posthumous" by using the curious phrase "I posthume as I breathe [*je posthume comme je respire*]" (BS2 174/248; D 26/28).[23] In the first place, the idea of posthuming is part of a critique of Descartes's cogito, which holds that "I think therefore I am and breathe." Derrida inverts this phrase to give "I breathe, therefore I think" (AA 86/121). In *L'Animal*, the Cartesian version is treated as removing the human mind, as rational, from embodied animality; the human as posthuming and sensing around in its environment questions the Cartesianism that Derrida also diagnoses in Robinson Crusoe (BS2 53/89, 199/280).

Sensing, *humer*, sniffing around for one knows not exactly what, is used here in the sense of "expecting without expectation"—death being the ultimate future to-come the living anticipate without being able to anticipate as such. On my reading, then, posthuming means relating to a future horizon that has mortal openings in it, like black holes one cannot see. Or we could say the horizon of expectation trembles like the quaking earth that engulfs life in a belly with holes in it. Intensifying this relation between animal sensing, as the feeling of being alive at all,[24] and the earth, Derrida then notes that the "h" in "posthumous" is a faulty addition that the *Académie française*, the organization that polices the French language, should, according to *Le Littré: Dictionnaire de la langue française*, like to see corrected: "posthumous" really derives from *posterus* ("what comes after or later") and should have no reference to "humus," to earth. However, Derrida notes, the mistaken addition is like the "a" in *différance*, deconstruction's most famous and more or less deliberate misspelling, *différance* naming "another way to posthume by differing or deferring life or, what comes down to the same thing, deferring death" (BS2 174/249).

The analogy indicates, it seems to me, that Derrida approves of the reference to "humus" or earth in "posthumous," despite the etymological error. By "posthumous," we mean of course some aftereffect of the dead concerning the living: what is posthumous is not dead and gone but, like the spectral, speaks to life from the dead as if from the future—the future already arriving and enveloping the living; but as *arrivant* or *revenant*, this future comes as an unanticipatable ghost. The posthumous is death's reach over the living. If we accept the misspelling, then the posthumous, the terrestrial postmortem future perfect, is a reach extended from the earth as the realm of death over the living—the posthumous is the world of lifedeath. And this reach is, for Derrida, also a claim, for it belongs to life to be "obsessed with the post-mortem, fascinated, worried and interpellated [*requis*]" (BS2 174/249).

In the analogy between "posthumous" and *différance*, I submit, there is more than a felicitous and revealing misspelling—otherwise, you could object that I rest my case here only on the analogy between two misspellings. Recall that Derrida says that both *différance* and posthuming live by deferring death, or die by deferring life, in a lifedeath or sur-vivance whose terrestrial and intergenerational significance we are elaborating throughout (BS2 174/249). Both "posthumous" and *différance* refer to the mortal future that affects, in co-constituting, the living present. We saw this when discussing the two futures into which double turning and double affirmation cast us: while life can only seek to live by stretching itself out to a future it affirms as the future of its self-preservation (perhaps all the way to imagining oneself immortal, as Freud suggests[25]), it thereby opens itself to the incalculable future to come that necessarily alters the self by routing it through its context, a context that cannot but reconstitute that self. *Différance* defers the living present to a future it cannot make its own, a future that hands the self over to an inappropriable alterity.

As we've seen, the corpse is Derrida's name for this exposure and deliverance to the other. In fact, "other" is, for Derrida, defined as that which or who will survive me. *Sur-vivance* as the structure of life (BS2 130–131/192–193) hands me over to others "with no possible defense" (BS2 126–127/188–189), in death as in life. There can be alterity only where there is no perfectly overlapping time, where we do not just belong to the same time block, the same generation block. Accordingly, the attempt to deny time is the attempt to erase alterity: sovereignty consists, as we have already seen, in the attempt to "kill time," to contract its own power into an instant, so as to turn around its own axis as a perfectly round wheel. Aristotle's unmoved mover represents the phantasmatic hallmark of Western notions of sovereignty: the actuality of pure motion, the pleasure of returning to oneself without encountering alterity, turning around itself and thereby setting others in motion without itself being moved by others (R 15/35). In general, while taking time implies receptivity to the outside, instantaneity and anaesthesia are, Derrida says, indissociable (DP1 226/308; see R 109/154). And the other from whom or from which the sovereign seeks immunity, as the analogy with the posthumous suggests, is not only the sovereign state that claims the right to kill, and to localize and manage the corpse, or the family and friends who organize my funeral—but also the *humus*, the earth. Correspondingly, the sovereign contraction of the instant, its faith in the masterability of death through its instantaneity, finds further expression in the attempt to master territory, in particular the site of burial, the territory of interring, as King Creon attempted with the corpse of Polyneices in Sophocles' *Antigone*.

Posthuming can also help us understand why my first two claims (lifedeath and the terrestrial claim to the corpse), elaborated in terms of *différance*, already imply the third claim (which I will unfold below): the earth claims and absorbs not only the dead but also the living body. That the claim of the differential context upon the body as corpse is not only restricted to the body's death but extends over its lifetime has already been seen in Derrida's association of *humus* with French *humer*, breathing in or smelling. Breathing is, no doubt, one of the principal connections between the life of the body and the earth, including air and climate, as its indispensable context—hence the widespread association of life itself with breath and spirit. In fact, the *respire* in *je posthume comme je respire* comes from *respirare*, *spirare*, also giving us the word "spirit." As we read in Genesis 2:7, "Then the Lord God formed man of dust from the ground, and breathed into his nostrils the breath of life (*nishmat chayyim*); and man became a living being." While here you may (but need not) discover a contrast between "dust" and "breath," between "ground" and "life," Derrida's use of "posthumous" does not separate breath and humus, air and earth. Whenever we breathe in and breathe out, perhaps especially when we are sniffing like an animal, we are close to the earth. The earth is also the earth of the dead, those buried and those cremated, like Blanchot, who had just died and was cremated when Derrida wrote: "The posthumous is becoming the very element, mixes in everywhere with the air we are breathing" (BS2 179/255).

It is this proximity between breathing life and mortal earth that I underlined in my reading of Derrida on earth. Elsewhere Derrida shows *humer* to be etymologically linked to humility and the humble, interpreting them to signify that which is close to the ground and the earth. "Humble," of course, stems from Latin *humilis*, "lowly, humble," literally "on the ground," from *humus*, "earth," which implies "not self-asserting" and "of low birth or rank," often implying servants and the class of peasants, working the earth (see the entry "humilis" in Lewis and Short's *A Latin Dictionary*[26]). That is why Derrida at times favors the moles and the hedgehogs, animals, he says, who are not erecting themselves in sovereign fashion over others, as the eagle and the lion (BS1 214/287), but who stay close to the ground, *terre-à-terre* (PI 325/335).

IV. Life Interred-Interring

In this section I elaborate the third claim: that the terrestrial absorption of life—the earth's claim to the body—does not merely happen at the so-called end of life, as if before then the body was in the firm possession of its living bearer. The two previous sections, "The *Différance* of the Earth" and "The Terrestrial Claim to the Corpse," already entailed and indicated this conclusion. *Différance* demands of every ipseity (such as a living individuality) that it be turned to a (necessarily) preceding context that shapes its being and remains inappropriable even as that being must appropriate from it to sustain its life. As I've argued, the inappropriability may be understood as the interpellation by, or claim of, the earth with respect to the mortal body.

If life is spaced out by having death inscribed in it, and this spacing out turns life to the earth as the differential context on life's inside, then earth claims life not only at death but as it lives. As habitat and history, earth here names that which precedes and exceeds life, that which provokes and gives birth to life, but also demands its dying. There are a few ways in which this natal and mortal connection between life and earth may be explored further. Though I cannot fully carry out this exploration here, I will sketch out what I see to be some of its most significant aspects.

(1) Evolution

I have defined earth as the self-differentiating force in the habitat and history of life. While I have mostly discussed earth as mortal habitat and one recipient of the corpse, fascinating work is being done on *différance* and the history of life (see Vitale 2014, 2015, 2018; Kirby 2018). Without an "itself," evolution can be thought as a differential force that speciates and individuates "itself" (without, of course, an "in itself") *in* the organism, in species, in habitats and biospheres. On this account, evolution is not a gradual, linear unfolding of complexity, nor is adaptation (or selection) a secondary operation between organism and earth; on this view, natural fitness is just another name for organism, its outside making up its very inside as the self-difference that I named earth. The differential complexity of the inside-outside relation may be of help in overcoming a mechanistic account of evolutionary biology, with its stress on efficient, external causes that enforce "adaptation" (see E. Thompson 2010, 131). This mechanical explanation reduces the organization of life to external forces without thinking life in terms of the self-other affirmation I have stressed.

(2) Excrement and Other Remains

Deconstruction has long been concerned with the remains that life as *sur-vivance* cannot but leave behind.[27] In view of the individual organism, we've seen that Derrida thinks its inside-outside connection first, as being tasty to earth others; second, as "posthuming" (a breathing in and breathing out that takes turns with the earth); and third, as the corpse that organismic life leaves to others and to the elements. Elsewhere in his oeuvre, however, this twisted tie to the earth during life is also thought metabolistically, as an intake of food that cannot but leave a remainder to earth others, hence Derrida's discussion of vomit and excrement. In "*Ja*, or the *Faux-Bond*," vomit symbolizes (and more than that, embodies) a living system's "unproduction" (PI 38/45), "nonreception," or "indigestion" (PI 41–42/48). In Derrida's 1990–91 seminar "Rhétorique du cannibalisme" (as recounted in Krell 2006), this unproduction or indigestion is figured by excrement. On this view, ipseity comes about only in responding to its mortality by affirming itself as separate from the environment, an environment first of all generated as its "world" in this perpetual separation. In response to mortal threats and contextual pressures, appropriation from the earth (principally in the form of breathing and eating) builds the fissured dividing line between ipseity and world, self and earth.

But the self, as discussed, never quite establishes itself, and for Derrida, vomit and excrement manifest this nonclosure, the deferral of wholeness and identity. Defecation ties the organism back to the environment it seeks to project as nonself. Excrement signifies the earth's nibbling away at life *qua* life. It figures the ex-appropriation or unproduction in the production of the self: namely, the involuntary engendering of waste inassimilable by the self. If every self-production is an unproduction, an inability, then it is also a production for the other-than-self, for others as fertilizer or food, for example. The natal-mortal nonpower that has always already turned life to the outside constrains it to produce its self also for the nonself and for what the self cannot ever make its own, appropriate, receive, and what it therefore leaves or gives to the earth.

(3) Robinson Crusoe's Possessive Individualism

As a third indicator for the claim of the earth upon life, let us return to Robinson Crusoe. Recall that Derrida stresses Crusoe's fear of being swallowed alive, of dying a living death. I have explained this fear by the fact that auto-affection entails encountering oneself in a preceding and exceeding context: in this case, the earth and the sea in particular. On the basis of the differential reading of auto-hetero-affection as requiring a larger context, we can now better understand why Derrida would say this fear of being devoured alive, or of already having been swallowed, and thus of dying a living death, is also a desire, and indeed *a reality*—for only in such an enveloping context can life live, even if that reality is also a *phantasmatic* reality (e.g., BS2 148–149/216–218; see also Rottenberg 2011).

Crusoe's fear and desire, then, respond to the "groundless ground of this quasi-transcendentality of living to death or of death as sur-vivance" (BS2 132/196), and it this structure that, I suggested above, inserts the living from the beginning into the earth as history and habitat of lifedeath. In seeking to build a bridge to the previous chapter on the nature of intergenerational time as turning (briefly mentioned in this context of survivance; BS2 130/193)—the living as turning to the earth and the earth as turning about the living—I want to examine briefly how, on Derrida's perceptive reading, Crusoe responds to the trembling, devouring earth. As we will see, for Crusoe and Derrida, the earth is hardly ever maternally comforting but often terrifying, for it trembles and opens up, threatening to swallow up "alive" what it has, in fact, always already engulfed despite the differential separation constitutive of life.

While living selves cannot be entirely removed from the earth, their iterated ex-appropriations and futural recontextualizations cannot but seek independence from it. Hence, we may say, we witness the attempt to stay sovereign in the face of nature. The attempt may take the form of seeking mastery over the elements—"the end of knowledge is power," Hobbes said after Bacon (Hobbes, cited in Hampton 1988, 46)[28]—or of seeking to avert or defer the return of one's corpse to the earth and its creepy creatures, by building airtight coffins, by cremation, by feeding it to the vultures from the Tower of Silence, or whatever. Much is at stake in how we respond to a fear-inspiring earth into which we are given over by the unpossessable and finite timespace of *différance*. But not all responses and sovereign self-affirmations are the same, and deconstruction should not be accused too quickly of disarmingly ontologizing Robinson Crusoe's fear and the history to which this novel belongs. This history is marked from the beginning of BS2 as one of carno-phallo-logo-centrism (see Baumeister 2017): carnivorous, sexist, individualistic, humanist, presentist, colonialist, and imperialist. I will pick out just a few of these attributes.

The First Session of volume 2 of *The Beast and the Sovereign* inserts the figure of Crusoe into the history of liberal individualism, which prompted Marx to ridicule the "Robinsonades" of classical political economy: the ahistorical, atemporal attempt to explain the emergence of market capitalism starting from Crusoe, the ideal embodiment of *homo economicus* and the textbook starting point for much economic theory (Eatwell et al. 2002; Söllner 2016): a single individual who fashions all economic values for himself, without inheritance and so having given birth to himself, sole proprietor of his island, sovereign ruler, but without any division between governor and governed or social classes (BS2 14/38, 23–29/49–59). By way of Rousseau, Derrida suggests that modern democracy shares this model of sovereignty as what C. B. Macpherson, the renowned Canadian political theorist, called "possessive individualism" (Macpherson 1962). Rousseau's ideal democracy is a Robinsonade, situated on an island with only one person occupying it. There is an element of the democratic ideal, the critical reading goes, that resembles *Robinson Crusoe*.[29]

Further, Derrida cites James Joyce on Robinson Crusoe as "the prefiguration of an imperialist colonialist sovereignty, the first herald of the British empire, the great island setting off to conquer other islands" (BS2

16/40; see also 134/197). Crusoe serves as a model for modern, Western imperialism: stranding on a foreign island, he immediately takes himself to be its sovereign ruler, an "auto-affirmation of sovereignty" (BS2 28/56) that Derrida's reading of the novel seeks to reveal as a response to the fear of being swallowed alive by wild beasts, the earth, or the sea. This reading teases out these possessive, virile, sovereign responses to the timespace of *différance*—that is to say, to time as finite and space as earthy.[30]

This critique of colonial, possessive subjectivity poses the question to us whether there are other ways of thinking human sovereignty. What would an interred-interring sovereignty look like? What if sovereignty took seriously both the in-earthed human condition and intergenerational natality and mortality—the condition by which one has to inter the remains of the other and be interred by others in turn, both at the level of the individual and the collective level of democracy, with and beyond the nation-state? How to respond, in Derrida's words, to

> the finite promise *of* the world, as world [*promesse finie du monde, comme monde*]: it is up to "us" to make the world survive; and we cannot say this question is not urgently important today; it always is and always will have been, any time it can be a matter—or not—of giving oneself death, that is to say the end of the world; it is thus up to "us" to make what "we" inadequately call the human earth survive, an earth that "we" know is finite, that it can and must exhaust itself in an end [*à 'nous' de faire que survive ce que 'nous' appelons inadéquatement la terre humaine, une terre dont 'nous' savons qu'elle est finie, qu'elle peut ou doit s'épuiser en une fin*]. (AV 47/39)

As the last two chapters argued, double turning with generations and earth may be understood as a more *humble* sovereignty, one that is closer to the earth, less like the lion or the wolf, the owl or the eagle, and more like the mole or the hedgehog, of which Derrida says they are, like us, *terre-à-terre*. A sovereignty that embodies (or even inters) the promise to let the earth survive as a human world, even if it will not live forever.

V. Conclusion

In the last two chapters I proposed double turning as one possible way to rethink sovereignty in light of earthly relatedness and intergenerational survivance. In its unconditional exposure to alterity, I argued sovereignty should be conceptualized as a *double turn-taking*: individually, humans are turned about by the earth with which, intergenerationally, they take turns among different overlapping and non-overlapping generations. The *in-earthed* condition signifies that humans come to be from, and pass away into, the earth, in breathing in and breathing out, eating and defecating, birthing and dying. The earth's turning with humans shakes up the linearity and the continuity of the spiraling line of generational turn-taking. The earth's turning sustains, but also crosses and interrupts the attempts of human sovereigns to remain sovereign despite the passing away of individuals.

Tour-à-tour, then, and *terre-à-terre*: such is the human condition, today: *tour-à-terre, terre-à-tour*.

Notes

CHAPTER I

1. The well-known 2006 *Stern Review* estimates that 90 percent or more of monetized climate change damages will occur after 2200. See http://webarchive.nationalarchives.gov.uk/20100407172811/http://www.hm-treasury.gov.uk/stern_review_report.htm); see also Jamieson 2013, 165.

2. See https://www.ipcc.ch/publications_and_data/publications_ipcc_first_assessment_1990_wg1.shtml (last accessed Oct. 27, 2017).

3. https://obamawhitehouse.archives.gov/the-press-office/2014/09/23/remarks-president-un-climate-change-summit (last accessed Feb. 20, 2017). Obama attributes the line cited to "one of America's governors."

4. My thanks to Tatsuyoshi Saijo for pointing me to the OLG model.

5. A crucial issue in this discussion is, of course, the question of what one takes existing morality to be, and on what basis one can claim to know what it is. As we will see, a good part of the blame for the difficulties goes to what Jamieson, for example, calls "our . . . commonsense morality" with its focus on individual responsibility, proximate and identifiable harm, and clear causal links (Jamieson 2014, 148). Others have argued that this conception of the self is too individualist (and too Western) to capture the collective responsibilities involved in global environmental problems. For example, to de-individualize and collectivize moral responsibility for climate change, Marion Hourdequin suggests that we adopt a relational (and more Confucian) conception of personhood (Hourdequin 2010). Though here I am mostly interested in the *generational* sociality of nonpresentist beings, in this and subsequent chapters I too offer a relational (indeed, differentially, thus agonistically, relational) conception of the person, for instance, in discussion with indigenous accounts of the gift (see esp. Chapter 3 on Mauss and Derrida, as well as the work of Strathern [1988]).

6. In addition to the nonexistence challenge, Gosseries discusses three further challenges for ascribing rights to future people: the nonidentity problem (see below), judicial nonactionability, and the challenge of self-sanction: sanctioning earlier generations for future rights violations may harm future generations themselves (Gosseries 2010, 108ff.).

7. See Fritsch, "Discourse Ethics and the Intergenerational Chain of Concern," unpublished manuscript.

8. See Jamieson for an expansion of this argument vis-à-vis climate change: the effects of present emissions are nonlinear (Jamieson 2014, 180ff.) and unpredictable with respect to which future generation will be affected (165; there he takes this to affect chain or community conceptions of IGJ, for these, he claims, can extend responsibility only to two or three future generations; see Chapter 3 for a response to this claim).

9. This point is sometimes put in terms of the inapplicability of Hume's circumstances of justice; see Barry 1978.

10. See also Wall 2003, as well as Attas 2009, where he argues, though on "pragmatic" rather than theoretical grounds, that the notion of a first generation seems contrived and empirically unrealistic (Attas 2009, 204). If we accept that a generation implies a preceding generation and a preceding context of inheritance (as I will argue in this chapter and throughout the book, esp. Chapter 3), then we could also say that the notion of a first generation is ontologically inadequate.

11. Have we today come so far from Heyd's diagnosis in 1988? Heyd wrote, "[I]t seems that no existing ethical theory lends itself to easy extension to the inter-generational dimension. Direct applications of utilitarianism (total, as well as average) lead to unacceptable conclusions. Kantian ethics and contract theories yield paradoxes, especially with regard to the determination of the scope and identity of the moral community (Kingdom of Ends) or that of moral membership (in the Original Position). All these theories must either be revised in a way that would incorporate the futuristic aspects of morality, or be replaced by completely new theories" (Heyd 1988, 152).

12. In response, note Stephen Gardiner on climate change: "In the perfect moral storm, our position is not that of idealized neutral observers but judges in our case, with no one to properly hold us accountable" (Gardiner 2011a, xii).

13. In this sense, my argument in this chapter and the ones to follow could be seen as making a move parallel to David Carr's phenomenological argument against the allegedly typical assumption, in approaches to history, of a "gap" between the living in the present and the past (see Carr 2014). In a different context, the denial of coevalness can, of course, also be oppressive, as when one subject or group takes itself to be more advanced than another (see Fabian 2014; McCarthy 2009). As a result of this insight into the relation between power and time, the assumption that time is nothing but an inert background to social life has been contested. A wide array of work across a range of disciplines suggests that varying understandings and embodied experiences of time are intimately intertwined with power and agency, for instance in postcolonial theory (e.g., Chatterjee 2001; Chakrabarty 2008), queer theory (e.g., Freeman 2010; Halberstam 2005), and feminist theory (e.g., Grosz 2004; Hemmings 2011).

14. In *Tous les hommes sont mortels*, Beauvoir not only suggests that immortality would gradually rob life of meaningfulness but also explores the other side, the battle against mortality and its threat of depleting life of meaning. She does this by portraying the erotic relationship between immortal Fosca and Régine, a mortal actress who fears her stage fame will be lost too soon in human memory. While Fosca seeks to derive meaning from Régine's ambitions, she hopes Fosca could sing her praises forever. She gradually comes to realize, however, that Fosca has nothing to give her and cannot love anyone, because choosing her does not rule out choosing other women or other pursuits. Moral agency and ethics, on this interpretation, make sense only for mortals, because mortals can win a game against the ever-present threat of failure. As Beauvoir puts in her *Ethics of Ambiguity*, "without failure, no ethics" (Beauvoir 1976, 8).

15. A lot has been written about Williams's claim that in an immortal life boredom will inevitably crop up. A common objection holds that boredom is not inevitable, especially not if the immortality could be voluntarily ended (see, e.g., Bortolotti and Nagasawa 2009; Metz 2003; Burley 2009). In particular, defenders of "human enhancement," in this case the hope that longer life spans or even immortality could be engineered, resist the connection between death and meaningfulness (e.g., Harris 2007), and portray death as the greatest evil (Bostrom 2005; de Grey and Rae 2007). For a rebuttal, see Hauskeller, forthcoming.

16. At this point, Nussbaum calls for works of literature that explore immortality, and while failing to refer to Beauvoir's *All Men Are Mortal*, she takes ancient Greek accounts of the gods to fit the bill. Williams discusses an immortal character in the play *The Makropulos Case*, by Karel Čapek. To add to this list, we can also mention Salman Rushdie's first novel, *Grimus*. It seems here, as in the corresponding case of lack of progeny, philosophical explorations stand to benefit from literature, especially science fiction. For literature on a sterile humanity—What would happen if humanity were to die out with the present generation? (a question to be explored, in my view, alongside immortality)—see P. D. James's *The Children of Men* (charged with homophobia in Edelman 2004) and Brian Aldiss's *Greybeard*. Nussbaum has reflected on the philosophy-literature interface in helpful ways (1990, 1997), arguing that the novel in particular expands our imagination and empathy, thus promoting sympathy for lives different from ours, though to my knowledge without specific regard for intergenerational questions.

17. For a critique of Heidegger's going on to privilege death over birth by making of the latter what authentic being-toward-death gives to itself, see Guenther 2008 and O'Byrne 2010.

18. See Heidegger 1962, §74, 436/385, where "generation" is placed in quotation marks and referenced to Dilthey for fuller discussion. See also, and especially, Heidegger 2002, his 1925 essay on Dilthey. Anne O'Byrne has analyzed

the reference to generation in *Being and Time* as a suppression of birth: "The mention of . . . 'generation' . . . marks the moment when Heidegger might have embarked on a new attempt to elucidate the whole of Dasein's being by finally broaching that being as specifically generational, which is to say, natal, historical, and essentially with others" (O'Byrne 2010, 35). See also McMullin 2013, and the discussion between Derrida, Nancy, and Lacoue-Labarthe in FSC (ch. 2).

19. Derrida, for example, argues that friendship and political sociality is thus structured by an "originary mourning" (A 61/111). In volume 2 of *The Beast and the Sovereign*, Derrida elaborates this insight by interpreting Paul Celan's line "The world is gone, I must carry you" in the direction of the relation to world as well as to the earth and the sea in which one will have to bury the other (see Chapter 5). While writing parts of this chapter in Japan, I learned that Japanese (as well as some other non-European languages) accentuate these temporal differences between persons even within birth cohorts by the use of personal pronouns. For instance, a male speaker will tend to use *wata(ku)shi* (literally, "privacy") to refer to himself in the presence of an older interlocutor, even if the age difference is minimal, while he normally uses *boku* (literally, "man-servant") instead in the presence of a younger interlocutor or one of the same age. (With thanks to Hiroshi Abe for clarification.)

20. Indirectly confirming the importance of intergenerational indirect (tripartite) reciprocity, Wade-Benzoni writes in this context: "Here, we suggest two potential avenues for enhancing intergenerational identification (and, consequently, intergenerational affinity and beneficence): emphasizing the role of past generations in producing present group identity and focusing on long-term group goals. First, theorists have argued that understandings of the past can have a powerful effect on feelings about the future (Sherif 1966). In intergenerational contexts, feeling identified with past generations may be more readily facilitated than directly enhancing identification with future others because past generations are more readily identified and specified. In addition, the role that members of past generations have played in creating the present group context makes the connection between past and present more easily clarified than the connection between the present and the future" (Wade-Benzoni 2009, 172; on the role of historical indebtedness in political motivation, see also Fritsch 2005). The second avenue Wade-Benzoni mentions lies in establishing long-term group goals that can only be realized by future people. The stress on identification with continuing groups should be balanced and supplemented with, on the one hand, the singular, capillary pathways connecting each person with past and future, and, on the other, with universal-egalitarian concerns.

21. Derrida makes this argument in *The Work of Mourning*, especially in "The Deaths of Roland Barthes" (see, in particular, WM 52/80).

CHAPTER 2

1. This sense of ethics as emerging with a heteronomic otherness and grounded in a command may conflict with a common but mistaken understanding of moral autonomy. In particular, in the modern, specifically Kantian lineage, it is often thought that morality requires an autonomous agent who freely accepts, or even self-imposes, its dictates. Here, however, normativity is seen to precede and (in part) to ground autonomy, so that there is always some unchosen and heteronomic aspect to autonomy. Kant himself, it may be worth pointing out, did not understand the moral law as depending on the autonomous agent accepting it autonomously: while particular norms may be issued autonomously by way of the categorical imperative, the moral imperative itself, as the law of reason, is strictly speaking without reason and we can only "comprehend its incomprehensibility" (*Groundwork of the Metaphysic of Morals*, B 128, referring to the second German edition. For this translation from the "Concluding Note," see Kant 1948, 131). For Kant, it remains a command with the corresponding necessitation (see Kant 2017, 155; 1900ff., 6:379). As Allen Wood, in particular, has pointed out, the idea of Kantian autonomy as itself grounding the moral law is a common misconception widely used by critics of Kantian ethics such as Anscombe and Rorty to discredit it (A. Wood 2008, 106ff.; see also Waldenfels 2006, 21ff.).

2. Wenzler 1984 is the postface to the German translation of Levinas's *Les Temps et l'autre*; Levinas himself said that he admired Wenzler's comprehensive account (see Cohen 1987, ix).

3. Later in these fascinating lectures, in discussing Kant on immortality, Levinas will put into question the attempt to "simply rank the hope of immortality among the derivatives of being-toward-death and therefore of the originary temporality of being-there" (GDT 63/75).

4. For Sternberger and Fink, see Hügli and Han 2001, 135. For the role of death in singularization, see Fritsch 2006b.

5. As Derrida writes in his discussion of sovereignty and capital punishment, "Time is sensibility or receptivity, affection (a major vein of philosophy from Kant to Heidegger . . .); time is suffering. . . . If you suppress time, you will suppress sensibility" (DP1 226/308). On Derrida's analysis, this link between time and suffering leads to the attempt to dissociate capital punishment from cruelty by way of the phantasm of instant killing: a killing that takes no time.

6. Little research has been done on the suggested correspondence between Levinasian responsibility and Arendtian natality. See Markovits 2009; Astell 2006; Fritsch 2017a; and Mensch 2015, 168–170.

7. See Heidegger, GA 20, 439–440/318, which reopens the contrast between *Mitsein* and dying.

8. The principle "ought implies can" would for Levinas come into play, and find its possibly rightful but always perilous place, with the arrival of the third party: as a secondary, political or legal definition that, while necessary, stands under the suspicion of passing over a prior responsibility.

9. "To be temporal is both to be for death and to still have time, to be against death," Levinas writes (TI 235/262). To live is to "die for the other," or "to die for the invisible," as Levinas says at times (TI 35/23).

10. There is some debate in the literature as to whether there is a substantive change from TI to OB that goes along with this terminological shift from paternity to maternity; for discussion, see Vasey 1992 (who claims OB's making of the maternal bearing of the other the model of responsibility makes Levinas a feminist); Sikka 2001; Brody 2001. Gürtler argues that maternity in OB is a new starting point (Gürtler 2001, 377), for there ethical substitution is said to begin with corporeal substitution, that is, with one giving her body for another; this now would mean that motherhood counts as full ethical substitution. By contrast, Severson claims the mother in OB is still a faceless matrix (Severson 2013, 274ff.), and that "a "subtle patriarchy . . . still inhabits [Levinas's] later thought" (271).

11. The caregiver's need for care and reliance on others is felicitously expressed by Kittay's "doulia" (Kittay 1999), whose intergenerational significance and "transitive reciprocity" I have attempted to elaborate further elsewhere (see Fritsch forthcoming).

12. The switching of roles that permits us to see the other (here, the child) as donor has already led some commentators to speak of an asymmetrical reciprocity in Levinas's face-to-face (Young 1997; Paradiso-Michau 2007; Tatransky 2008).

13. Paradiso-Michau offers a reading of Levinas on Kierkegaard, Buber, and Hegel on recognition in which he attributes the origin of the term "asymmetrical reciprocity" to Calvin Schrag's mobilization of contemporary feminist philosophers such as Luce Irigaray, Iris Marion Young, Patricia J. Huntington, and Drucilla Cornell (Paradiso-Michau 2007, 346).

14. On this transcendental or phenomenological reciprocity (I can stand in asymmetry to you only if I also recognize you as another me, in my likeness, etc.), see also the debate between Levinas and Ricoeur in Levinas and Ricoeur 1998. In her well-known "Questions to Levinas," Irigaray too reasserts a certain kind of reciprocity in fecundity. Repositioning woman as *amante* (as active lover and not just passive beloved), she writes, against Levinas: "Man and woman, woman and man can love each other in reciprocity as subjects, and not only in the transitive fashion whereby the man loves the woman" (Irigaray 1991, 185). As a result, the relation between lovers is already "fecund" for Irigaray, and not only with the introduction of the child, as in Levinas, for whom in the end the erotic relation is governed by need rather than ethical

transcencence. For a detailed discussion of Irigaray's critical (and here highly relevant) reading, see Guenther 2006a.

15. I discuss Benjamin's claim of the past upon the living in detail in Fritsch 2005.

16. Pointedly, Gürtler recalls further that in "Judaism and Woman" (in Levinas 1997), Levinas presents woman as not itself other but as operating at the border of nature and culture in preparing food. Woman is viewed as responsible for cooking and thus for transforming nature into edibles, but this subsistence labor is not seen as labor but as an ethical gift coming from an other (Gürtler 2001, 338).

17. This reading of *Totality and Infinity* should be seen as supplementing (rather than contesting) Butler's reading of *Otherwise than Being* on this point: "Levinas's references to subject formation do not refer to a childhood (Laplanche seems right that childhood would not factor for Levinas) and is given no diachronic exposition; the condition is, rather, understood as synchronic and infinitely recurring" (Butler 2005, 90; see also Perpich 2008, 141). It is true that for Levinas, in particular in his later works, every encounter with a face engages "subject formation" anew, as there is no point at which a "subject" could be said to be fully constituted. And yet "biological" relations of "maternity" and "paternity" retain a particular status impinging on the very ontology of being a subject, no matter how circumspect Levinas's use of "ontological" categories becomes over the years. As I will argue, if subject formation is transported entirely into a sphere that is "pre-ontological" (Butler 2005, 85), in a confrontation with an alterity that remains "outside of being," then no particular debts would be contracted in subject formation.

18. Levinas's determination of the "authentically human" as the "being-Jewish in every man" (Levinas 1988, 192) is hardly separable from his figuring Israel as an exemplary state beyond a state, a new form of politics that promises peace (see his "Zionisms," in *The Levinas Reader*, edited by Séan Hand, and for discussion, Beardsworth 1996, 142–144), but a peace in which some have claimed Jews are preferred over Palestinians (see the infamous interview "Ethics and Politics," also in *The Levinas Reader*; for a recent defense of Levinas's comments about Palestinians, see Eisenstadt and Katz 2016). Given his privileged references to "the Bible and the Greeks," and his offensive comments about China, Levinas has also often been accused of Eurocentrism (see the discussion in Morgan 2016).

CHAPTER 3

1. The reference is to the C. B. Macpherson, who chastises liberal political theory, especially the social contract doctrine from Hobbes to Locke, for its "possessive individualism," that is, the conception of individuals as sole proprietors of their talents and wealth, owing nothing to society for them (Macpherson 1962).

2. Proof of the continuing power of Mauss's work on the gift may be gleaned from studying the work of the so-called M.A.U.S.S. group of French scholars (*Mouvement anti-utilitariste dans les sciences sociales*) and their *Revue du MAUSS* (see www.revuedumauss.com). For a recent overview of the reception of Mauss, see *WestEnd*, special issue, 7(1) (2010): 63–132, including essays by Marcel Hénaff and Axel Honneth.

3. In developing his own virtue-based account of indirect reciprocity among generations, Lawrence Becker, too, refers to the *kula* ring (Becker 1986, 230), but without mentioning Mauss as a (likely) source of the widespread knowledge of the *kula* and the *potlatch* in the West.

4. Although Mauss does not hide the fact that in most of the societies studied, it is only men who can serve as representative of the clan and so have the power to give, I will often use gender-neutral language or indeed feminine pronouns to characterize donor and recipient. For some excellent discussion of the frequently overlooked role of women in accounts of gift-giving practices, see Strathern 1988 and Joy 2013. Derrida discusses women and the gift, with principal reference to Nietzsche, in Derrida 1979.

5. In an earlier essay (Mauss 1972), Mauss generalizes the idea of *mana* as a spiritual life force across all archaic cultures, thus as a universal origin of human society. This claim received the criticism of being an illicit generalization, by the famous historian of religion Mircea Eliade, for instance (Eliade 1996, 22; 1992, 127). Marcel Hénaff has recently criticized Derrida's reading of Mauss for allegedly taking over this illicit universalization in Hénaff 2009. I defend Derrida in Fritsch 2011a.

6. For a good overview, see Graeber 2001, ch. 6, esp. 163–183; the translation of *hau* as "natural generativity" is to be found on page 177.

7. Annette Weiner's notion of the "inalienable"—that aspect of a gift that still belongs to the giver even after having been given away (Weiner 1992)—may come closest to what I mean by the unpossessable, though her notion stresses continuing possession.

8. Strathern's concept, in *The Gender of the Gift* (Strathern 1988), of the "partible person" or "dividual" may be the best attempt to account for this aspect of Melanesian self-understanding.

9. See Gardiner (2009) on the "problem of initial generation" in contract theory. See also Derrida's claim that a generation is "necessarily second" and "originarily late and therefore destined to inherit" (SM 24/46).

10. As we saw in Chapter 2 with feminist readings of Levinas and Arendt on, in Lisa Guenther's terms, "being-from-others" (Guenther 2008); see also Derrida's discussion of birth, as elaborated, for example, by Boelderl 2006, 2012.

11. Derrida, too, notes that a gift that would be so purely generous and altruistic as not to obligate a return is impossible in the context of human historical

practices: "As soon as almsgiving is regulated by institutional rituals, it is no longer a pure gift—gratuitous or gracious, purely generous. It becomes prescribed, programmed, obligated, in other words bound. And a gift must not be *bound*, in its purity, nor even *binding*, obligatory or obliging" (GT 137/174).

12. Mauss 1971. See also Eliade 1954.

13. GT 20n10/34n1. A fuller study of the gift in Derrida should consult his seminar of the year 1977–78, from which *Given Time* is drawn (see GT ix/9).

14. Derrida says of *Specters*, much of which is devoted to a thinking of generations, that "[i]n a more general and more implicit manner, the present essay pursues earlier paths," and among these paths, he lists "the economy of debt and gift (*Given Time*)" (SM 225n3/24n1).

15. Use of the word "generation," as in this passage from the exordium to *Specters*—a rather privileged place—is rare. In *For Strasbourg*, in the context of a discussion (with Nancy and Lacoue-Labarthe) about Heidegger's use of the word in *Being and Time*, Derrida avers that "generation" is not a tenable philosophical concept (FSC 22). This is presumably because in the generic singular in particular, "generation" denies temporal disunity, dislocation, and the disjointure that play such a prominent role in his work, especially in *Specters*. This is a well-known, even if perhaps still underplayed, problem in the extant literature on intergenerational justice. My reading of Derrida, here and in Chapter 5, seeks to address both disjointure and a tenuous generational unity.

16. In this passage and in others, Derrida at times seems to privilege the dead over the unborn. In a note to his "Lyotard and Us," for example, he considers the claim that "[o]ne is under an unconditional obligation only to the dead. One can always negotiate conditions with the living." But of course, the dead are not accessible other than as conditioned by the living: "[W]hat is living conditions everything," the note continues (WM 223–224n3/268n2).

17. I have elaborated my reading of *différance* and related "infrastructures" in Fritsch 2011a and Fritsch 2005. "Infrastructures" is Rodolphe Gasché's well-known term (Gasché 1986).

18. This should be seen in connection with the notion of natality and mortality as discussed in the previous two chapters.

19. See also SM 26/48–49. In both *Specters* and *Given Time* (159n28), Derrida refers the idea of giving of what one does not have to Heidegger's account of the relation between time and justice in "Anaximander's Saying"; see GA 5.

20. Famously, Socrates refutes Cephalus's claim that justice is "giving back what one has taken from another" by the counterexample of having received a weapon from a friend who has gone mad in the meantime (331c; Plato 1991, 7).

21. Heidegger writes, "The attempt in *Being and Time*, section 70, to derive human spatiality from temporality is untenable" (GA 15, 23/29).

22. Highly relevant in this context would be Luce Irigaray's rereading of Heidegger's "es gibt Sein" ("it gives / there is being") as "elle donne—d'abord—l'air" ("she [mother, woman, nature] first gives air"), in Irigaray 1999, 28.

23. In fact, the passage from "Différance" just cited ("[*différance* as] temporalization and spacing, the becoming-time of space and the becoming-space of time, the 'originary constitution' of time and space") continues by distancing *différance* as temporization-spacing from Husserl's account: "the 'originary constitution' of time and space, as metaphysics or transcendental phenomenology would say, to use the language that here is criticized and displaced" (MP 8/8). The displacement consists precisely in questioning the division between an originary or transcendental level and its merely empirical manifestations, a gesture that Derrida called "ultra-transcendental" in *Of Grammatology* (OG 61/90), and later, "quasi-transcendental." *Given Time*, too, questions the "transcendental givenness" of conditions of (empirical) giving (GT 52–53/74–75). For more on the quasi-transcendental, permit me to refer again to Fritsch 2011a, together with Fritsch 2005.

24. I do not believe this account of the subject should be seen as a dogmatic premise, designed to help the aporetic conclusion (a pure gift is impossible yet necessary). Rather, Derrida points to various reasons for thinking subjectivity, even before any psychological speculation about egoism and altruism, as involving a quasi-circular temporality: given its noncoincidence with itself, its very being consists in seeking to re-turn to itself (see the next chapter for more on such turnings). He also refers to the hermeneutic circle (as discussed by Heidegger in GA 2, §§1, 32), according to which understanding operates by a precomprehension (e.g., as to what gift means) that we cannot escape but only return to for purposes of further explication (GT 11/23).

25. This is one of the reasons we should not accept the restricted focus on the family, a restriction found in many economists, such as Arrondel and Masson, who limit themselves to intergenerational reciprocities in the family, while excluding nonmaterial transfers such as care, education, tradition, and language. The family cannot be isolated entirely from wider contexts of the gift, including the gifts of nature, of inheritance, and of the economy of (monetary) signs (see Derrida's argument on this at GT 158–159). Levinas's seeming restriction to the family (father, son, maternity, etc.) could then be seen as equally problematic (a point Derrida in fact makes; see AEL 122/209–210, 144/165, 152/209–210; see also the readings of Levinas in Chanter 2001; Gürtler 2008; and others, as discussed in Chapter 2).

26. For the claim that *différance* includes an affirmation or commitment to the open-ended future, see Fritsch 2011a.

27. See Derrida's "Force of Law"; Fritsch 2006a, 2010.

28. See Nietzsche 2005, 121 (in the section "On Redemption"); for Heidegger, see his "Anaximander's Saying," as well as GA 8 85/89ff.; for Derrida, see SM 26/48–49. For a detailed treatment of anger, revenge, and time, see Sloterdijk 2008.

29. I take this to be the reason why Derrida rarely uses the word "generation." We cited the passage from *Specters* which calls for a "politics of generations" (SM xix/15), but it's also true that he claims, in *For Strasbourg* (FSC 22), that "generation" is an "untenable" concept (presumably because it denies temporal disunity, dislocation, disjointure). For Derrida on generation, see also Michael Naas's introduction to *The Work of Mourning* (WM 17–8/38–39).

30. For an argument that social obligations (in our account, obligations of reciprocity) attach to social roles (rather than individuals conceived as atoms), see Ames 2011. Drawing on what he calls Confucian role ethics, Ames discusses a number of basic roles, of which several are asymmetrical and some are intergenerational (such as parent-child, adult-parents, state-individual, older-younger siblings). See also Rosemont 1991.

31. Taking them seriously is also to recognize that, if the futural excess in every gift is co-constitutive of agency, then there is a reciprocity relation, however qualified, between present and future people, overlapping and non-overlapping. For the excess involved in natal mortality means that contemporaries cannot but draw an advance credit on the future, a future that they invest with a meaning and hope that contributes to the present. The claim that there is no reciprocity with future generations (see Chapter 1 on the nonreciprocity problem) is thus shown to be mistaken once we take this social-ontological level into account, beyond mere material transfers. However, it remains the case on this account that responsibility is profoundly asymmetrical in relation to the future in particular.

32. See Blumenberg 1983 and Habermas 1988 on modernity as having to draw its sources of normativity only from itself.

CHAPTER 4

1. Some economists have discussed taking turns as an efficient solution to action coordination problems under specific conditions (Leo 2017; my thanks to Tatsuyoshi Saijo for the reference). In linguistics, taking turns among conversation partners has been recognized as essential (Hayashi 2012). In philosophy, and apart from Aristotle, there is a brief reference to taking turns as addressing boundary disputes in Wood 2003, 229 (my thanks to Ted Toadvine for the reference). In the context of intergenerational justice, see the discussions of turn-taking in Fritsch 2011b and Habib 2013 (discussed in greater detail below).

2. Some of the data relevant to proving both current global warming and its anthropogenic nature are the comparison with the carbon release during

the so-called Paleocene-Eocene Thermal Maximum (about 55 million years ago, known through geological analysis of sedimentary rocks) and the study of ancient air (about 650,000 years ago, obtained by ice-core data).

3. Clark's anti-presentist diagnosis, like mine, draws on Derrida's work, but to the extent relations with future people are concentrated on environmental degradation, he goes on to claim that "these environmental issues do not fit the terms of Derrida's thinking" (Clark 2008, 64). While he recognizes that the deconstruction of presentism makes the dead and the unborn not secondary to the living, he believes that the environment is resistant even to this expanded notion of nonpresentist justice (47). It seems hard to sustain this claim if we remember that the disjointure of time, which gives rise to the intergenerationality of justice in *Specters of Marx*, depriveleges or de-presentifies not only the present, but also the human and its supposed sovereignty over the earth. For evidence, see BS1 110/157, as well as R 53/81.

4. Klein 2014 may be seen as making this point most visibly, and specifically with respect to global warming.

5. I treat some aspects of this account below, in the section on the ipsocratic turning (T1). For more details, I refer the interested reader to Fritsch 2008, 2012.

6. I think a careful reading of some texts by Heidegger on time, especially "Anaximander's Saying" (Heidegger 2002b; see also the recently published manuscript Heidegger 2010), may be taken to suggest turning or taking turns as ways of thinking time, even if Heidegger never uses these terms (perhaps because German lacks a single term, both verbal and nominative, for turn-taking, using instead the reflexive verb *sich abwechseln* and *an der Reihe sein*). See, in particular, the account of the present (*Anwesen*) as the "ek-static" unity of coming-to-be or genesis (*Ent-stehen*, which implies a *Stand* or standing up that resists mere flow) and passing-away (*Ent-gehen*), a discontinuous unity that Heidegger insists cannot simply be thought as becoming (Heidegger 2010, 115ff.). Perhaps Derrida's repeated readings of "Anaximander's Saying" prepared him for the trope of turning (see MP; SM).

7. Another such indication for thinking time in terms of turns might be the fact that Aristotle's *meros* (the word we translate as "part," as in the discussion of whether the now is a part of time) can also mean "turn." Neither Derrida's "Ousia and Grammē" nor (to my limited knowledge) other commentators on Aristotle's time treatise remark upon this fact.

8. See Kant, *Critique of Pure Reason*, B 474; see also B 561, B 582. For an excellent and detailed account of Kantian freedom as self-beginning, see Düsing 2002, esp. 214ff.

9. Particularly instructive in this context are different assessments of the references to divine sovereignty in founding a democratic republic, as in the US Declaration of Independence. Bonnie Honig (1991), for one, has instructively

compared Hannah Arendt's and Derrida's accounts of the performativity of founding political power.

10. We may of course argue, and I will below, that even eating does not consume its object in its entirety, for eating is inseparable from defecation. In general, the discussion of sharing here, and in particular the distinction between sharing by parts and sharing by turns, would benefit from Derrida's discussion of sharing in *Rogues*, where he insists that *le partage* means both sharing and division. To think differential sociality is to think of (democratic) sovereignty as shared in a way that divides power despite its appeal to sovereign indivisibility; to share is always to some extent to share the unshareable and to measure the immeasurable (see, in particular, R 44–49/69–75). I do not think, however, that these complications in sharing undermine the usefulness of the distinction between sharing by parts and by turns. Further, the distinction between two turnings is meant to do justice to the complexity of sharing.

11. As will become clear in what follows, my discussion of taking turns benefited greatly from Allen Habib (2013). Apart from Derrida's *Rogues*, Habib's essay remains, to my knowledge, the only article-long scholarly discussion of taking turns as a model of justice. I do not always indicate my departures from Habib's model, but I discuss one major disagreement below.

12. In a fascinating and convoluted passage on absolute monarchy, Aristotle seems to suggest that the need to apply the law already implies the idea of taking turns with law-executing offices. For if the human monarch applied the law to himself, he would still be above the law and thereby violate the very idea of the law as applying to all humans equally. Hence, law and taking turns are closely aligned, not only in democracy (which champions freedom and equality, and thus taking turns, the most; see Aristotle, *Politics* 1318a), but beyond it, too, wherever we want order and recognize that the human being, despite reason, has not just divine but also "beastly," desiring, and selfish characteristics (Aristotle, *Politics* 1287a). The very idea of constitutionalizing (i.e., legally constituting) sovereign political power entails sharing at least some offices (here, law-executing ones) by turns. The fact that humans are finite beings who do not divinely rotate around themselves, then, seems to imply turn-taking with others.

13. Indeed, I believe some of the moral and political concepts Derrida develops in his later work, such as unconditional and conditional hospitality, democracy-to-come, *aimance*, justice in its relation with law, and so on, can be productively thought of as also situated at this second level, for they are elaborated in view of certain areas of moral and political concern, even if Derrida tends to stress their quasi-ontological and, indeed, aporetic status (see Fritsch 2011a).

14. Despite this general relation of priority, and the criteria I gave above regarding the distinction between sharing by parts or by turns, the difficulties in deciding when reciprocity or turn-taking are most appropriate remain

formidable, and I don't claim to solve them here. Habib, for example, argues that a turn-based approach addresses the various problems associated with owing parts to the future; but in having to permit appropriations by the present generation as well as having to meet the demands of certain maintenance standards or threshold limits (like flourishing or the functionality of the natural world), turn-sharing would have to identify those aspects of the natural world constitutive of any turn. In order to allow substitutions within it, turn-sharing would have to adopt something like an ecological threshold, a minimum of essential aspects that must be owed to any turn.

15. Most famously, see Arne Naess's critique of the "man-in-environment" model in Naess 1973.

16. At one point in *Rogues* (R 60/90), precisely when opening political sovereignty beyond fraternity, nationality, and natural birth, Derrida invokes ethics as originating not with the like but with the unlike and the unrecognizable. And on this theme he recalls his seminar from that year (2001–2), which we now have as *The Beast and the Sovereign*, volume 1. If we follow up on his reference, we find the passage in which the (nonpresent) source of ethics is found in the death in life and in the living present that carries ethics not only toward nonpresent generations but also to the nonhuman (BS1 108–111/154–159).

CHAPTER 5

1. See http://www.footprintnetwork.org/ar/index.php/GFN/page/world_footprint/. I do not mean to suggest that all human earthlings should live in poverty. These comparative figures indicate the well-known need to balance sustainability and economic development, and, as suggested at the end of Chapter 3, to situate economics in earth and world.

2. Kant 2017, 56; see also 97. For a discussion of these references with respect to Kant's conceptions of property and cosmopolitan hospitality, see Oliver 2014. Oliver suggests a link in Kant between the shared terrestrial surface and the imaginary passage beyond earth in regarding humanity from the perspective of the universe, even as Kant admits that other planets are uninhabitable for humans. Kant writes in 1754: "Should the immortal [human] soul remain forever attached to this point in space, to our Earth for the whole infinity of its future duration, which is not interrupted by the grave itself, but only changed? Should it never obtain a closer view of the remaining wonders of creation? Who knows whether it is not intended to get to know at close quarters those distant spheres of the solar system and the excellence of their arrangements that already excite its curiosity so much from a distance?" (Kant 2012, 307; 1900ff., 1:367–368).

3. The moral law depends on the noumenal world of freedom, which, while merely thinkable, is unaffected by nature, for the latter is, for the Kant of the

first and second *Critiques*, the world of causality, whereas free (and thus possibly moral) action must be conceived as self-beginning (*Selbstanfang*) (*Critique of Pure Reason* B 474; Kant 1998, 484).

4. There are two places in which Derrida speaks of something like the promise of the earth. In the first, he speaks of the promise of the bond between singularities (singular people prior to citizenship), a noncommunal, spectral bond made up, he says, by the issues of life, animality, and earth (NII 241). In the second, one that we will examine in greater detail below, he speaks indeed of "the finite promise *of the* world," a promise according to which it is "up to 'us' to let survive that which 'we' inadequately call the human earth" (AV 47/39).

5. "If the autoposition, the automonstrative autotely of the 'I,' even in the human, implies the 'I' to be an other that must welcome within itself some irreducible hetero-affection (as I have tried to demonstrate elsewhere), then this autonomy of the 'I' can be neither pure nor rigorous; it would not be able to form the basis for a simple and linear differentiation of the human from the animal" (AA 133/95; see Lawlor 2007, 60ff.).

6. See Vicki Kirby on evolution and the environment as a force that speciates and individuates "itself" *in* the organism (Kirby 2018).

7. Derrida, "Eating Well," in *Points* (PI 268–269/282–284 et passim); see also TS 76–77. As commentators have pointed out, some of Derrida's metaphors and analogies in the last ten years of his writings, beginning in particular with "Faith and Knowledge" (FK), are also drawn from biology (e.g., autoimmunity).

8. "I am" Derrida writes, means "I am (not yet) born," and wonders "Who ever said that one was born just once?" (PI 339/349).

9. "La vie la mort" is the title of a Derrida seminar (so far unpublished in its entirety) on the notion of organic life from 1975, parts of which have been published in *The Postcard*. The term "lifedeath" appears frequently there, in a discussion of (Freud's) legacy and leaving remains more generally (PI 41, 273, 277, 284–285, 359–360, 367).

10. For Derrida, phantasms of self-beginning and self-birth are, at least implicitly, phantasms of matricide: "Birth, being born (not the being born nothing or from nothing, but always the being born from . . . or in two's, me and before me the other me): this is neither the beginning nor the origin nor even, save the phantasm, a point of departure. A dependency, no doubt, but not an origin or point of departure. A generation, perhaps, but without origin. The word generation is big with all these ambiguities" (NW 91). For more on Derrida on birth and maternity, see Boelderl 2006, 2012.

11. For instance (and I pick a passage from Session One that I see as typical): "[O]ne cannot keep from thinking that the death penalty, inasmuch as it puts an end, irreversibly, along with the life of the accused, to any perspective of the revision, reparation, redemption, even repentance, at least on earth and for someone

living . . . signifies that the crime it sanctions remains forever, on men's earth and in men's society, unforgivable" (DP1 45/78).

12. As in Genesis 3:19 (New International Version): "By the sweat of your brow / you will eat your food / until you return to the ground / since from it you were taken / for dust you are / and to dust you will return." See also Ecclesiastes 3:20: "All go to the same place; all come from dust, and to dust all return." These biblical lines must today be understood in the context of the dualism that is, of course, part of the long legacy of humanism: Ecclesiastes 12.17: "[A]nd the dust returns to the ground it came from, and the spirit returns to God who gave it."

13. Derrida's discusses "self-taste" further in one of the sessions of BS2 not published in the volume, but published separately as "Justices" (Derrida 2005). See the editorial note in BS2 xvin8/16n6.

14. My thanks to Ted Toadvine for pointing me to Hatley's wonderful essay.

15. "Provocation" is the word Derrida uses in interpreting Nietzsche's will-to-power and its dependence on obstacles; see "Nietzsche and the Machine" (at N 223–227).

16. For further details as to this connection between (quasi-)ontological concepts (world, self, identity) and normative ones (obligation, affirmation, promise), see Fritsch 2011a.

17. For an elaboration of the claim that vulnerability is not to be thought as a capacity, especially not in the context of environmental ethics, see my "An Eco-Deconstructive Account of the Emergence of Normativity in 'Nature'" (Fritsch 2018).

18. Note also the reference to *co-mourance*, dying together or shared mortality, in Derrida's conversation with Jean-Luc Nancy and Philippe Lacoue-Labarthe in *For Strasbourg*. Derrida there notes that if *Dasein* is always *Mitsein*, then Heidegger cannot conceive of dying in entirely solitary terms. To think this togetherness in dying, neither dying for the people (as in the infamous §74 of *Being and Time*) nor being a member of a generation quite suffices for Derrida (FSC 21–22). He then links dying together to what he calls a "testamentary desire, the desire that *something* survive" of me "that does not come back to me" (FSC 23), what psychologists call generativity, or the desire to leave a legacy. He then distances this desire from the Spinozist claim that "[w]e feel and know by experience that we are immortal," and says: "[N]aturally, I don't believe in immortality. But I know that there is an I, a *me*, a living being who is related to itself through auto-affection, who might be a bird, and who will feel alive like me. . . . When I am dead, there will be a bird, an ant, who will say 'me' for me, and when someone says 'me' for me, that's me" (FSC 26). Derrida thus conceives of co-dying in non-speciesist terms, and sees himself surviving, by proxy and without immortality, in the ant or the bird or another living being. We should connect this sense of co-dying to what we said above, with Derrida and Plumwood, about finding a third

way to conceive of the death-earth relation, beyond the reductive-naturalist and the spiritualist-distanced conceptions of death. (On Montaigne's *commourans*, see also Malabou and Derrida 2004, 7n2.)

19. Here it would be productive to relate this use of "world" in BS2 to Derrida's early work on Husserl on earth and world. In Derrida's introduction to Husserl's *Origin of Geometry*, for example, we read: "The language and consciousness of co-humanity are solidary possibilities and already given in the moment where the possibility of science is established. The horizon of co-humanity supposes the horizon of the world: it stands out and articulates its unity against [*se détache et articule son unité sur*] the unity of the world. Of course, the world and co-humanity here designate the single, but infinitely open totality of possible experiences and not this world here, this co-humanity here. . . . The consciousness of being-in-community within one and the same world establishes the possibility of a universal language" (IOG 74/79). Commenting on Husserl's use of "earth" to name this presupposition of a common world, Derrida goes on to suggest in that early text that earth provides the ground of a consciousness of "a pure and pre-cultural *we*" (IOG 76/81), a consciousness of belonging to "one and the same humanity, inhabiting one and the same world" (IOG 76/81). But of course, as in BS2, this presupposition cannot be accessed in pure form: "[P]re-cultural *pure Nature* is always already buried. So, as the ultimate possibility for communication, it is a kind of inaccessible infra-ideal" (IOG 77/81–82). My thanks to Phil Lynes for pointing me to these passages. See also Lynes 2018.

20. Derrida here associates this projection with the idea of a shared lifeworld and links it to Habermas's use of this idea, also in a quasi-transcendental argument, in his theory of communicative action (BS2 267/368). See also the afterword to *Limited Inc*, where Derrida claims that strong assumptions—for instance, that concept use must be governed by the logic of noncontradiction—are required for meaning. See in particular Derrida 1988 (114–130), which speaks of a "structural idealism" (120) that seems to me to be comparable to, though also different from, Habermas's universal pragmatics and its analysis of inevitable idealizations. For more on this proximity see Fritsch 2011a.

21. Kant's discussion of the "original possession in common [*ursprünglicher Gesamtbesitz*]" of "the earth's surface as spherical surface [*Erdfläche als Kugelfläche*]" is in his Doctrine of Right, particularly property law, in *The Metaphysics of Morals* (Kant 2017, 56; 1900ff., 6:262–263). See also Oliver 2014.

22. Note that the English edition, by translating *enterré* as "buried," loses the frequency of Derrida's references to earth as the recipient of the corpse; "inhumed" would be better, as in German *beerdigt*, both of which refer to the earth. In *Glas* Derrida uses *enseveli* more often than *enterré*, *ensevelir* being more formal and referring to shrouding and placing a body not in the earth but in a sepulchre (Latin *sepulturum, insepelire*), thereby protecting the body from terrestrial

elements. (In *Glas*, Derrida makes much of the fact that traditionally, it was the work of women to protect the sovereign separation of bodies from the earth, by cleaning and shrouding a corpse.) The contrast indicates that the discussion of the corpse in BS2 is earthier than in *Glas*. (Note: "terror," "terrified," etc. stem from PIE root **trem-* "to tremble" and so seem not to be etymologically related to Latin *terra*, source of the English "terrain," "territory," which stem from the PIE root **ters-* "to dry," as in "dry land" ("thirst" also comes from this root).

23. See also Cixous 2004: "[H]e who dies at the top of his lungs, a buried-alive supernatural . . . respire, respirare, it really is re- or post-humous, come back from the dead" (58–59/56–57).

24. For an excellent account of the history of this sense of life as sensing (rather than intuiting or thinking itself in consciousness), see Heller-Roazen 2007.

25. Derrida discusses this text by Freud in the second volume of *The Beast and the Sovereign*, concluding: "This is another way of saying, against Heidegger, that we never have any access to our own death *as such*, that we are incapable of it" (BS2 157/228). See also Hägglund 2012, 113ff.

26. http://www.perseus.tufts.edu/hopper/text?doc=Perseus:text:1999.04.0059:entry=humilis (last accessed Nov. 3, 2017).

27. See, e.g., Derrida 2002b. See also Miller 2006 and "Thinking What Remains," ed. Pleshette DeArmitt and Kas Saghafi, special issue, *Derrida Today* 9(2) (2016).

28. It would be useful in this context to consider Theodor Adorno and Max Horkheimer's analysis of this famous claim, made at the beginning of the modern epoch by Bacon and Hobbes, in Horkheimer and Adorno 2002 (1ff.).

29. Derrida comments that "[a]lthough it [the story of Robinson Crusoe] corresponds here to a myth or a legend, to a dated literary fiction, the structure that it describes . . . does correspond to what we still think of today when we speak of the absolute freedom of the citizen, who decides sovereignly, for example in a voting booth [*isoloir*] (the booth is an island)" (BS2 21/47).

30. In the interest of elaborating double turning in the context of indigenous struggles and land claims against settler colonialism, it would at this point be helpful to connect taking turns with indigenous survivance, for instance as developed so insightfully by Gerald Vizenor (Vizenor 1994, 2008, 2012). Drawing in part on Derrida's concept of lifedeath or *sur-vivance*, Vizenor and other indigenous writers have converted what looks, from the colonizer's viewpoint, to be a victim's mere survival into a self-affirmative intergenerational endurance, resistance, and active presence (Lee 2000; Breinig 2008; Kroeber 2008). I thank Lisa Guenther for directing me to Vizenor's fascinating work and hope to return to it in the future.

Bibliography

Ames, Roger. 2011. *Confucian Role Ethics: A Vocabulary*. Hong Kong: Chinese University Press.
Appiah, Kwame Anthony. 2005. *The Ethics of Identity*. Princeton, NJ: Princeton University Press.
Archard, David, and David Benatar, eds. 2010. *Procreation and Parenthood: The Ethics of Bearing and Rearing Children*. Oxford: Oxford University Press.
Arendt, Hannah. 1958. *The Human Condition*. Chicago: University of Chicago Press.
Aristotle. 1984. *Nichomachean Ethics, Politics,* and *Physics*. In *The Complete Works of Aristotle: The Revised Oxford Translation*, edited by Jonathan Barnes et al., 1729–1867, 1986–2129, 315–446. Princeton, NJ: Princeton University Press.
Arrondel, Luc, and André Masson. 2006. "Altruism, Exchange or Indirect Reciprocity: What Do the Data on Family Transfers Show?" In *Handbook of the Economics of Giving, Altruism and Reciprocity: Applications Volume 2*, edited by Serge-Christophe Kolm and Jean Mercier Ythier, 971–1053. Amsterdam: Elsevier.
Astell, Ann. 2006. "Mater-Natality: Augustine, Arendt, and Levinas." In *Analecta Husserliana 89*, edited by Anna Teresa Tymieniecka, 373–398. Dordrecht: Springer.
Attas, Daniel. 2009. "A Trans-Generational Difference Principle." In *Intergenerational Justice*, edited by Axel Gosseries and Lukas H. Meyer, 189–218. Oxford: Oxford University Press.
Baer, Paul. 2010. "Adaptation to Climate Change: Who Pays Whom?" In *Climate Ethics: Essential Readings*, edited by Stephen Gardiner, Simon Caney, Dale Jamieson, and Henry Shue, 247–262. Oxford: Oxford University Press.
Ball, Terence. 1985. "The Incoherence of Intergenerational Justice." *Inquiry* 28:321–337.
Bankovsky, Miriam. 2005. "Derrida Brings Levinas to Kant: The Welcome, Ethics, and Cosmopolitical Law." *Philosophy Today* 49(2): 156–170.
Barro, Robert J., and Xavier Sala-i-Martin. 2004. "Appendix: Overlapping-Generations Models." In *Economic Growth*, 190–199. New York: McGraw-Hill, 190–200.

Barry, Brian. 1978. "Circumstances of Justice and Future Generations." In *Obligations to Future Generations*, edited by R. Sikora and B. Barry, 204–248. Philadelphia: Temple University Press.

Barry, Brian. 1989. *Theories of Justice: A Treatise on Social Justice*. Vol. 1. Berkeley: University of California Press.

Barry, Brian. 1991. *Liberty and Justice: Essays in Political Theory II*. Oxford: Clarendon Press.

Bastian, Michelle, and Thom van Dooren. 2017. "Editorial Preface: The New Immortals: Immortality and Infinitude in the Anthropocene" *Environmental Philosophy* 14(1): 1–9.

Baumeister, David. 2017. "Derrida on Carnophallogocentrism and the Primal Parricide." *Derrida Today* 10(1): 51–66.

Beardsworth, Richard. 1996. *Derrida and the Political*. London: Routledge.

Beauvoir, Simone de. 1976. *The Ethics of Ambiguity*. Translated by Bernard Frechtman. New York: Citadel Press.

Becker, Gary S., and Robert J. Barro. 1986. "Altruism and the Economic Theory of Fertility." In *Population and Development Review* 12:69–76.

Becker, Lawrence. 1986. *Reciprocity*. Oxford: Oxford University Press.

Beckerman, Wilfred. 1999. "Sustainable Development and Our Obligations to Future Generations." In *Fairness and Futurity*, edited by Andrew Dobson, 71–92. New York: Oxford University Press.

Beckerman, Wilfred, and J. Pasek. 2001. *Justice, Posterity and the Environment*. Oxford: Oxford University Press.

Beckman, Ludvig, and Edward A. Page. 2008. "Perspectives on Justice, Democracy, and Global Climate Change." *Environmental Politics* 17(4): 527–535.

Bedorf, Thomas. 2003. *Dimensionen des Dritten: Sozialphilosophische Modelle zwischen Ethnischem und Politischem*. Munich: Wilhelm Fink Verlag.

Benjamin, Walter. 1968. "Theses on the Philosophy of History." In *Illuminations: Essays and Reflections*, translated by Harry Zohn, 253–264. New York: Schocken.

Bensussan, Gérard. 2008. *Éthique et expérience: Levinas politique*. Strasbourg: La Phocide.

Bergo, Bettina. 2003. *Levinas between Ethics and Politics: For the Beauty That Adorns the Earth*. Duquesne: Duquesne University Press.

Bernasconi, Robert. 1988. "The Trace of Levinas in Derrida." In *Derrida and Differance*, edited by David Wood and R. Bernasconi, 13–29. Coventry, UK: Parousia.

Bernasconi, Robert. 1997. "What Goes Around Comes Around: Derrida and Levinas on the Economy of the Gift and the Gift of Genealogy." In *The Logic of the Gift: Towards an Ethics of Generosity*, edited by Alan D. Schrift, 256–273. New York: Routledge.

Bernasconi, Robert. 1998. "Different Styles of Eschatology: Derrida's Take on Levinas's Political Messianism." *Research in Phenomenology* 28:3–19.
Birnbacher, Dieter. 1977. "Rawls' Theorie der Gerechtigkeit und das Problem der Gerechtigkeit zwischen den Generationen." *Zeitschrift für philosophische Forschung* 31:385–401.
Birnbacher, Dieter. 1988. *Verantwortung für zukünftige Generationen*. Stuttgart: Reclam.
Blanchard, Olivier Jean, and Stanley Fischer. 1989. "The Overlapping Generations Model." In *Lectures on Macroeconomics*, 91–152. Cambridge, MA: MIT Press.
Bloch, Ernst. 1985. *Das Prinzip Hoffnung*. Vol. 1. Frankfurt: Suhrkamp.
Blumenberg, Hans. 1983. *The Legitimacy of the Modern Age*. Translated by Robert M. Wallace. Cambridge, MA: MIT Press.
Bockover, Mary I., ed. 1991. *Rules, Rituals, and Responsibility: Essays Dedicated to Herbert Fingarette*. La Salle, IL: Open Court.
Boelderl, Artur. 2006. *Von Geburts wegen: Unterwegs zu einer philosophischen Natologie*. Würzburg: Koenigshausen und Neumann.
Boelderl, Artur. 2012. "Derridas Mutter: Sexuelle Differenz, intergenerative Differenz." In *In statu nascendi: Geborensein und intergenerative Dimension des menschlichen Miteinanderseins*, edited by Tatiana Shchyttsova, 121–145. Nordhausen: Bautz.
Bortolotti, Lisa, and Yujin Nagasawa. 2009. "Immortality without Boredom." *Ratio* 22–23:261–277.
Bostrom, Nick. 2005. "The Fable of the Dragon Tyrant." *Journal of Medical Ethics* 31:273–277.
Bowles, Samuel, and Herbert Gintis. 2013. *A Cooperative Species: Human Reciprocity and Its Evolution*. Princeton, NJ: Princeton University Press.
Breinig, Helmbrecht. 2008. "Native Survivance in the Americas." In *Survivance: Narratives of Native Presence*, edited by Gerald Vizenor, 39–60. Lincoln: University of Nebraska Press.
Brumlik, Micha. 2004. *Advokatorische Ethik: Zur Legitimation pädagogischer Eingriffe*. Berlin: Philo.
Burley, Mikel. 2009. "Immortality and Meaning: Reflections on the Makropulos Debate." *Philosophy* 84:529–547.
Butler, Judith. 2005. *Giving an Account of Oneself*. New York: Fordham University Press.
Butler, Judith. 2012. "Precarious Life, Vulnerability, and the Ethics of Cohabitation." *Journal of Speculative Philosophy* 26(2): 134–151.
Bykvist, Krister. 2009. "Preference Formation and Intergenerational Justice." In *Intergenerational Justice*, edited by Axel Gosseries and Lukas H. Meyer, 301–322. Oxford: Oxford University Press.

Calder, Gideon. 2008. "Ethics and Social Ontology." *Analyse & Kritik* 30(2): 427–443.
Caney, Simon. 2010a. "Cosmopolitan Justice, Responsibility, and Global Climate Change." In *Climate Ethics: Essential Readings*, edited by Stephen Gardiner, Simon Caney, Dale Jamieson, and Henry Shue, 122–145. Oxford: Oxford University Press.
Caney, Simon. 2010b. "Climate Change, Human Rights and Moral Thresholds." In *Climate Ethics: Essential Readings*, edited by Stephen Gardiner, Simon Caney, Dale Jamieson, and Henry Shue, 163–177. Oxford: Oxford University Press.
Caney, Simon. 2016. "Political Institutions for the Future: A Five-Fold Package." In *Institutions for Future Generations*, edited by Inigo Gonzalez-Ricoy and Axel Gosseries, 135–155. Oxford: Oxford University Press.
Caputo, John D. 1988. *Radical Hermeneutics. Repetition, Deconstruction, and the Hermeneutic Project*. Bloomington: Indiana University Press.
Carr, David. 2014. *Experience and History: Phenomenological Perspectives on the Historical World*. Oxford: Oxford University Press.
Cavarero, Adriana. 2000. *Relating Narratives: Storytelling and Selfhood*. London: Routledge.
Cavarero, Adriana. 2014. "'A Child Has Been Born unto Us': Arendt on Birth." *philoSOPHIA* 4(1) (Winter): 12–30.
Chakrabarty, Dipesh. 2009. "The Climate of History: Four Theses." *Critical Inquiry* 35: 197–222.
Chanter, Tina. 1988. "Feminism and the Other." In *The Provocation of Levinas: Rethinking the Other*, edited by Robert Bernasconi and David Wood, 32–56. London: Routledge.
Chanter, Tina. 2001. *Time, Death, and the Feminine: Levinas with Heidegger*. Stanford, CA: Stanford University Press.
Chatterjee, Piya. 2001. *A Time for Tea: Women, Labor, and Post/Colonial Politics on an Indian Plantation*. Durham, NC: Duke University Press.
Ciaramelli, Fabio. 1998. "The Posteriority of the Anterior." *Graduate Faculty Philosophy Journal* 20/21(2/1): 409–427.
Cixous, Hélène. 2004. *Portrait of Jacques Derrida as Young Jewish Saint*. New York: Columbia University Press.
Clark, Timothy. 2008. "Towards A Deconstructive Environmental Criticism." *Oxford Literary Review* 30:45–68.
Cohen, Richard. 1987. "Translator's Note." In Emmanuel Levinas, *Time and the Other*, translated by Richard A. Cohen, vii–ix. Pittsburgh: Duquesne University Press.
Cohen, Richard. 2006. "Levinas: Thinking Least about Death; Contra Heidegger." *International Journal for Philosophy of Religion* 60(1–3): 21–39.

Coope, Ursula. 2005. *Time for Aristotle*. Oxford: Oxford University Press.
Cornell, Drucilla. 2005. "Derrida: The Gift of the Future." *Differences: A Journal of Feminist Cultural Studies* 16(3): 68–75.
Critchley, Simon. 1992. *The Ethics of Deconstruction: Derrida and Levinas*. Oxford: Blackwell.
Critchley, Simon. 2009. *Ethics-Politics-Subjectivity: Essays on Derrida, Levinas and Contemporary French Thought*. London: Verso.
Dahlstrom, Daniel. 2001. *Heidegger's Concept of Truth*. Cambridge: Cambridge University Press.
Daly, Herman E. 2008. *A Steady-State Economy*. Sustainable Development Commission, UK (April 24, 2008), accessed March 12, 2014. http://www.sd-commission.org.uk/publications.php?id=775.
Davidson, Scott, and Diane Perpich, eds. 2012. *Totality and Infinity at 50*. Pittsburgh: Duquesne University Press.
de Grey, Aubrey, and Michael Rae. 2007. *Ending Aging*. New York: St. Martin's Press.
de Shalit, Avner. 1995. *Why Posterity Matters: Environmental Policies and Future Generations*. London: Routledge.
Derrida, Jacques. 1979. *Spurs: Nietzsche's Styles*. Translated by Barbara Harlow. Chicago: University of Chicago Press.
Derrida, Jacques. 1984. "No Apocalypse, Not Now (Full Speed Ahead, Seven Missiles, Seven Missives)." *Diacritics* 14(2): 20–31.
Derrida, Jacques. 1987. *The Post Card: From Socrates to Freud and Beyond*. Translated by Alan Bass. Chicago: University of Chicago Press.
Derrida, Jacques. 1988. *Limited Inc*. Translated by Elisabeth Weber. Evanston, IL: Northwestern University Press.
Derrida, Jacques. 1995a. *The Gift of Death*. Translated by David Wills. Chicago: University of Chicago Press.
Derrida, Jacques. 1995b. *On the Name*. Edited by Thomas Dutoit. Stanford, CA: Stanford University Press.
Derrida, Jacques. 1996. "Remarks on Deconstruction and Pragmatism." In *Deconstruction and Pragmatism*, edited by Chantal Mouffe, 79–90. London: Routledge.
Derrida, Jacques. 2000a. "Foreigner Question." In Jacques Derrida and Anne Dufourmantelle, *Of Hospitality*, translated by Rachel Bowlby, 3–74. Stanford, CA: Stanford University Press.
Derrida, Jacques. 2000b. "Hostipitality." Translated by Barry Stocker and Forbes Morlock. *Angelaki* 5(3): 3–18.
Derrida, Jacques. 2002a. "Faith and Knowledge." In *Acts of Religion*, edited by Gil Anidjar, 40–101. London: Routledge.
Derrida, Jacques. 2002b. "Reste-le maitre ou le supplement d'infini." *Le genre humain* 37 (April): 25–64.

Derrida, Jacques. 2005a. "Justices." Translated by Peggy Kamuf. *Critical Inquiry* 31(3): 689–721.
Derrida, Jacques. 2005b. "Shibboleth: For Paul Celan." In *Sovereignties in Question: The Poetics of Paul Celan*, edited by Thomas Dutoit and Outi Pasanen, 1–64. New York: Fordham University Press.
Derrida, Jacques. 2007a. *Psyche: Inventions of the Other*. Vol. I. Edited by Peggy Kamuf and Elizabeth Rottenberg. Stanford, CA: Stanford University Press.
Derrida, Jacques. 2007b. "A Certain Impossible Possibility of Saying the Event." Translated by Gila Walker. *Critical Inquiry* 33:441–461.
Derrida, Jacques. 2010. *Parages*. Edited by John P. Leavey Jr. Stanford, CA: Stanford University Press.
Derrida, Jacques. 2011. *Voice and Phenomenon: Introduction to the Problem of the Sign in Husserl's Phenomenology*. Translated by Leonard Lawlor. Evanston, IL: Northwestern University Press.
Derrida, Jacques. 2013. "The Night Watch (over 'the book of himself')." Translated by Pascale-Anne Brault and Michael Naas. In *Derrida and Joyce: Texts and Contexts*, edited by Andrew J. Mitchell and Sam Slote, 87–108. Albany, NY: SUNY Press.
Derrida, Jacques, and Geoffrey Bennington. 1999. *Derrida*. Chicago: University of Chicago Press.
Derrida, Jacques, and Anne Dufourmantelle. 2000. *Of Hospitality*. Translated by Rachel Bowlby. Stanford, CA: Stanford University Press.
Derrida, Jacques, and Maurizio Ferraris. 2001. *A Taste for the Secret*. Cambridge: Polity Press.
Derrida, Jacques, and Bernard Stiegler. 2002. *Echographies of Television: Filmed Interviews*. Translated by Jennifer Bajorek. Cambridge: Polity Press.
Dilthey, Wilhelm. 1990. *Die geistige Welt: Einleitung in die Philosophie des Lebens; Erste Hälfte; Abhandlungen zur Grundlegung der Geisteswissenschaften*, edited by Georg Misch, published as *Gesammelte Schriften Band V.* Kornwestheim: Vandenhoeck and Ruprecht.
Diprose, Rosalyn. 2009. "Women's Bodies Giving Time for Hospitality." *Hypatia* 24(2): 142–163.
Diprose, Rosalyn, and Ewa Płonowska Ziarek. 2013. "Time for Beginners: Natality, Biopolitics, and Political Theology." *philoSOPHIA* 3(2): 107–120.
Dobson, Andrew. 1996. "Representative Democracy and the Environment." In *Democracy and the Environment: Problems and Prospects*, edited by W. M. Lafferty and J. Meadowcroft, 125–148. Cheltenham, UK: Edward Elgar.
Drabinski, John. 2000. "The Possibility of an Ethical Politics: From Peace to Liturgy." *Philosophy and Social Criticism* 26(4): 49–73.
Drabinski, John. 2011. *Levinas and the Postcolonial: Race, Nation, Other*. Edinburgh: Edinburgh University Press.

Dryzek, John. 1996. *Democracy in Capitalist Times*. Oxford: Oxford University Press.
Durst, Margaret. 2004. "Birth and Natality in Hannah Arendt." In *Does the World Exist?*, Analecta Husserliana 79, edited by Anna Teresa Tymieniecka, 777–797. Dordrecht: Kluwer.
Düsing, Klaus. 2002. *Subjektivitaet und Freiheit: Untersuchungen zum Idealismus von Kant bis Hegel*. Stuttgart: Bad Cannstatt.
Dyke, Heather, ed. 2003. *Time and Ethics: Essays at the Intersection*. Dordrecht: Kluwer Academic.
Eatwell, John, Murray Milgate, Peter K. Newman, and Robert Harry Inglis. 2002. "Robinson Crusoe." In *The New Palgrave: A Dictionary of Economics*, 4:5629–5630. New York: Palgrave.
Eckersley, Robyn. 2004. *The Green State: Rethinking Democracy and Sovereignty*. Cambridge, MA: MIT Press.
Edelglass, William, and Christian Diehm, eds. 2012. *Facing Nature: Levinas and Environmental Thought*. Pittsburgh: Duquesne University Press.
Edelman, Lee. 2004. *No Future: Queer Theory and the Death Drive*. Durham, NC: Duke University Press.
Eisenstadt, Oona, and Claire Elise Katz. 2016. "The Faceless Palestinian: A History of an Error." *Telos* 174 (Spring): 9–32.
Eliade, Mircea. 1954. *Cosmos and History: The Myth of the Eternal Return*. Translated by W. R. Trask. Princeton, NJ: Princeton University Press.
Eliade, Mircea. 1992. *Myths, Dreams and Mysteries: The Encounter between Contemporary Faiths and Archaic Realities*. Magnolia, MA: Peter Smith.
Eliade, Mircea. 1996. *Patterns in Comparative Religion*. Lincoln: University of Nebraska Press.
Elias, Amy J. 2000. "Holding Word Mongers on a Lunge Line: The Postmodernist Writings of Gerald Vizenor and Ishmael Reed." In *Loosening the Seams: Interpretations of Gerald Vizenor*, edited by A. Robert Lee, 85–108. Bowling Green, KY: Bowling Green State University Press.
Fabian, Johannes. 2014. *Time and the Other: How Anthropology Makes Its Object*. New York: Columbia University Press.
Fagenblat, Michael. 2010. *A Covenant of Creatures: Levinas's Philosophy of Judaism*. Stanford, CA: Stanford University Press.
Feiler, Daniel, and Kimberly A. Wade-Benzoni. 2009. "Death and Intergenerational Behavior: A Tale of Power and Immortality." In *The Impact of 9/11 on Psychology and Education*, edited by Matthew Morgan, 187–200. London: Palgrave Macmillan.
Feinberg, Joel. 1970. "The Nature and Value of Rights." *Journal of Value Inquiry* 4:243–257.

Fishkin, James S., and Robert E. Goodin, eds. 2009. *Population and Political Theory*. Chichester, UK: Wiley-Blackwell.
Floyd, Jonathan. 2016. "Analytics and Continentals: Divided by Nature but United by Praxis?" *European Journal of Political Theory* 15(2): 155–171.
Freeman, Elizabeth. 2010. *Time Binds: Queer Temporalities, Queer Histories*. Durham, NC: Duke University Press.
Freud, Sigmund. 1946. "Our Attitude towards Death." In *Thoughts for the Times on War and Death*, edited and translated by James Strachey, 289–300. London: Hogarth Press. Originally published as "Unser Verhältnis zum Tode," in *Zeitgemäßes über Krieg und Tod* (Frankfurt am Main: S. Fischer, 1915).
Fritsch, Matthias. 2000. "Levinas on Ethical Responsibility after a History of Violence." *International Studies in Philosophy* 32(1): 123–145.
Fritsch, Matthias. 2005. *The Promise of Memory: History and Politics in Marx, Benjamin, and Derrida*. Albany, NY: SUNY Press.
Fritsch, Matthias. 2006a. "Equal Consideration of All—an Aporetic Project?" *Philosophy and Social Criticism* 32(3): 299–323.
Fritsch, Matthias. 2006b. "Cura et Casus: Heidegger and Augustine on the Care of the Self." In *The Influence of Augustine on Heidegger: The Emergence of an Augustinian Phenomenology*, edited by Craig J. N. de Paulo, 89–113. New York: Edwin Mellen Press.
Fritsch, Matthias. 2007. "Wide Reflective Equilibrium and Critical Social Theory." In *Reason and Emancipation: Essays in Honour of Kai Nielsen*, edited by Michel Seymour and Matthias Fritsch, 95–110. New York: Humanity Books.
Fritsch, Matthias. 2008. "Antagonism and Democratic Citizenship (Schmitt, Mouffe, Derrida)." *Research in Phenomenology* 38(2): 174–197.
Fritsch, Matthias. 2010. "Equality and Singularity in Justification and Application Discourses." *European Journal of Political Theory* 9(3): 328–346.
Fritsch, Matthias. 2011a. "Deconstructive Aporias: Both Quasi-Transcendental and Normative." *Continental Philosophy Review* 44(4): 439–468.
Fritsch, Matthias. 2011b. "Taking Turns: Democracy to Come and Intergenerational Justice." *Derrida Today* 4(2): 148–172.
Fritsch, Matthias. 2012. "Derrida on the Death Penalty." *Southern Journal of Philosophy* 50:56–73.
Fritsch, Matthias. 2013a. "Europe's Constitution for the Unborn." In *Europe after Derrida*, edited by Agnes Czajka and Bora Isyar, 80–94. Edinburgh: Edinburgh University Press.
Fritsch, Matthias. 2013b. "Sources of Morality in Habermas's Recent Work on Religion and Freedom." In *The Limits of Secularism: Engagements with Jürgen Habermas on Religion and the Public Sphere*, edited by Craig Calhoun, Eduardo Mendieta, and Jonathan VanAntwerpen, 277–300. Cambridge: Polity Press.

Fritsch, Matthias. 2015. "Rational Justification and Human Vulnerability: On the 'All-Affected' Principle in Discursive Ethics." *Political Theory* 43(6): 805–821.
Fritsch, Matthias. 2017a. "Between Generational Presentism and Reproductive Futurism: How to Be Concerned about the Future of Children without Becoming Repressively Heteronormative." In *Responsabilità verso le generazioni future: Una sfida al diritto, all'etica e alla politica*, edited by Fabio Ciaramelli and Ferdinando G. Menga, 63–88. Naples: Editoriale Scientifica.
Fritsch, Matthias. 2017b. "'La Justice doit porter au-delà de la vie présente': Derrida on Ethics between Generations." *Symposium* 21(1): 231–253.
Fritsch, Matthias. 2018. "An Eco-Deconstructive Account of the Emergence of Normativity in 'Nature.'" In *Eco-Deconstruction: Derrida and Environmental Philosophy*, edited by Matthias Fritsch, Philippe Lynes, and David Wood, 279–302. New York: Fordham University Press.
Fritsch, Matthias. Forthcoming. "Asymmetrical Reciprocity in Intergenerational Justice." In *Future Design: Incorporating Preferences of Future Generations for Sustainability*, edited by Tatsuyoshi Saijo. Berlin: Springer.
Fritsch, Matthias, Philippe Lynes, and David Wood, eds. 2018. *Eco-Deconstruction: Derrida and Environmental Philosophy*. New York: Fordham University Press.
Fritsch, Matthias, and Ferdinando Menga. 2017. "Phenomenology and Responsibility toward Future Generations." Editors' introduction to "Phenomenology and Intergenerational Justice," special issue, *Metodo: International Studies in Phenomenology and Philosophy* 5(2): 7–16.
Fritsche, Johannes. 1994. "The Unity of Time in Aristotle." In "In Memoriam David Rapport Lachterman," special issue, *Graduate Faculty Philosophy Journal* 17(1–2): 101–125.
Gaertner, David. 2013. "'Redress as a Gift': Historical Reparations and the Logic of the Gift in Roy Miki's Redress." In *Tracing the Lines: A Symposium to Honour Roy Miki*, edited by Christine Kim, Maia Joseph, Larissa Lai, and Chris Lee, 67–75. Vancouver: Talonbooks.
Gaertner, David. 2014. "Gift Theory and the Settler State." *Novel Alliances: Allied Perspectives on Literature, Art, and New Media* (blog). https://novelalliances.com/2014/11/18/gift-theory-and-the-settler-state/.
Gardiner, Stephen. 2006. "A Perfect Moral Storm: Climate Change, Intergenerational Ethics and the Problem of Moral Corruption." *Environmental Values* 15(3): 397–413.
Gardiner, Stephen. 2009. "A Contract on Future Generations?" In *Intergenerational Justice*, edited by Axel Gosseries and Lukas H. Meyer, 77–118. Oxford: Oxford University Press.
Gardiner, Stephen. 2011a. *A Perfect Moral Storm: The Ethical Tragedy of Climate Change*. Oxford: Oxford University Press.
Gardiner, Stephen. 2011b. "Is No One Responsible for Global Environmental

Tragedy? Climate Change as a Challenge to Our Ethical Concepts." In *The Ethics of Global Climate Change*, edited by D. G. Arnold, 38–59. Cambridge: Cambridge University Press.

Gardiner, Stephen, Simon Caney, Dale Jamieson, and Henry Shue, eds. 2010. *Climate Ethics: Essential Readings*. Oxford: Oxford University Press.

Gardiner, Stephen, and David Weisbach. 2016. *Debating Climate Ethics*. Oxford: Oxford University Press.

Garvey, James. 2008. *The Ethics of Climate Change*. London: Continuum.

Gasché, Rodolphe. 1986. *The Tain of the Mirror: Derrida and the Philosophy of Reflection*. Cambridge, MA: Harvard University Press.

Gauthier, David. 1986. *Morals by Agreement*. Oxford: Clarendon Press.

Gethmann, Carl F. 1993. *Dasein: Erkennen und Handeln; Heidegger im phänomenologischen Kontext*. Berlin: De Gruyter.

Giddens, Anthony. 2009. *The Politics of Climate Change*. Cambridge: Polity Press.

Gilligan, Carol. 1982. *In A Different Voice: Psychological Theory and Women's Development*. Cambridge, MA: Harvard University Press.

Gonzalez-Ricoy, Inigo, and Axel Gosseries, eds. 2017. *Institutions for Future Generations*. Oxford: Oxford University Press.

Goodin, Robert. 2003. *Reflective Democracy*. Oxford: Oxford University Press.

Gosseries, Axel. 2001. "What Do We Owe the Next Generation(s)?" *Loyola of Los Angeles Law Review* 35(1): 293–354.

Gosseries, Axel. 2009. "Three Models of Intergenerational Reciprocity." In *Intergenerational Justice*, edited by Axel Gosseries and Lukas H. Meyer, 119–146. Oxford: Oxford University Press.

Gosseries, Axel. 2010. "On Future Generations' Future Rights." In *Population and Political Theory*, edited by James S. Fishkin and Robert E. Goodin, 104–134. Chichester, UK: Wiley-Blackwell.

Gosseries, Axel, and Lukas H. Meyer. 2009. "Intergenerational Justice and Its Challenges." In *Intergenerational Justice*, edited by Axel Gosseries and Lukas H. Meyer, 1–22. Oxford: Oxford University Press.

Gosseries, Axel, and Lukas H. Meyer, eds. 2009. *Intergenerational Justice*. Oxford: Oxford University Press.

Graeber, David. 2001. *Toward An Anthropological Theory of Value: The False Coin of Our Own Dreams*. New York: Palgrave.

Gratton, Peter, and Marie-Eve Morin, eds. 2012. *Jean-Luc Nancy and Plural Thinking: Expositions of World, Ontology, Politics, and Sense*. Albany, NY: SUNY Press.

Grosz, Elizabeth. 2004. *The Nick of Time: Politics, Evolution, and the Untimely*. Durham, NC: Duke University Press.

Guenther, Lisa. 2006a. *The Gift of the Other: Levinas and the Politics of Reproduction*. Albany, NY: State University of New York Press.

Guenther, Lisa. 2006b. "'Like a Maternal Body': Emmanuel Levinas and the Motherhood of Moses." *Hypatia* 21(1): 119–136.
Guenther, Lisa. 2008. "Being-from-Others: Reading Heidegger after Cavarero." *Hypatia* 23(1): 99–118.
Guenther, Lisa. 2012. "Fecundity and Natal Alienation: Rethinking Kinship with Emmanuel Levinas and Orlando Patterson" *Levinas Studies* 7:1–19.
Gürtler, Sabine. 2001. *Elementare Ethik: Alterität, Generativität und Geschlechterverhältnis bei Emmanuel Lévinas.* Munich: Wilhelm Fink Verlag.
Habermas, Jürgen. 1987. *Theorie des kommunikativen Handelns.* 2 vols. Frankfurt: Suhrkamp. Translated by Thomas McCarthy as *Theory of Communicative Action*, 2 vols. (Boston: Beacon Press, 1987).
Habermas, Jürgen. 1988. *The Philosophical Discourse of Modernity.* Translated by Frederick G. Lawrence. Cambridge, MA: MIT Press.
Habermas, Jürgen. 1998. *The Inclusion of the Other.* Edited by Ciaran Cronin and Pablo de Greiff. Cambridge, MA: MIT Press.
Habib, Allen. 2013. "Sharing the Earth: Sustainability and the Currency of Inter-Generational Environmental Justice." *Environmental Values* 22:751–764.
Hägglund, Martin. 2004. "The Necessity of Discrimination: Disjoining Derrida and Levinas." *Diacritics* 34(1): 40–71.
Hägglund, Martin. 2008. *Radical Atheism: Derrida and the Time of Life.* Stanford, CA: Stanford University Press.
Hägglund, Martin. 2012. *Dying for Time: Proust, Woolf, Nabokov.* Cambridge, MA: Harvard University Press.
Hägglund, Martin. 2016. "The Trace of Time: A Critique of Vitalism." *Derrida Today* 9(1): 36–46.
Halberstam, Judith. 2005. *In a Queer Time and Place: Transgender Bodies, Subcultural Lives.* New York: New York University Press.
Hampton, Jean. 1988. *Hobbes and the Social Contract Tradition.* Cambridge: Cambridge University Press.
Hanson, Jeffrey. 2010. "Returning (to) the Gift of Death: Violence and History in Derrida and Levinas." *International Journal for Philosophy of Religion* 67(1): 1–15.
Harari, Yuval Noah. 2014. *Sapiens: A Brief History of Humankind.* Toronto: McClelland and Stewart.
Haraway, Donna. 2016. *Staying with the Trouble: Making Kin in the Chthulucene.* Durham, NC: Duke University Press.
Harcourt, J. L., G. Sweetman, A. Manica, and R. A. Johnstone. 2010. "Pairs of Fish Resolve Conflicts over Coordinated Movement by Taking Turns." *Current Biology* 20(2): 156–160.
Hardin, Garrett. 1968. "The Tragedy of the Commons." *Science* 162(3859): 1243–1248.

Harris, John. 2007. *Enhancing Evolution: The Ethical Case for Making Better People*. Princeton, NJ: Princeton University Press.
Harvey, David. 1990. *The Condition of Postmodernity*. Oxford: Blackwell.
Hatley, James. 2004. "The Uncanny Goodness of Being Edible to Bears." In *Rethinking Nature: Essays in Environmental Philosophy*, edited by Bruce Foltz and Robert Frodeman, 13–31. Bloomington: Indiana University Press.
Hauskeller, Michael. Forthcoming. "Death and Meaning." In *Trans-Humanism and the Philosophy of Immortality*, edited by Stephen Burwood, Daniel Came, and Alexander Ornella. Oxford: Oxford University Press.
Hayashi, Makoto. 2012. "Turn Allocation and Turn Sharing." In *The Handbook of Conversation Analysis*, edited by Jack Sidnell and Tanya Stivers, 167–190. Chichester, UK: John Wiley and Sons.
Heath, Joseph. 1997. "Intergenerational Cooperation and Distributive Justice." *Canadian Journal of Philosophy* 27(3): 361–376.
Heath, Joseph. 2008. *Following the Rules: Practical Reasoning and Deontic Constraint*. Oxford: Oxford University Press.
Heidegger, Martin. 2002a. "Wilhelm Dilthey's Research and the Struggle for a Historical Worldview." In *Supplements: From the Earliest Essays to "Being and Time" and Beyond*, edited by John van Buren, 147–176. Albany, NY: SUNY Press.
Heidegger, Martin. 2002b. "Anaximander's Saying." In *Off the Beaten Track*, translated and edited by Julian Young and Kenneth Haynes, 242–281. Cambridge: Cambridge University Press.
Heidegger, Martin. 2010. *Der Spruch des Anaximander*. Gesamtausgabe 78. Frankfurt: Klostermann.
Held, Virginia. 2006. *The Ethics of Care: Personal, Political, and Global*. Oxford: Oxford University Press.
Heller-Roazen, Daniel. 2007. *The Inner Touch: Archaeology of a Sensation*. New York: Zone Books.
Hemmings, Clare. 2011. *Why Stories Matter: The Political Grammar of Feminist Theory*. Durham, NC: Duke University Press.
Hénaff, Marcel. 2009. "The Aporia of Pure Giving and the Aim of Reciprocity: On Derrida's *Given Time*." In *Derrida and the Time of the Political*, edited by Pheng Cheah and Suzanne Guerlac, 215–234. Durham, NC: Duke University Press.
Heyd, David. 1988. "Procreation and Value: Can Ethics Deal with Futurity Problems?" *Philosophia* 18(2–3): 151–170.
Heyward, Clare. 2008. "Can the All-Affected Principle Include Future Persons? Green Deliberative Democracy and the Non-Identity Problem." *Environmental Politics* 17(4): 625–643.
Holland, Alan. 1997. "Substitutability: Or Why Strong Sustainability Is Weak

and Absurdly Strong Sustainability Is not Absurd." In *Valuing Nature?*, edited by John Foster, 119–134. London: Routledge.

Holland, Alan. 1999. "Sustainable Development: Should We Start from Here?" In *Fairness and Futurity*, edited by Andrew Dobson, 46–68. Oxford: Oxford University Press.

Honig, Bonnie. 1991. "Declarations of Independence: Arendt and Derrida on the Problem of Founding a Republic." *American Political Science Review* 85:97–113.

Horkheimer, Max. 1974. *Eclipse of Reason*. London: Continuum.

Horkheimer, Max, and Theodor Adorno. 2002. *Dialectic of Enlightenment*. Translated by Edmund Jephcott. Stanford, CA: Stanford University Press.

Hourdequin, Marion. 2010. "Climate, Collective Action, and Individual Ethical Obligations." *Environmental Values* 19(4): 443–464.

Howarth, Richard B. 1992. "Intergenerational Justice and the Chain of Obligation." *Environmental Values* 1(2): 133–140.

Hügli, Anton, and Byung Chul Han. 2001. "Heideggers Todesanalyse." In *Martin Heidegger: Sein und Zeit; Klassiker Auslegen*, edited by Thomas Rentsch, 133–148. Berlin: Akademie Verlag.

Humphrey, Mathew. 2009. "Mapping the Moral Future: Environmental Problems and What We Owe to Future Generations." *Res Publica* 15:85–95.

Irigaray, Luce. 1993a. "The Fecundity of the Caress: A Reading of Levinas, *Totality and Infinity*, "Phenomenology of Eros." In *An Ethics of Sexual Difference*, 185–217. Ithaca, NY: Cornell University Press.

Irigaray, Luce. 1993b. *An Ethics of Sexual Difference*. Translated by Carolyn Burke and Gillian C. Gill. Ithaca, NY: Cornell University Press.

Irigaray, Luce. 1999. *The Forgetting of Air in Martin Heidegger*. Translated by Mary Beth Mader. Austin: University of Texas Press.

Jamieson, Dale. 2002. "Ethics, Public Policy, and Global Warming." In *Morality's Progress*, 31–42. Oxford: Clarendon Press.

Jamieson, Dale. 2013. "Jack, Jill, and Jane in a Perfect Moral Storm." *Philosophy and Public Issues*, n.s., 3(1): 1–17.

Jamieson, Dale. 2014. *Reason in a Dark Time: Why the Struggle against Climate Change Failed—and What It Means for Our Future*. Oxford: Oxford University Press.

Johnson, Genevieve Fuji. 2007. "Discursive Democracy in the Transgenerational Context." *Contemporary Political Theory* 6:67–85.

Jonas, Hans. 1984. *The Imperative of Responsibility: In Search of Ethics for the Technological Age*. Translated by Hans Jonas and David Herr. Chicago: University of Chicago Press.

Jonas, Hans. 1996. *Mortality and Morality: A Search for Good after Auschwitz*. Edited by Lawrence Vogel. Evanston, IL: Northwestern University Press.

Joy, Morny, ed. 2013. *Women and the Gift*. Bloomington: Indiana University Press.

Kamuf, Peggy. 2012. "Protocol: Death Penalty Addiction." *Southern Journal of Philosophy* 50(1): 5–19.

Kant, Immanuel. 1900ff. *Gesammelte Schriften*. Edited by Preussische Akademie der Wissenschaften (Akademie-Ausgabe). 24 vols. Berlin: De Gruyter.

Kant, Immanuel. 1948. *Groundwork of the Metaphysics of Morals*. Translated by H. J. Paton. New York: Harper.

Kant, Immanuel. 1992. *Critique of Practical Reason*. Edited and translated by Paul Guyer and Allen W. Wood. Cambridge: Cambridge University Press.

Kant, Immanuel. 1996. "Perpetual Peace." In *Practical Philosophy*, edited and translated by Mary J. Gregor, 311–352. Cambridge: Cambridge University Press.

Kant, Immanuel. 1998. *The Critique of Pure Reason*. Edited and translated by Paul Guyer and Allen W. Wood. Cambridge: Cambridge University Press.

Kant, Immanuel. 2012. "Universal Natural History and a Theory of the Heavens." In *Natural Science*, edited by Eric Watkins, translated by Olaf Reinhard et al. Cambridge: Cambridge University Press.

Kant, Immanuel. 2017. *The Metaphysics of Morals*. Edited by Lara Denis and translated by Mary J. Gregor. Cambridge: Cambridge University Press.

Kass, Leon. 2002. "L'Chaim and Its Limits: Why Not Immortality?" In *Life, Liberty and the Defence of Dignity: The Challenge for Bioethics*, 257–274. San Francisco: Encounter.

Kass, Leon. 2003. "Ageless Bodies, Happy Souls: Biotechnology and the Pursuit of Perfection." *New Atlantis* 1:9–28.

Kavka, Gregory. 1981. "The Paradox of Future Individuals." *Philosophy and Public Affairs* 11(2): 93–112.

Kittay, Eva Feder. 1999. *Love's Labor: Essays on Women, Equality and Dependency*. London: Routledge.

King, Anthony, and Ivor Crewe. 2014. *The Blunders of Our Governments*. London: Oneworld.

Kingston, Ewan. 2014. "Climate Change as a Three-Part Ethical Problem: A Response to Jamieson and Gardiner." *Science and Engineering Ethics* 20 (4): 1129–1148.

Kirby, Vicki. 2018. "Un/limited Ecologies." In *Eco-Deconstruction: Derrida and Environmental Philosophy*, edited by Matthias Fritsch, Philippe Lynes, and David Wood, 81–98. New York: Fordham University Press.

Klein, Naomi. 2014. *This Changes Everything: Capitalism vs. the Climate*. Toronto: Knopf Canada.

Kleinberg, Ethan. 2012. "Back to Where We've Never Been: Heidegger, Levinas, and Derrida on Tradition and History." *History and Theory* 51(4): 114–135.

Klun, Branko. 2007. "Der Tod als Grenze: Zu einer Schlüsselfrage von Emmanuel Levinas." *Prolegomena* 6(2): 253–266.
Köveker, Dietmar. 2004. "Levinas als Kritiker Heideggers." *Dialektik: Zeitschrift für Kulturwissenschaft* 2:88–101.
Kolm, Serge-Christophe. 2006. "Reciprocity: Its Scope, Rationales and Consequences." In *Handbook of the Economics of Giving, Altruism and Reciprocity*, vol. 1, edited by S. Kolm and J. Mercier Ythier, 371–541. Amsterdam: Elsevier.
Kramvig, Britt. 2015. "Gifts of Dreams." In *Idioms of Sami Health and Healing*, edited by Barbara Helen Miller, 183–208. Edmonton: University of Alberta Press.
Krell, David Farrell. 2006. "All You Can't Eat: Derrida's Course 'Rhétoriques du Cannibalisme (1990–1991).'" *Research in Phenomenology* 36:130–180.
Kroeber, Karl. 2008. "Why It's a Good Thing Gerald Vizenor Is Not an Indian." In *Survivance: Narratives of Native Presence*, edited by Gerald Vizenor, 25–38. Lincoln: University of Nebraska Press.
Krupat, Arnold. 1987. "Post-Structuralism and Oral Literature." In *Recovering the Word: Essays on Native American Literature*, edited by Arnold Krupat and Brian Swann, 113–128. Berkeley: University of California Press.
Kuokkanen, Rauna Johanna. 2007. *Reshaping the University: Responsibility, Indigenous Epistemes, and the Logic of the Gift*. Vancouver: University of British Columbia Press.
Lawlor, Leonard. 2007. *This Is Not Sufficient: An Essay on Animality and Human Nature in Derrida*. New York: Columbia University Press.
Lenman, James. 2000. "Consequentialism and Cluelessness." *Philosophy and Public Affairs* 29(4): 342–370.
Leo, Greg. 2017. "Taking Turns." *Games and Economic Behavior* 102:525–547.
Lévi-Strauss, Claude. 1987. *Introduction to the Work of Marcel Mauss*. Translated by Felicity Baker. London: Routledge.
Levinas, Emmanuel. 1988. *À l'heure des nations*. Paris: Minuit.
Levinas, Emmanuel. 1995. *Outside the Subject*. Translated by Michael Smith. Stanford, CA: Stanford University Press.
Levinas, Emmanuel. 1997. *Difficult Freedom: Essays on Judaism*. Translated by Séan Hand. Baltimore: Johns Hopkins University Press.
Levinas, Emmanuel. 2001. *Is It Righteous to Be? Interviews with Emmanuel Levinas*. Edited by Jill Robbins. Stanford, CA: Stanford University Press.
Levinas, Emmanuel, and Paul Ricoeur. 1998. "Entretien Levinas—Ricoeur." In *Emmanuel Levinas: Philosophe et Pedagogue*, 9–28. Paris: Nadir.
Li, Victor. 2007. "Elliptical Interruptions: Or, Why Derrida Prefers Mondialisation to Globalization." *CR: The New Centennial Review* 7(2): 141–154.
Liebsch, Burkhard. 2001. "Überlieferung als Versprechen: Rudimente einer Ethik des weitergegebenen Wortes in der gegenwärtigen Phänomenologie

und Hermeneutik." In *Vernunft im Zeichen des Fremden: Zur Philosophie von Bernhard Waldenfels*, edited by Matthias Fischer, Hans-Dieter Gondek, and Burkhard Liebsch, 304–344. Frankfurt am Main: Suhrkamp.

Liebsch, Burkhard. 2017. "Generativität, Generationen und generative, intergenerationelle Solidarität." In "Phenomenology and Intergenerational Justice," edited by Matthias Fritsch and Ferdinando Menga, special issue, *Metodo: International Studies in Phenomenology and Philosophy* 5(22): 124–160.

Lin, Yael. 2013. *The Intersubjectivity of Time: Levinas and Infinite Responsibility*. Pittsburgh: Duquesne University Press.

Llewelyn, John. 1991. *The Middle Voice of Ecological Conscience: A Chiasmic Reading of Responsibility in the Neighbourhood of Levinas, Heidegger and Others*. London: Macmillan.

Locke, John. 1988. *Two Treatises of Government*. Edited by Peter Laslett. Cambridge: Cambridge University Press.

Lynes, Philippe. 2018. "The Posthuman Promise of the Earth." In *Eco-Deconstruction: Derrida and Environmental Philosophy*, edited by Matthias Fritsch, Philippe Lynes, and David Wood, 63–80. New York: Fordham University Press.

Macpherson, C. B. 1962. *The Political Theory of Possessive Individualism: Hobbes to Locke*. Oxford: Clarendon Press.

Malabou, Catherine, and Jacques Derrida. 2004. *Counterpath: Traveling with Jacques Derrida*. Translated by David Wills. Stanford, CA: Stanford University Press.

Margel, Serge. 1995. *Le Tombeau du dieu artisan*. Paris: Minuit, 1995. Translated by Philippe Lynes as *The Tomb of the Artisan God: On Plato's "Timaeus"* (Minneapolis: University of Minnesota Press, forthcoming).

Markovits, Elizabeth. 2009. "Birthrights: Freedom, Responsibility, and Democratic Comportment in Aeschylus' *Oresteia*." *American Political Science Review* 103(3): 427–441.

Mauss, Marcel. 1972. *A General Theory of Magic*. Translated by Robert Brain. London: Routledge.

MacKenzie, Michael K. 2016. "Institutional Design and Sources of Short-Termism." In *Institutions for Future Generations*, edited by Inigo Gonzalez-Ricoy and Axel Gosseries, 24–48. Oxford: Oxford University Press.

McCarthy, Thomas. 2009. *Race, Empire, and the Idea of Human Development*. Cambridge: Cambridge University Press.

McCormick, Hugh. 2009. "Intergenerational Justice and the Non-Reciprocity Problem." *Political Studies* 57:451–458.

McMullin, Irene. 2013. *Time and the Shared World: Heidegger on Social Relations*. Evanston, IL: Northwestern University Press.

Mei, Todd S. 2017. *Land and the Given Economy. The Hermeneutics and Phenomenology of Dwelling.* Evanston, IL: Northwestern University Press.
Mensch, James. 2015. *Levinas's Existential Analytic: A Commentary on "Totality and Infinity."* Evanston, IL: Northwestern University Press.
Metz, Thaddeus. 2003. "The Immortality Requirement for Life's Meaning." *Ratio* 16:161–177.
Meyer, Lukas, and H. Dominic Roser. 2009. "Enough for the Future." In *Intergenerational Justice*, edited by Axel Gosseries and Lukas H. Meyer, 219–248. Oxford: Oxford University Press.
Miller, J. Hillis. 2006. "Derrida's Remains." *Mosaic: An Interdisciplinary Critical Journal* 39(3): 197–211.
Mills, Charles. 2014. "White Time: The Chronic Injustice of Ideal Theory." *Du Bois Review: Social Science Research on Race* 11(1): 27–42.
Moellendorf, Darrel, and Heather Widdows, eds. 2015. *The Routledge Handbook of Global Ethics.* London: Routledge.
Moore, Jason W., ed. 2016. *Anthropocene or Capitalocene? Nature, History, and the Crisis of Capitalism.* Oakland, CA: PM Press.
Morgan, Kenneth. 2008. "Slave Women and Reproduction in Jamaica, ca. 1776–1834." In *Women and Slavery: The Modern Atlantic*, vol. 2, edited by Gwyn Campbell, Suzanne Miers, and Joseph Calder Miller, 27–53. Athens: Ohio University Press.
Morgan, Matthew, ed. 2009. *The Impact of 9/11 on Psychology and Education.* New York: Palgrave MacMillan.
Morgan, Michael. 2007. *Discovering Levinas.* Cambridge: Cambridge University Press.
Morgan, Michael. 2016. *Levinas's Ethical Politics.* Bloomington: Indiana University Press.
Mulgan, Tim. 2015. "Population." In *The Routledge Handbook of Global Ethics*, edited by Darrel Moellendorf and Heather Widdows, 428–440. London: Routledge.
Myers, Tim Christion. 2015. "Review of Dale Jamieson, *Reason in a Dark Time.*" *Environmental Philosophy* 12(1): 126–130.
Naas, Michael. 2008. *Derrida from Now On.* New York: Fordham University Press.
Naess, Arne. 1973. "The Shallow and the Deep, Long-Range Ecology Movement." *Inquiry* 16:95–100.
Nagel, Thomas. 1979. *The Possibility of Altruism: Revised Edition.* Princeton, NJ: Princeton University Press.
Nancy, Jean-Luc. 2007. *The Creation of the World, or Globalization.* Translated by François Raffoul and David Pettigrew. Albany, NY: SUNY Press.

Nielsen, Kai. 1993. "Relativism and Wide Reflective Equilibrium." *The Monist* 76(3): 316–332.

Nietzsche, Friedrich. 2005. *Thus Spoke Zarathustra*. Translated by Graham Parkes. Oxford: Oxford University Press.

Noddings, Nel. 2002. *Starting at Home: Caring and Social Policy*. Berkeley: University of California Press.

Nolt, John. 2011. "Greenhouse Gas Emissions and the Domination of Posterity." In *The Ethics of Global Climate Change*, edited by Denis Arnold, 61–76. Cambridge: Cambridge University Press.

Nowak, Martin, and Robert Highfield. 2011. *Supercooperators: Why We Need Each Other to Succeed*. New York: Simon and Schuster.

Nozick, Robert. 1974. *Anarchy, State and Utopia*. Oxford: Blackwell.

Nussbaum, Martha. 1990. *Love's Knowledge: Essays on Philosophy and Literature*. Oxford: Oxford University Press.

Nussbaum, Martha. 1994. *Therapy of Desire: Theory and Practice in Hellenistic Ethics*. Princeton, NJ: Princeton University Press.

Nussbaum, Martha. 1997. *Poetic Justice: The Literary Imagination and Public Life*. Boston: Beacon Press.

Nussbaum, Martha. 1999. "The Feminist Critique of Liberalism." In *Women's Voices, Women's Rights: Oxford Amnesty Lectures*, edited by A. Jeffries, 13–56. Boulder, CO: Westview Press.

Nussbaum, Martha. 2001. "The Enduring Significance of John Rawls." *Chronicle of Higher Education*, Section 2, July 20, B7–B9.

Nussbaum, Martha. 2006. *Frontiers of Justice*. Cambridge, MA: Harvard University Press.

Nussbaum, Martha. 2013. "The Damage of Death." In *The Metaphysics and Ethics of Death*, edited by James Stacey Taylor, 25–43. Oxford: Oxford University Press.

O'Byrne, Anne. 2010. *Natality and Finitude*. Bloomington: Indiana University Press.

Oliver, Kelly. 2014. "The Excesses of Earth in Kant's Philosophy of Property." *The Comparatist* 38:23–40.

Oliver, Kelly. 2015. *Earth and World: Philosophy after the Apollo Mission*. New York: Columbia University Press.

Oliver, Kelly. 2018. "Earth: Love It or Leave It." In *Eco-Deconstruction: Derrida and Environmental Philosophy*, edited by Matthias Fritsch, Philippe Lynes, and David Wood. New York: Fordham University Press.

Osborne, Peter. 1995. *The Politics of Time: Modernity and Avant-Garde*. London: Verso.

Page, Edward A. 2006. *Climate Change, Justice, and Future Generations*. Cheltenham, UK: Edward Elgar.

Page, Edward A. 2007. "Fairness on the Day after Tomorrow: Justice, Reciprocity, and Global Climate Change." *Political Studies* 55(1): 225–242.
Paradiso-Michau, Michael. 2007. "Ethical Alterity and Asymmetrical Reciprocity: A Levinasian Reading of *Works of Love*." *Continental Philosophy Review* 40(3): 331–347.
Parfit, Derek. 1984. *Reasons and Persons*. Oxford: Clarendon Press.
Partridge, Ernest. 1978. "Beyond 'Just Savings.'" Unpublished manuscript. www.igc.org/gadfly/papers/swsabf.htm.
Passmore, J. A. 1974. *Man's Responsibility for Nature*. New York: Scribner.
Perpich, Diane. 2008. *The Ethics of Emmanuel Levinas*. Stanford, CA: Stanford University Press.
Peters, Philip G. 2009. "Implications of the Nonidentity Problem for State Regulation of Reproductive Liberty." In *Harming Future Persons: Ethics, Genetics and the Nonidentity Problem*, edited by Melinda A. Roberts and David T. Wasserman. Berlin: Springer.
Pitcher, George. 1984. "The Misfortunes of the Dead." *American Philosophical Quarterly* 21:183–188.
Plato. 1997. *Complete Works*. Edited by John M. Cooper and D. S. Hutchinson. Indianapolis: Hackett.
Plato. 1991. *Plato's Republic*. Translated by Allan Bloom. 2nd ed. New York: Basic Books.
Plumwood, Val. 2012. *The Eye of the Crocodile*. Edited by Lorraine Shannon. Canberra: Australian National University E-Press.
Pogge, Thomas. 1995. "How Should Human Rights Be Conceived?" *Jahrbuch für Recht und Ethik* 3:103–120.
Przeworski, Adam. 2010. *Democracy and the Limits of Self-Government*. New York: Cambridge University Press.
Przeworski, Adam, and Michael Wallerstein. 1988. "Structural Dependence of the State on Capital." *American Political Science Review* 82:11–29.
Raffoul, François. 2010. *The Origins of Responsibility*. Bloomington: Indiana University Press.
Rawls, John. 1971. *A Theory of Justice*. Cambridge, MA: Harvard University Press.
Rawls, John. 1996. *Political Liberalism*. New York: Columbia University Press.
Raworth, Kate. 2017. *Doughnut Economics: Seven Ways to Think like a 21st-Century Economist*. White River Junction, VT: Chelsea Green.
Ricoeur, Paul. 1992. *Oneself as Another*. Translated by Kathleen Blamey. Chicago: University of Chicago Press.
Roberts, Melinda A., and David T. Wasserman, eds. 2009. *Harming Future Persons: Ethics, Genetics and the Nonidentity Problem*. Berlin: Springer.
Rolland, Jacques. 1998. "Death in Its Negativity." *Graduate Faculty Philosophy Journal* 20(2): 461–494.

Rosa, Hartmut. 2010. *Alienation and Acceleration: Towards a Critical Theory of Late-Modern Temporality*. Ann Arbor: University of Michigan Press.

Rosa, Hartmut. 2012. *Weltbeziehungen im Zeitalter der Beschleunigung: Umrisse einer neuen Gesellschaftskritik*. Frankfurt: Suhrkamp.

Rosemont, Henry. 1991. "Rights-Bearing Individuals and Role-Bearing Persons." In *Rules, Rituals, and Responsibility: Essays Dedicated to Herbert Fingarette*, edited by Mary I. Bockover. La Salle, IL: Open Court.

Rosenthal, Irene. 2016. "Ontology and Political Theory: A Critical Encounter between Rawls and Foucault." *European Journal of Political Theory*. DOI: https://doi.org/10.1177/1474885116659633.

Rottenberg, Elizabeth. 2011. "Devouring Figures. The Last Seminars of Jacques Derrida." *Philosophy Today* 55:177–182.

Routley, Richard. 1973. "Is There a Need for a New, an Environmental, Ethic?" *Proceedings of the XVth World Congress of Philosophy* 1:205–210.

Routley, Richard, and Val Routley. 1979. "Nuclear Energy and Obligations to the Future." *Inquiry* 21:133–179.

Ruddick, Sarah. 1989. *Maternal Thinking: Toward a Politics of Peace*. New York: Ballantine Books.

Ruin, Hans. 2005. "Contributions to Philosophy." In *A Companion to Heidegger*, edited by Hubert L. Dreyfus and Mark A. Wrathall. London: Blackwell.

Rutte, Claudia, and Thomas Pfeiffer. 2009. "Evolution of Reciprocal Altruism by Copying Observed Behaviour." *Current Science* 97(11): 1572–1573.

Saghafi, Kas. 2016. "The Master Trembles: Sacrifice, Hierarchy, and Ontology in Derrida's 'Remain(s).'" *Derrida Today* 9(2): 124–138.

Sahlins, Marshall. 1972. *Stone Age Economics*. Chicago: Aldine.

Sallis, John. 1999. *Chorology. On Beginning in Plato's "Timaeus."* Bloomington: Indiana University Press.

Sanford, Stella. 2001. "Masculine Mothers? Maternity in Levinas and Plato." In *Feminist Interpretations of Emmanuel Levinas*, edited by Tina Chanter, 180–202. University Park: Penn State University Press.

Scheuerman, William. 2004. *Liberal Democracy and the Social Acceleration of Time*. Baltimore: Johns Hopkins University Press.

Serres, Michel. 2012. *Biogea*. Translated by Randolph Burks. Minneapolis: Univocal.

Severson, Eric. 2013. *Levinas's Philosophy of Time: Gift, Responsibility, Diachrony, Hope*. Pittsburgh: Duquesne University Press.

Severson, Eric. 2017. "In Defense of Reverence: Levinas, Responsibility and Future Generations." In "Phenomenology and Intergenerational Justice," edited by Matthias Fritsch and Ferdinando Menga, special issue, *Metodo: International Studies in Phenomenology and Philosophy* 5(2): 83–102.

Shearman, David, and Joseph Wayne Smith. 2007. *The Climate Change Challenge and the Failure of Democracy*. Westport, CT: Greenwood Press.
Sheridan, Mary, Ajay Sharma, and Helen Cockerill. 2014. *From Birth to Five Years: Children's Developmental Progress*. 4th ed. London: Routledge.
Sherif, Muzafer. 1966. *In Common Predicament: Social Psychology of Intergroup Conflict and Cooperation*. Boston: Houghton Mifflin.
Shrader-Frechette, Kristin. 2002. *Environmental Justice: Creating Equality, Reclaiming Democracy*. Oxford: Oxford University Press.
Sikka, Sonia. 2001. "The Delightful Other: Portraits of the Feminine in Kierkegaard, Nietzsche, and Levinas." In *Feminist Interpretations of Emmanuel Levinas*, edited by Tina Chanter, 96–118. University Park: Penn State University Press.
Sikora, Richard I., and Brian Barry, eds. 1978. *Obligations to Future Generations*. Philadelphia: Temple University Press.
Singer, Peter. 1998. "Ethics." *Encyclopædia Britannica Online*, accessed February 3, 2016, http://www.britannica.com/topic/ethics-philosophy.
Singer, Peter. 2002. *One World: The Ethics of Globalization*. New Haven, CT: Yale University Press.
Singer, Peter. 2006. "Ethics and Climate Change: A Commentary on MacCracken, Toman and Gardiner." *Environmental Values* 15(3): 415–422.
Sloterdijk, Peter. 2008. *Zorn und Zeit*. Frankfurt: Suhrkamp.
Smith, Mick. 2011. *Against Ecological Sovereignty: Ethics, Biopolitics and Saving the Natural World*. Minneapolis: University of Minnesota Press.
Söllner, Fritz. 2016. "The Use (and Abuse) of Robinson Crusoe in Neoclassical Economics." *History of Political Economy* 48(1): 35–64.
Steiner, Hillel. 1983. "The Rights of Future Generations." In *Energy and the Future*, edited by D. MacLean and P. G. Brown, 151–165. Totowa, NJ: Rowman and Allanheld.
Steiner, Hillel, and Peter Vallentyne. 2009. "Libertarian Theories of Intergenerational Justice." In *Intergenerational Justice*, edited by Axel Gosseries and Lukas H. Meyer, 50–76. Oxford: Oxford University Press.
Stiegler, Bernard. 2010. *Taking Care of Youth and of the Generations*. Translated by Stephen Barker. Stanford, CA: Stanford University Press.
Stone, Alison. 2010. "Natality and Mortality: Rethinking Death with Cavarero." *Continental Philosophy Review* 43(3): 353–372.
Strathern, Marilyn. 1988. *The Gender of the Gift: Problems with Women and Problems with Society in Melanesia*. Berkeley: University of California Press.
Tatransky, Tomáš. 2008. "A Reciprocal Asymmetry? Levinas's Ethics Reconsidered." *Ethical Perspectives* 15(3): 293–307.
Taylor, Charles. 1995. "Cross-Purposes: The Liberal-Communitarian Divide." In *Philosophical Arguments*, 181–203. Cambridge, MA: Harvard University Press.

Thompson, Dennis F. 2005. "Democracy in Time: Popular Sovereignty and Temporal Representation." *Constellations* 12(2): 245–261.

Thompson, Dennis F. 2010. "Representing Future Generations: Political Presentism and Democratic Trusteeship." *Critical Review of International Social and Political Philosophy* 13(1): 17–37.

Thompson, Evan. 2010. *Mind in Life: Biology, Phenomenology, and the Sciences of Mind.* Cambridge, MA: Harvard University Press.

Thompson, Janna. 2006. *Intergenerational Justice.* New York: Routledge.

Thompson, Janna. 2009. "Identity and Obligation in a Transgenerational Polity." In *Intergenerational Justice*, edited by Axel Gosseries and Lukas H. Meyer, 25–49. Oxford: Oxford University Press.

Thompson, Janna. 2013. "Intergenerational Relations and Moral Motivation." Paper read at "Nature Time Responsibility" conference, University of Macau, China.

Tremmel, Jörg Chet, ed. 2006. *Handbook of Intergenerational Justice.* Cheltenham, UK: Edward Elgar.

Tremmel, Jörg Chet. 2013. "The Convention of Representatives of All Generations under the 'Veil of Ignorance.'" *Constellations* 20(3): 483–502.

Tremmel, Jörg Chet, and Ned Chambers. 2010. "Review of Melinda A. Roberts and David T. Wasserman (eds.), *Harming Future Persons: Ethics, Genetics and the Nonidentity Problem.*" *Notre Dame Review of Books.* http://ndpr.nd.edu/review.cfm?id=19327.

Unnerstall, Herwig. 1999. *Rechte zukünftiger Generationen.* Würzburg: Königshausen und Neumann.

Vasey, Craig. 1992. "Faceless Women and Serious Others: Levinas, Misogyny, and Feminism." In *Ethics and Danger: Essays on Heidegger and Continental Thought*, edited by Arleen B. Dallery and Charles E. Scott, 317–330. Albany, NY: SUNY Press.

Vitale, Francesco. 2014. "The Text and the Living: Jacques Derrida between Biology and Deconstruction." *Oxford Literary Review* 36(1): 95–114.

Vitale, Francesco. 2015. "Life Death and Differance: Philosophies of Life between Hegel and Derrida." *CR: The New Centennial Review* 15:93–112.

Vitale, Francesco. 2018. *Biodeconstruction: Jacques Derrida and the Life Sciences.* Translated by Mauro Senatore. Albany, NY: SUNY Press.

Vizenor, Gerald. 1994. *Manifest Manners: Narratives on Postindian Survivance.* Middletown, CT: Wesleyan University Press.

Vizenor, Gerald, ed. 2008. *Survivance: Narratives of Native Presence.* Lincoln: University of Nebraska Press.

Vizenor, Gerald, J. Doerfler, and D. E. Wilkins, eds. 2012. *The White Earth Nation: Ratification of a Native Democratic Constitution.* Lincoln: University of Nebraska Press.

Voelkl, B., S. J. Portugal, M. Unsöld, J. R. Usherwood, A. M. Wilson, and J.

Fritz. 2015. "Matching Times of Leading and Following Suggest Cooperation through Direct Reciprocity during V-Formation Flight in Ibis." *Proc. Natl. Acad. Sci. USA* 112(7): 2115–2120.
Wade-Benzoni, Kimberly A. 2002. "A Golden Rule over Time: Reciprocity in Intergenerational Allocation Decisions." *Academy of Management Journal* 45(5): 1011–1028.
Wade-Benzoni, Kimberly A. 2009. "The Egoism and Altruism of Intergenerational Behavior." *Personality & Social Psychology Review* 13(3): 165–193.
Waldenfels, Bernhard. 2006. *Schattenrisse der Moral*. Frankfurt: Suhrkamp.
Waldenfels, Bernhard. 2017. "Antworten auf Ansprüche Nachkommender." In "Phenomenology and Intergenerational Justice," edited by Matthias Fritsch and Ferdinando Menga, special issue, *Metodo: International Studies in Phenomenology and Philosophy* 5(2): 19–45.
Wall, Steven. 2003. "Just Savings and the Difference Principle." *Philosophical Studies* 116:79–102.
Weiner, Annette. 1992. *Inalienable Possession: The Paradox of Keeping-While-Giving*. Berkeley: University of California Press.
Weiss, Edith Brown. 1989. *In Fairness to Future Generations: International Law, Common Patrimony, and Intergenerational Equality*. Dobbs Ferry, NY: Transnational Publishers.
Wenzler, Ludwig. 1984. "Zeit als Nähe des Abwesenden." In Emmanuel Levinas, *Die Zeit und der Andere*, translated by Ludwig Wenzler, 67–92. Hamburg: Meiner.
White, Stephen. 2000. *Sustaining Affirmation: The Strengths of Weak Ontology in Political Theory*. Princeton, NJ: Princeton University Press.
Williams, Bernard. 1973. "The Makropulos Case: Reflections on the Tedium of Immortality." In *Problems of the Self*, 82–100. Cambridge: Cambridge University Press.
Wood, Allen. 2008. *Kantian Ethics*. Cambridge: Cambridge University Press.
Wood, David. 2003. "What Is Eco-Phenomenology?" In *Eco-Phenomenology: Back to the Earth Itself*, edited by Charles S. Brown and Ted Toadvine, 211–234. Albany, NY: SUNY Press.
Wood, David. 2007. "Specters of Derrida: On the Way to Econstruction." In *Ecospirit: Religions and Philosophies for the Earth*, edited by Laurel Kearns and Catherine Keller, 264–290. New York: Fordham University Press.
Wood, Paul M. 2008. "Sustainability Impeded: Ultra Vires Environmental Issues." *Environmental Ethics* 30(2): 159–174.
Woodward, James. 1986. "The Non-Identity Problem." *Ethics* 96:804–831.
Young, Iris Marion. 1997. "Asymmetrical Reciprocity." *Constellations* 3(3): 340–363.
Zwartheod, Danielle. 2015. "Cheap Preferences and Intergenerational Justice." *Revue de philosophie économique* 16(1): 69–101.

Index

Abel, 77
Adaptive preferences, 32–33
Agency: anachrony of time as ground of, 10–11, 41, 70, 72, 75–77, 90; futural structure of, 45–46, 68–69, 75–76; gift as constitutive of, 101; inheritance as constitutive of, 61, 93; mortality linked to, 9–10, 44–46, 68–69, 72; natality linked to, 48–49, 89–90
All affected principle, 27
Althusser, Louis, 128
Altruism, 113, 142–43. *See also* Dynastic altruism
Animals: as component of nature, 114, 117, 135, 137; ethics and, 126; extension of ethics to, 199–200; humans distinguished from, 157, 160–61; justice and, 39; rights of, 26
Anthropocene, 5–6, 157
Anthropocentrism, 183
Arendt, Hannah, 7, 48–50, 71, 89–90
Aristotle, 47, 143, 161, 164, 166, 173–75, 207; *Physics*, 162; *Politics*, 155, 173, 227n12
Arrondel, Luc, 112–13, 120–21, 138, 143
Asymmetrical reciprocity, 4, 8; altruism and, 143; defined, 11–12, 57–58, 108; inappropriability as characteristic of, 95; indirect reciprocity compared to, 12, 57–59, 108, 146–47; Levinas and, 91–106; past and future commingled in, 58–59; serial chain models compared to, 139–41; symmetrical vs., 144–45; temporal relations in, 147–51; turn-taking in relation to, 181–82
Asymmetry, in moral interactions, 31, 57
Auto-hetero-affection, 186, 189, 195, 200, 205, 211

Baby Boomers, 21
Bacon, Francis, 212
Barry, Brian, 120
Barter, 110
Barthes, Roland, 128
Bataille, Georges, 152
Baudelaire, Charles, "La fausse monnaie," 133, 136
Beauvoir, Simone de, 7, 44
Becker, Lawrence, 25
Beckerman, Wilfred, 26
Being-for-beyond-my-death, 10, 47, 50, 67, 75, 78, 79, 148, 181
Benjamin, Walter, 93
Best, Elsdon, 123
Biodeconstruction, 192
Bioethics, 33
Biology, 87–88, 94–95
Birth. *See* Natality
Blanchot, Maurice, 208
Bloch, Ernst, 75
Brumlik, Micha, 57
Butler, Judith, 50, 92, 221n17

Cain, 77
Caney, Simon, 159–60
Capitalism, 110, 123

Capital punishment, 146, 156–57, 190, 194, 219n5, 229n11
Care, 45, 47–48, 70–71, 101, 120, 143, 147, 152, 220n11
Cavarero, Adriana, 10, 49–50
Chain: of concern, 20, 24; intergenerational, 12, 50, 57, 61, 81–82, 108, 111–13, 122, 124, 139–41
Chambers, Ned, 35
Chanter, Tina, 101
Choice theory of rights, 26
Clark, Timothy, 158
Climate change and environmental crises: applicability of extant moral theories to, 17–18; generation defined by, 23–24; historical uniqueness of current, 157; intergenerational justice made salient by, 5–6; intergenerational obligations concerning, 180; moral renewal called for by, 1–2; timing of damage expected from, 140; as world-constituting, 36
Collective action problems, 29–30, 57, 160
Communitarianism, 54
Consequentialism, 35, 36
Contractualist ethics, 30–31, 34. *See also* Social contract tradition
Corpse, 77, 188, 189, 194–202, 205, 207–8
Crewe, Ivor, 160
Crusoe, Robinson. *See* Defoe, Daniel, *Robinson Crusoe*
Cuarón, Alfonso, *The Children of Men*, 54

Daly, Herman, 153
Death and mortality: agency linked to, 9–10, 44–46, 68–69, 72; alterity of, 69, 73–74; *co-mourance*, 202, 230n18; Derrida and, 146, 156–57, 189, 219n5; Heidegger and, 45–48, 50, 68–70, 72–75, 89, 189; humans and nonhumans sharing, 202; instantaneity of, 146, 156–57, 190, 207–8, 219n5; and intergenerational being, 7; interpersonality of, 71, 73–74; Levinas and, 46–48, 69–70, 73–78, 95–97, 189; life implicated in, 51, 189–90, 192–93, 195–98; meaning grounded in, 44–45, 47, 68–69, 74; not mere nothingness, 73–78; overview of, 44–47; politics and, 156–57; posthuming and, 205–9; sovereignty and, 168; sovereignty over, 15, 146, 156–57, 189–90, 190, 219n5; totality vs. singularity concerning, 95–96; understanding of, 45–46, 73–78, 190, 199; and vulnerability, 10, 46. *See also* Capital punishment; Lifedeath; Natal mortality
Death penalty. *See* Capital punishment
Declaration of the Human Rights of Future Generations, 25
Deconstruction, 7–8, 44, 160–61, 168, 191, 203, 210. *See also* Phenomenology
Defoe, Daniel, *Robinson Crusoe*, 189, 195–96, 204–6, 211–13
Deliberative democracy, 26–27
Democracy: deliberative, 26–27; extension of, 167; presentism of, 156–61, 166; sovereignty in, 155–56, 158, 160, 161, 164, 166–67, 185; turn-taking in, 155–56, 161, 167–70, 173–75, 178, 227n12
Democracy-to-come, 160, 190–91
Derrida, Jacques, 7, 11–13, 15, 58, 92, 95; *Adieu*, 105–6; *The Animal That Therefore I Am*, 196, 198–200, 206; *Aporias*, 126; *The Beast and the Sovereign*, 126, 188, 189, 197, 228n16; *The Beast and the Sovereign*, volume 2 (BS2), 77, 189, 193–95, 199, 202–3, 205, 212, 231n19; on Crusoe, 195–96, 204–6, 211–13; and death, 146, 156–57, 189, 190, 219n5, 229n11; *The Death Penalty*, 190; on democracy,

155–56, 160, 161; "Différance," 134; and the earth, 205–9; on earth-world relation, 188; and the gift, 120–21, 125–37, 141–43; *Given Time*, 125, 131, 133–34, 152; *Glas*, 196, 231n22; *Of Grammatology*, 165; on inheritance, 149; *Limited Inc*, 231n20; on Mauss, 108–9, 114–15, 125–27; "Ousia and Gramm," 134, 162; *The Politics of Friendship*, 169; and reciprocity, 141; *Rogues*, 13, 126, 156, 161, 189–90, 228n16; "Shibboleth," 163; *Specters of Marx*, 52, 125, 169, 223n14; and time, 127, 133–35, 145, 163; "Violence and Metaphysics," 103–4; *For What Tomorrow*, 126; world concept in, 62

Descartes, René, 206

Descartes effect, 138

Différance: concept of, 132; of earth, 191–95, 198, 212; evolution and, 209–10; and the gift, 109; of the gift, 128–37, 142; and identity, 127, 129; posthuming in relation to, 206–7; reciprocity and, 147; subjectivity and, 104–5; time and, 127; timespace and, 146, 164–65

Dilthey, Wilhelm, 20, 22

Diprose, Rosalyn, 49

Discourse ethics, 26–27, 34

Distributive justice, 27–28

Domination, 33, 60

Double affirmation, 105–6, 156, 165–66, 181

Double turn-taking, 158, 166–72, 213–14

Dynastic altruism, 139

Earth/nature: as context of life, 189–90, 194–201, 208–13; corpse claimed by, 194–95; Derrida and, 132–37, 205–9; *différance* of, 191–95, 198, 212; excessive/unpossessable nature of, 205; fear of, 137, 195, 204–5, 211–12; the gift and, 109, 111–12, 114–19, 122–24, 132–37; as hetero, 186, 189; as holistic object, 14, 175; as home of the self, 99–100; humanist conception of, 14, 183, 187–90, 196; Levinas's concept of elemental, 98–99; lifedeath and, 204–5; Mauss and, 109, 111–12, 114–19, 122–24; resources of, 187–88; sovereignty over, 190; subjectivity in relation to, 137; world in relation to, 187–91, 202–5; as world preceding generations, 22. *See also* Terrestrial turn-taking; World

Earth Overshoot Day, 187

Ecological crises. *See* Climate change and other environmental crises

Economy and economics, 109, 151–53, 212, 224n25

Elemental earth, 98–99

Enkelmann, Wolf Dieter, 152–53

Environment, concept of, 183–84

Environmental crises. *See* Climate change and other environmental crises

Environmental turning. *See* Terrestrial turn-taking

Epistemic access, as moral criterion, 27–29, 55–57, 65–66

Ethics. *See* Intergenerational justice; Morality

Evolution, 209–10

Ex-appropriation, 129, 137, 177, 185, 201, 211, 212

Excess: in nature of gifts, 12, 58–59, 108–9, 118–20, 122, 127–37, 149; of obligation to the future, 12, 59, 62; world as, in relation to the self, 184–85

Exchange, gifts compared to, 12, 141–43, 145, 151–52

Excrement, 210–11

Exoplanets, 187

Extensionism, 38–39, 41

Fagenblat, Michael, 83

Family, 20, 98, 106, 143, 152, 224n25; and the State, 83–86

Fecundity, 10, 47, 53, 56, 71, 83, 86–91, 93–95, 103
Feminine, the, 98–103
Feminism, and critique of Levinas, 10–11, 99–102
Fink, Eugen, 70
First Scientific Assessment Report (IPCC), 5
Forgiveness, 89–90
Foucault, Michel, 128
Fraternity, 84–85
French Resistance, 85
Freud, Sigmund, 199
Fritsche, Johannes, 162
Futural structure: of agency, 45–46, 68–69, 75–76; excess associated with, 12, 59, 62, 67; of inheritance, 54, 149; the past in relation to, 11; of responsibility/obligation, 53; of subjectivity, 10, 46–47, 78
Future people: applicability of extant moral theories to, 8, 17–18, 25–27, 38–40, 216n11; creation of, 33, 36; defined, 20; epistemic problems concerning, 27–29, 55–57; interaction problems concerning, 29–31; Levinas and, 67–68; nonexistence of, as problem in morality/justice for, 25–27, 51–55; nonidentity problem involving, 33–36; responsibility/obligation to, 3, 8–9, 24–38, 51, 80; rights of, 25–26; as source of meaning, 53, 76, 89, 148; spectral presence of, 52–54, 81; subjectivity in relation to, 10; turn-taking with regard to, 179–83; world-constitution problems concerning, 31–37, 53–54, 59–63. *See also* Generational time; Intergenerational justice

Gardiner, Stephen, 1–4, 7, 29–31, 158, 172
Generational beings: humans as, 4–5, 19, 50; justice linked to human nature as, 18
Generational overlap: abstraction from, 41–42, 55–56; ethical significance of, 24; features of, 20; reciprocity associated with, 11, 57, 139–40; time and, 52–53; turn-taking and, 179
Generational time: as critical component in intergenerational justice, 7–8, 9, 18, 169–70; turn-taking emerging out of, 176–79. *See also* Future people; Natal mortality
Generational turn-taking, 8, 15, 162, 170–79
Generations: beginning/ending of, 4–5, 21–22, 118, 178–79; climate change as historical event defining, 23–24; cultural aspect of, 21–22; defining, 19–24; historical aspect of, 21, 23
Generation X, 21
Generation Y, 21–22
Genetic manipulation, 33
Gifts: ambivalence of, 121, 125; asymmetrical, 11–12; cyclical character of, 108–9, 114, 118, 122–23, 132–33; Derrida and, 125–37, 141–43; donors inseparable from, 108–9, 114, 115–16; excessive/unpossessable nature of, 12, 58–59, 108–9, 118–20, 122, 127–37, 149; exchanges compared to, 12, 141–43, 145, 151–52; and formation of subjectivity, 101; intergenerational, 11, 111–12, 115–22, 124–27, 137–38; Mauss and, 109–24; obligations elicited by, 111, 113–22, 128–30; of one's time, 79; spirit of, 108–9, 114, 116–19, 123–24; subjectivity constituted by, 111, 124, 142; time and, 127, 133–35, 145; world as context for, 116–18. *See also* Reciprocity
Globalization, 187
Global warming. *See* Climate change and environmental crises
Gosseries, Axel, 25–26, 215n6
Graeber, David, 115
Guenther, Lisa, 11, 50, 90

Habermas, Jürgen, 34
Habib, Allen, 13–14, 174, 177, 179, 180, 182
Harari, Yuval, 200
Hatley, James, 196
Hau (spirit), 108, 110, 114–17, 119, 123–24
Hauntology, 131, 161, 173, 176
Heidegger, Martin, 7, 9–10, 87, 131; and agency, 44, 46; and birth, 47–48; and care, 45, 71; and death, 45–48, 50, 68–70, 72–75, 89, 189; and the gift, 125; and responsibility, 199; and revenge, 146; and time, 134, 226n6; world concept in, 60, 62
Hemingway, Ernest, 21
Heyd, David, 32, 216n11
History, 95–106
Hobbes, Thomas, 110, 212
Holistic/quasi-holistic objects, 12–14, 174, 177–83
Homo economicus, 110, 212
Hope, 75
Humanism/human exceptionalism, 14, 156–57, 160, 183, 187–90, 196–99
Humility, 175, 177, 208, 213
Husserl, Edmund, 7, 231n19
Huxley, Aldous, *Brave New World*, 32

Identity: *différance* and, 127–28, 146–47; turn-taking as constitutive of, 13, 163–64, 166–67; world as partly constitutive of, 62, 197. *See also* Subjectivity and the self
IGJ. *See* Intergenerational justice
Immortality, 44, 45, 47, 69, 189, 217n14, 217n15, 217n16
Indirect reciprocity, 11–12, 58–59, 108, 112–13, 146–47
Individualism, 4, 84–85, 110, 195, 211–12, 221n1
Infinity: of responsibility/obligation, 79, 81–82, 86, 97–98, 103; totality and, 95–96, 103–5
Inheritance: agency grounded in, 61, 93; culture as, 22, 61; futural structure of, 54, 149; of present generation from the past, 38, 61, 91–97. *See also* Natality
Institutions, 4–5, 85–86, 155–56, 166–68, 172–78; presence of future people in, 53–54
Interest theory of rights, 26, 28
Intergenerational justice (IGJ): antihumanism and, 18; climate change as motivation for, 5–6; definition of generation significant for, 19; epistemic problems concerning, 27–29, 55–57; as extension or special case of ethics and justice, 8, 17–18, 25–27, 38–40, 216n11; generational time as critical component in, 7–8, 9, 18, 169–70; interaction problems concerning, 29–31; intra- vs., 9, 18, 21, 38, 41, 59, 61–62, 125–26; Levinas's relevance for, 64–73; need to address, 2; nonexistence challenge to, 25–27, 51–55; ontological approach to, 24–38, 40–43; ontological problems in, 8–9; population size as topic in, 32; presentism as hindrance to, 2–4; psychology of, 3; scholarship on, 6–7; temporal alterity as ground of, 51–52, 58; world-constitution problems concerning, 31–37, 59–63. *See also* Asymmetrical reciprocity; Future people; Morality
Intergenerational ties: gifts as embodying, 11, 111–12, 115–22, 124–27, 137–38; Heidegger and, 48; past-present vs. present-future, 218n20; reciprocities in, 91–97; recognition and acknowledgment of, 3–4
Intergenerational turning. *See* Generational turn-taking
Intergovernmental Panel on Climate Change (IPCC), 5
Interment, 14–15, 188–90, 213
IPCC. *See* Intergovernmental Panel on Climate Change

Irigaray, Luce, 10, 99

James, P. D., *The Children of Men*, 54
Jamieson, Dale, 28–29, 33, 35, 37, 60, 140
Jonas, Hans, 6, 26, 32, 50, 57
Joyce, James, 212
Justice: assumptions of symmetry in, 31, 57; ontological and normative demands of, 42–43. *See also* Intergenerational justice (IGJ); Reciprocity

Kamuf, Peggy, 190
Kant, Immanuel, 30, 66, 77, 166, 187, 219n1, 228n2
King, Anthony, 160
Kittay, Eva, 57, 88–89
Knowledge. *See* Epistemic access, as moral criterion

Lacan, Jacques, 128, 131, 197
Learning to live, 169
Leroi-Gourhan, André, 165
Letting the other live, 10, 46–47, 77–78, 87, 199
Levinas, Emmanuel, 7, 9–11, 64–106; and death, 46–48, 69–70, 73–78, 95–97, 189; and fecundity, 86–91, 95; and the feminine, 98–103; feminist critique of, 10–11, 99–102; and the gift, 125; and history, 95–106; and intergenerational reciprocities, 91–97; on meaning derived from future people, 53; *Otherwise than Being*, 86, 220n10; and presentism, 67, 80–81; and reciprocity, 141; on responsibility/obligation, 53, 55–56, 62, 65–67, 78, 80, 199; and subjectivity, 221n17; and temporality, 65–68, 70–71; on the third party, 83–86; *Time and the Other*, 73–74, 86, 87, 99; *Totality and Infinity*, 65, 74, 79, 86, 97, 99–100, 220n10; world concept in, 62. *See also* Being-for-beyond-my-death

Lévi-Strauss, Claude, 108–9, 114, 128, 131
Liebsch, Burkhard, 111
Life: auto-hetero-affection as defining, 186; death implicated in, 51, 189–90, 192–93, 195–98; *différance* and, 192–95; earth as context of, 189–90, 194–201, 208–13; interment as condition of, 188. *See also* Lifedeath; Natal mortality
Lifedeath, 137, 155, 156, 161, 165, 189, 191–93, 204–5, 211, 229n9. *See also* Natal mortality
Lifeworld. *See* World
Locke, John, 117; *Second Treatise of Government*, 189
Lost Generation, 21
Lucretius, 44, 73

Macbeth, 77
Macpherson, C. B., 110, 212, 221n1
Maintenon, Madame de, 131
Malinowski, Bronislaw, 111
Mana (spirit), 108, 114–17, 222n5
Marx, Karl, 212
Masson, André, 112–13, 120–21, 138, 143
Maternity, 49–50, 84–87, 91, 97–103, 220n10, 229n10
Mauss, Marcel, 11–12; *Essai sur le don*, 58, 108–10; and the gift, 109–24; on political economy, 110–13; on return obligation, 113–22
McKenzie, Michael, 158
Meaning: death/mortality as source of, 44–45, 47, 68–69, 74; future people as source of, 53, 76, 89, 148
Millennials, 21–22
Mills, Charles, 145
Mondialisation, 187
Morality: agency linked to, 9–10, 44–46; asymmetry and, 31, 57; autonomy and, 219n1; commonsense notion of, 28–29, 37, 38, 215n5; epistemic problems concerning, 27–29, 55–57; extension of, to the nonhuman, 197–200; first-person perspective on, 66;

and future people, 3, 8–9, 24–38, 51; nonidentity problem and, 33–36; ontological issues in, 17–18, 24–38; scope of, 3; time in relation to, 18–19; world disclosure dependent on fact of, 45. *See also* Intergenerational justice; Responsibility/obligation

Mortality. *See* Death and mortality

Mother. *See* Maternity

Murder, 76–77

"My" time, 75, 78

Naas, Michael, 190

Naess, Arne, 191

Nancy, Jean-Luc, 164, 187

Natality: agency linked to, 48–49, 89–90; and asymmetrical social relations, 49–50; defined, 10; and intergenerational being, 7; overview of, 47–51; sovereignty and, 168; women and, 49–50. *See also* Inheritance; Natal mortality

Natal mortality: defined, 24; and epistemic access, 55–57; and interaction problems, 57–59; moral subjectivity grounded in, 43, 50; and nonexistence, 51–55; and ontological problems, 65; and world constitution, 59–63. *See also* Generational time; Lifedeath

Nature. *See* Earth/nature

Nietzsche, Friedrich, 145–46

Noncoincidence: agency and, 10–11, 70, 72, 75–77; future arising from, 76; identity and, 54, 163, 167; time and, 163. *See also Différance*

Nonexistence, of future people, 25–27, 51–55

Nonhuman. *See* Animals; Earth/nature

Nonidentity problem, 33–36

Nonreciprocity argument, 30, 57

Nozick, Robert, 117, 120

Nussbaum, Martha, 44–45, 47, 57

Obama, Barack, 5

Obligation. *See* Responsibility/obligation

O'Byrne, Anne, 22, 50

Ontology: approaches to IGJ based on, 40–43; issues in IGJ, 8–9, 24–38. *See also* Hauntology

Other, the: alterity of, 56, 65–67, 72, 76–77; death as/and, 73–74; earth as, 186, 189; letting the other live, 10, 46–47, 77–78, 87, 199; responsibility/obligation to, 65–67; subjectivity in relation to, 10, 46–47, 104–6; turning toward, 167–71; vulnerability of, disclosed by mortality, 10

"Ought implies can," 41, 55, 77, 220n8

Overlapping generations (OLG) model, 20–21. *See also* Generational overlap

Parfit, Derek, 34–36

Pasek, J., 26

Paternity, 10, 47, 86–87, 97–99

Person-affecting view of morality, 33–35

Personal/impersonal, 83–86

Phenomenology, 7–8, 44. *See also* Deconstruction

Plato, 90, 98, 133, 161, 166; *Republic*, 133; *Timaeus*, 98

Plumwood, Val, 196–97

Political legitimacy, 27

Population size, 32, 36

Posthuming, 205–9

Presentism: as collective action problem, 29–30; critique of, 2–4; democracy and, 156–61, 166; humanism linked to, 198; Levinas and, 67, 80–81; as modern industrial artifact, 3–4

Propagation effect, 139

Quasi-holistic objects. *See* Holistic/quasi-holistic objects

Rawls, John, 30, 36, 39, 42, 145

Rebound effect, 138

Reciprocal altruism, 143

Reciprocity: altruism in relation to, 113; assumptions of symmetry in, 31, 49, 57, 144–45; critiques of, 141–53; indirect, 11–12, 58–59, 108, 112–13, 146–47; intergenerational, 11, 57, 91–97; moral obligation dependent on, 30; serial chain model of, 139–41; in small-group situations, 3; time in relation to, 145–46; turn-taking compared to, 12–13, 154–55; types (motivations/directions) of, 137–39. *See also* Asymmetrical reciprocity; Gifts

Renter model, 14

Responsibility/obligation: fecundity as model for, 86–88; futural structure of, 53; to future people, 3, 8–9, 24–38, 51, 80; gifts as eliciting, 111, 113–22, 128–30; infinity of, 79, 81–82, 86, 97–98, 103; Levinas and, 53, 55–56, 62, 65–67, 78, 80; lifedeath and, 199; to the other, 65–67; "ought implies can," 41, 55, 77, 220n8; society grounded in, 111

Restance, 175

Revenge, 145–46

Ricoeur, Paul, 92

Rights, 25–26, 28

Rosa, Hartmut, 159

Rousseau, Jean-Jacques, 109, 212

Routley, Richard, 75

Sahlins, Marshall, 110

Sartre, Jean-Paul, 126

Saussure, Ferdinand de, 191

Scanlon, T. M., 34

Self. *See* Subjectivity and the self

Serres, Michel, 14

Severson, Eric, 98

Sharing, by parts vs. by turns, 12–14, 155, 173–75, 177, 179–80, 182, 227n10, 227n14

Singularization, 83–85, 95–96

Social contract tradition, 65, 89, 110–11, 133, 144, 221n1. *See also* Contractualist ethics

Sovereignty: Crusoe and, 213; over death, 15, 146, 156–57, 189–90, 190, 219n5; democratic, 155–56, 158, 160, 161, 164, 166–67, 185; divine, 166–67; as double turn-taking, 214; over earth, 190; finite nature of, 175, 184; human, 15, 137, 156–58, 161, 184, 213; individual, 145–46, 166; over nature, 137, 158; over the nonhuman, 157, 161; over otherness, 207; turn-taking as means of, 166–69

Space, time in relation to, 127, 134–35, 137, 139, 144, 146–48, 150, 164–65

State, and the family, 83–86

Stein, Gertrude, 21

Steiner, Hillel, 26

Sternberger, Dolf, 70

Stewardship, 14, 183

Strathern, Marilyn, 222n7

Subjectivity and the self: futural structure of, 10, 46–47, 78; as generational beings, 4–5, 19, 50; gifts as constitutive of, 101, 124, 142; Levinas and, 221n17; mortality and, 45–46; "my" time, 75, 78; nature in relation to, 137; others in relation to, 10, 46–47, 104–6; past as constitutive of, 91–97; relational conception of, 67, 71, 215n5; role of the feminine in the constitution of, 99–102; temporal component of, 43, 70–71; turn-taking as constitutive of, 169–70; world as context of, 184–85. *See also* Identity

Survivance, 156, 170, 193, 207, 210, 232n30

Taste, 196

Tatransky, Tomáš, 92

Taylor, Charles, 2

Temporality. *See* Time and temporality

Terrestrial turn-taking, 14–15, 15, 171–72, 183–85

Third party, 83–86

Thompson, Dennis, 158

Thompson, Janna, 4, 53
Time and temporality: abstraction from role of, in social relations, 41–42; agency grounded in anachrony of, 70, 72, 75–77; alterity/anachrony of, 41, 51–52, 58, 70, 72, 75–77, 90; Aristotle on, 162; asymmetrical reciprocity and, 147–51; death penalty and, 146; Derrida on, 127, 133–35, 145, 163; *différance* and, 127, 134–35; as embodied in turn-taking, 13; gifts and, 127, 133–35, 145; Heidegger and, 134, 226n6; Levinas and, 65–68, 70–71; morality in relation to, 18–19; nature of, 162–63; reciprocity in relation to, 145–46; space in relation to, 127, 134–35, 137, 139, 144, 146–48, 150, 164–65; subjectivity and, 43, 70–71; turn-taking as a conception of, 162–63. *See also* Generational time
Tocqueville, Alexis de, *Democracy in America*, 167
Totality, 95–96, 103–4
Tragedy of the commons, 29–30, 160
Tremmel, Jörg Chet, 35
Trusteeship, 14
Turn-taking: advantages of, as model of sharing, 175–79; asymmetrical reciprocity in relation to, 181–82; commonsense nature of, 176; as a conception of time, 162–63; conditions for, 12–14; content of justice in, 14; in democracy, 155–56, 161, 167–70, 173–75, 178, 227n12; fairness in, 179–83; future people as subject of, 179–83; generational, 162, 170–79; Heidegger and, 226n6; with holistic objects, 12–14, 174, 177–83; identity constituted by, 13, 163–64, 166–67; toward the other, 167–71; reciprocity compared to, 12–13, 154–55; sovereignty achieved by, 166–69; subjectivity constituted by, 169–70; time as embodied in, 13; in various fields, 225n1. *See also* Double turn-taking; Generational turn-taking; Sharing, by parts vs. by turns; Terrestrial turn-taking

Universalization, 83–85
Utilitarianism, 36, 110

Valéry, Paul, 126
Vitale, Francesco, 192
Vizenor, Gerald, 232n30
Vomit, 210
Vulnerability: agency and, 50; morality and, 52, 71, 77, 84, 169; mortality and, 10, 45–46, 198, 202; of the other, 199; of subjectivity, 43, 190

Wade-Benzoni, Kimberly A., 3, 218n20
Waste, 153, 210–11
Weiner, Annette, 222n7
Williams, Bernard, 44
Will theory of rights, 26
Women: Levinas's ontologization of, 101; and natality, 49–50. *See also* Maternity
World: climate change as constitutive of, 36; Derrida on Husserl's notion of, 231n19; earth in relation to, 187–91, 202–5; excessive nature of, 62–63; expectation of the future, 148; gifts as embedded in, 116–18; as ground/precedent for generations, 22, 62, 148; humans and nonhumans sharing, 202–5; inheritance of, from past generations, 61; as island, 203–4; mortality as essential to disclosure of, 45; natal mortality and constitution of, 59–63; plurality of worlds, 62–63; as setting for interaction with future people, 31–37, 53–54, 59–63; subjectivity in context of, 184–85. *See also* Earth/nature

Ziarek, Ewa, 49

The authorized representative in the EU for product safety and compliance is:
Mare Nostrum Group
B.V Doelen 72
4831 GR Breda
The Netherlands

www.ingramcontent.com/pod-product-compliance
Lightning Source LLC
Chambersburg PA
CBHW022003220426
43663CB00007B/936